ACCEPTABILITY IN LANGUAGE

Contributions to the Sociology of Language

17

Joshua A. Fishman
Editor

MOUTON PUBLISHERS . THE HAGUE . PARIS . NEW YORK

Acceptability in Language

Sidney Greenbaum
Editor

MOUTON PUBLISHERS . THE HAGUE . PARIS . NEW YORK

ISBN: 90-279-7623-6
Jacket design by Jurriaan Schrofer

Printed in the Netherlands

For Sholem and Arieh
with affection

Preface

This volume contains twelve previously unpublished papers, with markedly different orientations, reporting on diverse aspects of research into grammaticality and acceptability in language. Although the volume appears in a series on the sociology of language, the contents are relevant also to readers interested in general linguistics and psycholinguistics.

I am grateful to Joshua Fishman for suggesting that I undertake the editing of this collection of papers. The work was supported by a grant from the College of Letters and Science of the University of Wisconsin-Milwaukee. Thanks are due to Isaac D. Corré for reading the proofs.

Milwaukee, October 1976 Sidney Greenbaum

Contents

SIDNEY GREENBAUM

1

Introduction

Sociolinguists, like other social scientists, concern themselves with societally patterned variation in behavior and attitudes and seek the factors that explain and predict such variation (Fishman 1971: 9; 1972: 10). Within the sociology of language a broad distinction has been drawn between macro-level and micro-level analyses (Fishman 1972: 29–54). The study of the macro-level, often considered the sociology of language *par excellence,* deals with large-scale relationships between language and society; for example, as manifested in multilingual societies, in diglossic communities, or through language planning, language maintenance and language standardization. The study of the micro-level, often identified with sociolinguistics proper, is primarily concerned with societally patterned variation in areas that are traditionally the domain of linguistics: phonetics, phonology, morphology, syntax, lexicology and semantics. In contrast with most linguists, sociolinguists have recognized sociocontextual units as well as the traditional units abstracted from the use of language. Some linguists too have advocated a functional approach to language description (*cf.* Greenbaum 1976), but rigorous studies involving quantitative and statistical analyses primarily date from the rise of sociolinguistics as a separate discipline. The hope has been expressed by both sociolinguists and linguists that one day all linguists will accept the new broader goals of linguistic description; when that day arrives, the study of the micro-level will rightly be recognized as an integral part of linguistics (Fishman 1971: 8f.; Labov 1972: 184–202; Fillmore 1973; Bailey 1973b: 23).

Within the context of this volume, the macro-level concerns attitudes towards the acceptability of a language or of a variety within a language, whereas the micro-level concerns the acceptability of specific linguistic features. The two levels intersect in an investigation of features across varieties. Most of the papers in this volume deal exclusively or principally with the micro-level, but several focus on the macro-level. Afolayan discusses the acceptability of the English language in the diglossia situation that obtains in Nigeria, where English is the language of law, administration and formal education, and is also used as a neutral language for inter-ethnic communication. The language situation in Nigeria is typical of that in African and Asian countries that were at one time British territories in that there is ambivalence toward the English language. On the one hand, English is politically more acceptable than any indigenous language because the indigenous languages are associated with particular ethnic components of the population. In addition, the retention of an international language has obvious advantages for external trade and, perhaps more significantly, for higher education: vocabulary resources are available for use in science and technology, and numerous textbooks and journals are published in the language. On the other hand, there is political resistance to the English language on patriotic grounds, since it is associated with the former colonial oppressors, and its rejection is seen as an assertion of national independence. The resolution of the ambivalence is likely to come through the emergence of distinct regional varieties of the English language that can be claimed as national languages. Afolayan notes that a Nigerian variety of English is developing though it is still some way from achieving standardization and institutional status or the local prestige of American and British English with which Nigerian forms are compared.

Rabin's paper also touches on language acceptability and diglossia, though in a very different context: the revival of Hebrew as a first language. Rabin relates problems of acceptability in contemporary Israeli Hebrew to attempts on the part of normative writers to restore to the language the characteristics it once had as a purely written language in a diglossia situation. We see the development of a normative tradition that establishes prescriptive and proscriptive rules at variance with general usage in present-day Hebrew. New rules are constantly being formulated and disseminated, to the confusion of most native speakers. As a result, even the educated are linguistically insecure when they write, and native speakers are reluctant to make acceptability judgments. Rabin's description presents an extreme situation that has its analogues in the normative traditions associated with more established languages, where spoken and written varieties have diverged, and discrepancies exist between explicit norms and actual usage. The Israeli situation contributes to our understanding of the ways in which norms are developed.

Bickerton's paper also poses questions about the way in which a 'new' community establishes norms. He discusses the nature of grammaticality and acceptability in the pidgin-creole cycle, including the two processes which commonly affect creoles: decreolization and repidginization. We shall later have occasion to consider the contrast that many linguists make between grammaticality and acceptability. Bickerton distinguishes between the underlying system in the language (speech output conforming to the system is designated as grammatical) and the acceptability judgments of individual speakers. He suggests that norms do not exist in early pidgins, with the result that everything is acceptable and nothing is grammatical. At the other extreme, 'in the process of decreolization that produces creole continua, almost everything may be grammatical while, for given individuals, much less may be acceptable'. The distinctions that Bickerton makes for the pidgin-creole cycle are relevant to our understanding of the nature of grammaticality and acceptability in 'natural' languages, which can be regarded as belonging to the end of the cycle, and should also throw light on other areas of activity in society where there is extensive variation.

Tottie's paper refers to a practical problem on the macro-level: what variety of English should the foreign student be taught? The question suggests parallels with more familiar problems of language planning. In the past the answer was obvious. British English (often in the Received Pronunciation) was the natural choice for one or more reasons: geographical proximity (as in Europe), British occupation (as in the former British colonies in Africa and Asia), commercial relations with Britain (as in Latin America), British political power and British cultural prestige. Furthermore, there has been a widespread popular belief that the variety spoken in the original location of English speakers must be correct and the most pure. But, particularly since the end of the Second World War, British political and economic influence has been declining rapidly, and the British Empire has disintegrated; during the same period the United States has emerged as a superpower, bestowing prestige on American English. As a result, British and American English have been competing in many parts of the world, including Europe and former British territories (for example, Nigeria, as Afolayan reports). We may expect competition from other English standards when countries such as Canada and Australia grow in influence. The adoption for foreign language teaching of one among several competing standard varieties involves extralinguistic factors analogous to those that determine the adoption of a standard variety from among several competing varieties.

Tottie also mentions an approach that avoids a choice between existing regional standards, though she rejects it: a mixed form of English that draws on the dominant standard varieties but is not identical with any variety used by native speakers. Such an approach involves decisions on the micro-level, since it requires that criteria be established for choosing between variants among linguistic features (*cf.* Greenbaum 1974: 253f.). A solution along those lines, which would produce a neutral English *lingua franca,* would have to be imposed by education authorities and is therefore practicable only in countries with a strongly centralized education administration. And unless there is international cooperation, several different forms of 'neutral' English are likely to develop.

Language variation is by no means limited to the differences between standard regional varieties, and even within the standard varieties there is variation. Several of the papers in this volume address themselves to this issue with reference to the acceptability judgments of native speakers. During the last few decades acceptability judgments have assumed crucial significance in linguistic theory and practice, particularly among transformational-generative linguists. The data for linguistic analysis have been the intuitions of native speakers of the language, most importantly their judgments of the acceptability of sentences. Linguists have often found it convenient to refer to their own intuitions, but it is dangerous for a linguist to depend on his introspection as a means of obtaining data: lengthy exposure to a set of examples is likely to blur his judgments, and his reactions will inevitably be prejudiced by his general theoretical position and by the specific hypotheses that predict acceptability judgments (*cf.* Spencer 1973). Even when linguists are not personally involved in formulating hypotheses on acceptability, their reactions often differ from those of nonlinguists, as Snow and Meijer demonstrate in their paper in the present volume. If acceptability judgments are to constitute part of the data for linguistic analysis, it is imperative that linguists collect the data from native informants rather than relying on their own intuitions. As Labov has argued, 'linguists cannot continue to produce theory and data at the same time' (Labov 1972: 199).

More recently it has been claimed that the primary data for linguistics must be speech samples, a view espoused here in the papers by Bickerton, Snow and Meijer, and Tottie. Bickerton is typical of the trend among sociolinguists to question the validity and reliability of intuitive judgments as primary data (*cf.* also Labov 1972: 192–201; Bailey 1973b: 32). At the same time, those three papers maintain that there is intrinsic as well as practical value in investigating linguistic intuitions, particularly intuitions about acceptability. The practical value has usually been the main reason for resorting to acceptability judgments: it derives from the difficulty of collecting sufficient information from speech samples of all but the most frequent linguistic features, a problem that is particularly acute in syntactic analysis and that has therefore led to the development of techniques for eliciting features (Labov 1972: 204f.; *cf.* Greenbaum and Quirk 1970: 1–7). The intrinsic value is more debatable. It has been recognized that acceptability intuitions and language behavior do not necessarily coincide and that informant reactions do not always reflect actual usage. As van Dijk points out, an act of acceptability is implicit in the speaker's production of utterances, yet the producible is not always identical with the acceptable. But command of a language is evidenced by more than actual usage. It includes potential usage (what one might use if the opportunity presented itself, Greenbaum and Quirk 1970: 2); comprehension of variants that others use (Labov 1973); and evaluation of language features in one's own usage and in the usage of others. The evaluations include beliefs about one's own use and that of others, attitudes towards linguistic features and the appropriate linguistic and situational contexts for their use and recognition of norms. Sociolinguists in particular have been insistent on taking account of attitudes. For example, both Fishman and Labov have recognized shared evaluations as criterial for membership of the same speech community. For Fishman a speech community is defined as one in which all members 'share at least a single speech variety and the norms for its appropriate use' (Fishman 1972: 22). While insisting on the primacy of speech samples as data, Labov paradoxically goes so far as to say that 'a speech community cannot be conceived as a group of speakers who all use the same forms; it is best defined as a group who share the same norms in regard to language' (Labov 1972: 158; *cf.* also Bailey 1973a: 175f.). Linguists have generally continued to use intuitions, especially intuitions about acceptability, as primary data for syntactic analysis.

Within theoretical linguistics a distinction has been made between *acceptability,* a concept denoting the reactions of native speakers, and *grammaticality,* denoting what linguists working within a particular theory find feasible, convenient or relevant to account for in their grammar (*cf.* Chomsky 1965: 10–15). The distinction is explicity discussed in the papers by Bickerton, van Dijk, Lakoff and (to a lesser extent) Afolayan. Grammaticality, as Lakoff points out, implies a binary decision on what should be included or excluded from the data accounted for by the grammatical rules. Or, at least, it has implied a binary decision for the kinds of formal rules that linguists have devised during the last couple of decades. Acceptability, on the other hand, does not require a binary distinction between the acceptable and the unacceptable: we can recognize a continuum from the most acceptable to the least acceptable. Furthermore, a given piece of language need not be inherently acceptable or unacceptable. Its acceptability may depend on sociological or psychological factors, such as the social status of the participants in the discourse and their relationship to the situation and the speaker's assumptions (Lakoff 1969).

Several of the papers deal with such factors. Van Dijk cites ample evidence for his claim that a sentence-based grammar cannot predict the acceptability of sentences in a discourse or in a pragmatic situation, since the acceptability of an utterance is relative to the verbal and non-verbal contexts (including the interaction of the participants) in which it is placed. Snow and Meijer make a related point when they assert, on the basis of experimental evidence, that 'Judges seem to be trying to find a situation in which they would use the test sentence; if they cannot find one, then they call it ungrammatical'. This claim is the basis of the paper by Levelt *et al.,* as we shall see later.

Other papers are more concerned with the status of the participants, more specifically the status of the speaker. McDavid and O'Cain, utilizing material on South Carolina from the *Linguistic Atlas of the Middle and South Atlantic States,* analyze the sociolinguistic comments of informants on a number of lexical, phonological and grammatical items and correlate the comments with elicited reports on the usage of those items. The informants are cross-classified by two sets of binary distinctions: cultivated/uncultivated (education) and White/Negro (ethnic group). One of the authors' findings on attitudes and usage is relevant to the current preoccupation of some sociolinguists with Black English: 'Those forms that are labelled Negroisms are not infrequently widely distributed in white speech and are not necessarily predominant among Negroes'. Scholars still disagree as to whether there is a variety (or set of varieties) that is characteristic of Black speakers of American English. Speaking generally, the contenders are divided along the lines of the traditional discipline of dialectology and the newer school of sociolinguistics. Sociolinguists (such as Labov) tend to claim that there is a Black English, while dialectologists (such as McDavid) tend to deny the existence of a distinctive Black English (*cf.* Bailey and Robinson 1973: 237). The authors also point out that attitudes do not necessarily change at the same rate as usage.

Two other papers also refer to education as a factor influencing acceptability: the papers by Svartvik and Wright and by Eagleson. Svartvik and Wright used a series of different types of elicitation tests, most of them developed at the Survey of English Usage, University College London. (Some of these tests are briefly discussed by Tottie.) Their subjects were teenage students living in an area close to London and divided into three groups according to educational ability. Svartvik and Wright demonstrate that the modal auxiliary *ought (to)* is disappearing from the language and is being replaced by *should,* particularly in non-assertive contexts such as questions and negative statements. The experiments were repeated with similar groups three years later; the results indicated that the process of change was continuing at a rapid pace. The investigation therefore provides evidence of a change in *apparent* time (the difference between teenage usage and what is known about adult usage of the same period) and in *real* time (the difference that manifests itself over a three-year interval) (*cf.* Labov 1972: 275). Of particular interest is their finding that the process of change is most advanced in the group with the lowest educational level. This difference in the rate of change affecting a syntactic feature parallels the instances that Labov cites of innovations in pronunciation that spread from a lower class to an upper class (Labov 1972: 286f.). There does not appear to be any social value related to the syntactic change; the linguistic motivation seems to be the elimination of an anomalous construction.

Eagleson's study of certain features in Australian English is also based on the same types of elicitation tests. He too notes that educational differences correlate with choices of syntactic variables, but in his study the educational differences are combined with socio-economic differences. Once again, changes are discernible, and they appear to be initiated in the lower classes. Eagleson reports another effect of education, a differentiation based on the kind of education informants receive at the university level: science students tend to be less conservative than humanities students. This result is in harmony with Rabin's observation that science students are less aware of normative prescriptions.

A different facet of the speaker's identity is discussed in Lakoff's paper. She enumerates the linguistic features that are characteristic of women's language and explains them as related to women's distinctive perceptions of social and psychological contexts. Hence, a consideration of acceptability in language must take account of both the sex of the speaker and the social and psychological context of what is said. Lakoff points to a dilemma for women: whether to conform to the markers of women's language and be treated differently from men, or to adopt men's language (the prestige norm – the standard – in society) and be rejected as speaking deviantly. Language is only one instance of the problem: such a dilemma faces women in all aspects of social behavior where there are different norms for men and women.

Some language variation does not correlate with societal patterning and cannot be ascribed to the status of the speaker or the style of the speech. At least, no evidence of such correlation has been found for some language variation. Even so, it has been suggested that non-societal variation is also systematic and patterned (Bailey 1973a: 164–170). Sociolinguists and psycholinguists, as well as general linguists, need to be aware of that type of variation. One example appears in Mohan's paper.

Mohan's paper brings evidence from acceptability testing to support the claims of a particular theory of grammar. The theory is George Lakoff's 'fuzzy grammar', which is intended to account for non-societal variation. Lakoff's model claims that there is an ordinal scale of acceptability within a speech community such that all the speakers will agree on the relative acceptability of a given set of sentences. They may disagree on a binary distinction between the acceptable and the unacceptable, but that is because speakers may have different acceptability thresholds. Mohan's analysis indicates that variation in acceptability judgments for given sets of sentences is indeed systematic and that there is evidence for ordinal scale hierarchies. If Lakoff's model continues to acquire empirical support, there is an important implication for sociolinguistics. We can define a speech community as a set of speakers sharing the same hierarchies of acceptability.

As Mohan points out, George Lakoff's model invites comparison with Labov's model of variable rules. But Labov's model is intended to account for variable frequency (his variable rules incorporate a rule application probability), whereas Lakoff's model is intended to account for variable acceptability. Hence, the data for Labov's model are speech samples, whereas the data for Lakoff's rules assume acceptability judgments on isolated sentences. Furthermore, Labov's model accounts for sociological factors that influence the applicability of the rules, whereas such factors are not recognized in Lakoff's model. It will be an interesting subject for empirical research to determine how far sociological factors account for all the variation among speakers, both in actual usage and in evaluations of acceptability.

At least some variation seems to depend on personality differences. Mohan cites evidence from his experiments to show that acceptability data include a 'yea-saying' factor, a tendency to accept sentences regardless of what the sentences are. Levelt *et al.* also point to psychological factors in acceptability data. They suggest that a subject's judgment depends on his ability to imagine a context for the sentence or phrase he is judging (*cf.* Bolinger 1968; 1971), and that therefore his reaction will be influenced both by how fertile his imagination is and also by how readily the test material triggers his imagination. Levelt *et al.* demonstrate that concrete ('high imagery') material facilitates judgments more than abstract ('low imagery') material: concrete material tends to be rated higher and to be judged faster. Moreover, paraphrasing time is also faster for concrete material, in conformity with the hypothesis that finding a possible interpretation is in effect finding a possible context. Levelt *et al.* note that the data strongly suggest that before judgments are made only preliminary checks rather than full interpretations take place. These checks are analogous to the sociolinguistic checks that give a listener the clue to the speaker's status and relationship to himself before a full interpretation is made.

It is important for an investigator to be aware of psychological factors of the type discussed by Levelt *et al.* Material included in acceptability experiments is intended to be canonical – representative of a far larger body of material. But the results can be misinterpreted if some or all of the material has some unrepresentative feature. That is a motivation for providing more than one token of the type being tested. Aberrations can then be more easily detected.

In their experiments Snow and Meijer introduced four versions for each sentence type for another reason: to investigate the reliability of acceptability judgments, whether individual subjects rated sentence types consistently. They found a relatively high degree of consistency for acceptability judgments on a three-term scale, though they caution against taking the results at their face value, since 'the asymmetrical scoring tendencies of the subjects inflate their apparent reliability'. Snow and Meijer also asked subjects to rank sets of six sentences in order of acceptability. Though they did not investigate the reliability of ranking judgments, they suggest that the ranking procedure is preferable because subjects can distinguish more than three levels of acceptability. We can meet this argument by asking subjects to judge sentences on a scale that allows for more than three levels, and indeed Mohan provided a 10-point scale in his experiment. Mohan found a greater correlation between the rating and ranking tasks than did Snow and Meijer; presumably, his better result was due to the more discriminating rating scale that he allowed. Note that the preference for ranking over rating tests is not required by the view that acceptability judgments are essentially relative, a view expressed by Levelt *et al.* and inherent in George Lakoff's model of fuzzy grammar. Mohan shows that rating on a multi-point scale yields information also on relative acceptability. All the papers incorporating experimental data point to the need for continuing research into the methodology of acceptability testing and measurement techniques. We have elsewhere demonstrated that results may be affected by the order in which sentences are presented and by the acceptability status of a preceding sentence (Greenbaum 1973, 1977).

Further research is also needed into the nature of acceptability judgments. Snow and Meijer cite evidence from their experimental data to support the contention that the ability to produce acceptability intuitions about a language is distinct from the capacity to speak and understand the language (*cf.* Bever 1970: 341–352). Thus, the group of native nonlinguist speakers bore a closer resemblance in their acceptability intuitions to the group of nonnative bilingual speakers than it did to the group of native linguist speakers. We need to know much more about the variability of acceptability intuitions and its relation to the variability of speech behavior. Both are inherent in human language. Both have, at least in part, their sociological correlates.

REFERENCES

Bailey, R. W., and Robinson, J. L., Eds. (1973), *Varieties of Present-Day English.* New York, Macmillan.

Bailey, C-J. N. (1973a), 'The patterning of language variation', pp. 156–189 in R. W. Bailey, and J. L. Robinson, Eds., *Varieties of Present-Day English.* New York. Macmillan.

– (1973b), *Variation and Linguistic Theory.* Arlington, Virginia, Center for Applied Linguistics.

Bever, T. G. (1970), 'The cognitive basis for linguistic structures', pp. 312–348 in J. R. Hayes, Ed., *Cognition and the Development of Language.* New York, John Wiley.

Bolinger, D. (1968), 'Judgments of grammaticality', *Lingua,* 21, pp. 34–40.

– (1971), 'Semantic overloading: A restudy of the Verb *remind', Language,* 47, pp. 522–547.

Chomsky, N. (1965), *Aspects of the theory of syntax.* Cambridge, Mass., M.I.T. Press.

Fillmore, C. J. (1973), 'A grammarian looks to sociolinguistics', pp. 273–287 in R. W. Shuy, Ed.

Fishman, J., Ed. (1971), *Advances in the Sociology of Language,* Vol. 1: *Basic Concepts, Theories and Problems: Alternative Approaches.* The Hague, Mouton. Reprinted 1976.

– (1972), *The Sociology of Language.* Rowley, Massachusetts, Newbury House.

Greenbaum, S. (1973), 'Informant elicitation of data on syntactic variation', *Lingua,* 31, pp. 201–212.

– (1974), 'Problems in the negation of modals', *Moderna Språk, 68,* pp. 244–255.

– (1976), 'Syntactic frequency and acceptability', *Lingua, 40, pp. 99–113.*

– (1977), 'Contextual influence on acceptability judgements', *International Journal of Psycholinguistics.*

Greenbaum, S., and Quirk, R. (1970), *Elicitation Experiments in English: Linguistic Studies in Use and Attitude.* London and Coral Gables, Florida, Longman and University of Miami Press.

Labov, W. (1972), *Sociolinguistic Patterns*. Philadelphia, University of Pennsylvania Press.
– (1973), 'Where do grammars stop?', pp. 43–88 in R. W. Shuy, Ed.
Lakoff, R. (1969), 'Some reasons why there can't be any *some-any* rules', *Language*, 45, pp. 608–615.
Shuy, R. W., Ed. (1973), *Georgetown University Monograph Series on Languages and Linguistics*, 23. Washington, D. C., Georgetown University Press.
Spencer, N. J. (1973), 'Differences between linguists and nonlinguists in intuitions of grammaticality-acceptability', *Journal of Psycholinguistic Research*, 2, pp. 83–98.

ADEBISI AFOLAYAN

Acceptability of English as a Second Language in Nigeria

A consideration of the degree of acceptability of English in Nigeria raises sociological issues in the broadest sense. Such issues are at once political, educational, economic and social; and there are not only factors that facilitate acceptability but also forces that restrict it.

The political realities of Nigeria by and large facilitate the acceptability of English. Nigeria is a multilingual federation of twelve states. The exact number of languages used in the country is not yet determined, as there is still much linguistic description to be done before the situation can be clear. A recent linguistic investigation (*cf.* Williamson 1968), for example, revealed that what had hitherto been regarded as dialects of one single Ijo language in the Rivers State are in fact different languages, and as many as seventeen of them have now been identified. Yet the Rivers State had always been recognized as one of the multilingual states of the Federation.

From the linguistic point of view, the twelve states belong to three categories: the unilingual (for example, West, Kano and East Central) the multilingual with a dominant language (for example, Lagos, North Central and South-East) and the multilingual with no dominant language (for example Kwara, Mid-West and Rivers). Thus, with the multiplicity of languages[1] the low rate of literacy in English among her citizens, and the use of English as the only medium of her national politics, it is generally true to say that, as a single political entity, Nigeria today has barely passed that stage of deserving the epithet 'a colonial geographical expression'. It is true she has recently[2] fought successfully a civil war 'to keep the country one'.[3] It is true she has been actively pursuing a program of post-civil-war rehabilitation and reconstruction. But it is equally true that she is still a nation of nations, amalgamated into a political unit by Britain sixty years ago and held together by the language then imposed upon her.

Ethnicity rather than one strong nationality is the centripetal force most noticeable among the peoples of the Federation. The various ethnic languages are therefore the greatest and most forceful political media. Yet ethnicity with its accompanying diverse languages cannot be a direct, potent agency for forging out a common and strong nationality. Consequently, the Federal Government in promoting national unity and strength has always pursued a practical language policy. The number of the indigenous languages of the country makes it impracticable to adopt any one of them as the national language. English therefore by its neutrality recommends itself as the only choice available for adoption as a national language. No one ethnic group can feel cheated through its use as it naturally would if the language of another ethnic group were adopted. Thus before and after independence the English language has been generally accepted as the only possible national language in practice, though it is not so recognized in the written constitution of the country. It is accepted as the language of the nation's legislature, judiciary and administration.

The sociological acceptance of English in Nigerian education has been nearly complete, more so, probably, than in any other aspect of the national life. There is politics without English. There is trade without it. Administration takes place at the local level without it. But there cannot be any pretence at formal education wherever and whenever English cannot be used as the medium of instruction or at least taught as a subject. All existing nursery schools are English-medium. In certain places primary education begins with English as the medium and remains English-medium throughout. In some others primary education, which begins in the first two or three years in a local language,[4] is fully developed, completed and examined only in the English language. Secondary education is given and examined throughout in English; it cannot be regarded as successful without a pass in the English language.[5] As would be expected, university education is given and examined in the English language alone, and, as the level of attainment in the language is being generally noted in the country to be inadequate for scholarship, the necessity for a compulsory 'Use of English' course for all undergraduates before certification is increasingly being felt and met. Thus formal education in Nigeria is taken to be synonymous with a knowledge of English. Whoever has no access to English has no access to formal education.

Economically, the multilingual situation also facilitates the acceptability of English, although to a lesser extent than in the fields of politics or education. Unlike the political and education fields, the economic field, marked chiefly by the employment of labor, commercial and trading activities, does not necessarily demand literacy. Here is a field where activities may be grouped under two heads: external and internal. Those activities involving Nigeria and any other country are external, and those involving component parts of the country as partners are internal. The internal then sub-divides into two: interethnic and intraethnic. Economic activities among members of an ethnic group are thus intraethnic, while those across ethnic boundaries are interethnic. Of the three final (sub)sets of activities – external, interethnic and intraethnic – only the external would always require the use of an international language. External economic activities are controlled at national (Federal) rather than the local (State, Province, Divisional or District) level, and English is the accepted international language. The interethnic activities do not necessarily require the use of English and indeed do so on a rather restricted scale. For example, cattle is one of the main objects of interethnic economic activity in Nigeria, and the process of buying and selling is hardly ever conducted in English. Non-Hausa-speaking Nigerians who trade in a commodity such as cattle produced and sold by Hausa-speaking people usually learn to use Hausa. Similarly other Nigerians who seek employment in the labor market owned, manned and directed by members of another speech community usually learn to use the language of the community.

The intraethnic economic activities are independent of the use of English. This is not to suggest that English is sociologically banned in such intraethnic activities. On the one hand, certain activities, particularly in the trades, involve much borrowing from English into the local language. The Yoruba carpenters, for example, make use of *sukurudireba* (screw-driver), *dosipleni* (dutch-plane) and *soo* (saw). On the other hand, increasing urbanization and population movement mean the destruction of the homogeneity of speech-communities through the introduction of other ethnic groups as non-negligible elements within the speech communities.

This is true of most state capitals and particularly of Lagos, the Federal capital. The co-existence of members of different ethnic groups in a location necessarily creates a mini-state of interethnic economic activities rather than purely intraethnic. And as such the activities may sometimes permit the use of English as the medium, although the use of the local language of the speech community (that is, the language of the majority and native element of the community) is the norm.

And this brings us to social aspects. Any bilingual or multilingual situation usually requires the specialization of roles of the different languages involved. Although the language situation in Nigeria has been referred to as multilingual, it can be said that the practical norm is bilingual. This is because, in any given situation demanding a language act, two choices are normally available for use: the local indigenous Nigerian language and the English language. Generally the English language is reserved for official activities and the local languages for the nonofficial, though code-switching, partial or full,[6] is common practice in all situations. However, the presence of members of several different ethnic groups at any given location for whatever purpose demands the use of English throughout, and, in such circumstances, only English is acceptable. The use of any local language by any sub-group of the audience will appear distasteful. Since the occurrence of such situations is unavoidable in cosmopolitan centers as well as national institutions, it can be said that the social situation of the country facilitates the acceptability of the English language. Undoubtedly the facilitating influence of this social condition is less than is the political, educational or economic condition.

The sociological factors not only *facilitate* the acceptability of English. Their influence may also be negative.

Politics can hinder the acceptability of English. Some nationalists cannot accept that the sovereignty of the nation is complete if it has to depend on a foreign language for the conduct of their internal and external affairs. Nigeria is not without this type of nationalistic feeling, and, since independence, she has never lacked agitation for the adoption nationally of an indigenous language. Although the government has not yielded to this pressure, it has been giving more recognition to the indigenous language. This is particularly true in the field of education.

Educationally, the acceptance of the English language has not been altogether healthy. This is particularly true at the primary school level. There is no doubt that most of the products of primary education will live and die in their local communities. It is among those who go beyond primary education that the main crop of contributors to the national life of the country will come, and primary education is terminal for most of the children who experience it. Even the Universal Primary Education program is not aimed at producing radical changes in this connection, since it is not envisaged that anything beyond some vocational training after primary education will be the norm. Indeed one of the main objectives of the program is the control of rural-urban population movement through the development of rural areas and the consequent retention of the citizens of such areas within them. If properly executed, the Universal Primary Education program will ensure that most pupils will live and die within their own local speech communities. Worthwhile education for such people should give them permanent literacy and the opportunity for further self-education. Certainly such permanent literacy is more easily obtained for everybody in the mother tongues of the people than in a foreign language. It seems correct to declare:

> It is axiomatic that the best medium for teaching a child is his mother-tongue. Psychologically, it is the system of meaningful signs that in his mind works automatically for expression and understanding. Sociologically, it is a means of identification among the members of the community to which he belongs. Educationally, he learns more quickly through it than through an unfamiliar linguistic medium.[7]

Thus it would seem that the more the authorities agree to make fundamental education effective and functional, the more acceptable the indigenous Nigerian languages and the less acceptable the English language as the medium. This resultant reduction in the acceptability of the English language within the field of education seems right and desirable as long as it is restricted to fundamental education. But a multilingual country like Nigeria cannot afford to reduce the role of English in secondary and tertiary education. Indeed it would seem that if the use of *each* local indigenous Nigerian language as the medium of primary education is promoted wherever practicable, and if only specialist teachers are employed for the teaching of English as a second language and materials are specially constructed for that purpose, then better and more effective English may result.[8] The present situation whereby ill-equipped teachers lacking proficiency in the language teach English would therefore disappear. Also, as the pupils come in contact with better teachers or are under the pressure of a national or academic demand for minimum intelligibility of their own form of English, a stop would be put to the wasteful process whereby pupils can learn bad habits. Similarly, the indefensible and impracticable assumption underlying the present practice of making every primary teacher not only teach the language but also teach in it would be halted. The assumption is that every teacher is capable of learning a second language and becoming so proficient in it that he can effectively impart it to others. This is implausible: we can assume such proficiency only if the language is the mother tongue of the teachers. That the existing policy is wrong-headed is borne out by the fact that all efforts by the Ministries of Education and the British Council to improve the teaching of English in the country through various courses have produced minimum positive results. If now, instead of the present unproductive practice, at that stage of basic education the question of acquiring the English language for some specialist functions could be separated from the learning of basic knowledge and skills, it would seem that the result would be a primary education that gives better enlightenment while at the same time providing a more solid foundation for learning and using English effectively. After all, few teachers (about a quarter of the total strength[9]) would be needed as specialist English teachers, and an efficient process of selecting and training of those with a flair for learning a second language would ensure success.

There is also negative economic and social influence, though it is less than the political and educational. The language most suited to the expression of local cultural matters is undoubtedly the language that accompanies and forms a part of the total culture. On the other hand, an attempt to use English to express such cultural matters would lead to the enrichment of the language itself. Indeed if a multilingual society such as Nigeria has to use the English language to express her culture, the inevitable result will be the emergence of a new dialect of the language. Such a development is bound to have an influence on the acceptability of the English language in such a community. Thus one can envisage that social considerations are bound to enhance, in the long run, the acceptability of the language in Nigeria. The economic influence is less than the social, and economic independence does not necessarily affect language directly.

This takes us to the purely linguistic aspect of our topic. From the linguistic point of view, acceptability is related to grammaticality. In this respect, acceptability is associated with the intuition the users of a language have about the appropriateness or correctness of any utterance in the language. Directly or indirectly this intuition is related to what Chomsky (1965) would refer to as competence. It would seem that if we follow his concept of competence, we cannot talk about the acceptability of English forms to Nigerian speakers. It is true that the distinction is made that 'acceptability is a concept that belongs to the study of performance, whereas grammaticality belongs to the study of competence' (Chomsky 1965: 11). But it is equally true that the point is well made that 'investigation of performance will proceed only so far as understanding of underlying competence permits', and effective and concrete performance studies have to be 'based on assumptions about underlying competence' (Chomsky 1965: 10). That is the crux of the matter. Classical presentation of competence sees it as something that can only be associated with the native speakers of a language; and consequently any concrete generalization in performance studies such as acceptability seems to be ruled out in a community using a language as a second one. However, we would not like to draw such a conclusion about English in Nigeria. It would seem that bilingual experience suggests that competence is transferable from one's mother tongue to a second language. It would therefore seem more fruitful to conceive competence in universalistic rather than particularistic terms.

Conceptually, competence goes with native speakers, but native speakers constitute a sociological phenomenon with no serious biological, racial or geographical implications. A person's mother tongue is his primary and most intimate language. It is the language in which he has the greatest facility. The curious feature of bilingualism is the possibility of role-changing between the two languages involved. In the life of a bilingual, it is possible for his sequentially first and second languages to take turns in being his mother tongue.[10] This being so it is clear that competence insofar as it really exists in an individual speaker is not significantly different from the ideal performance of that speaker in the language. Again, it should be noted that, as far as individuals are concerned, competence does not exist in the ideal form but in varying degrees. A stage may be reached, therefore, at which the second language learner of English in Nigeria may have developed a special intuition in the language as a result of his having obtained so high a level of performance in it that he can be seen to have acquired a degree of competence found in some native speaker of the language. A demonstration or application of this degree of competence in social contexts implies a demonstration of acceptability.

For us, then, competence in any given language can be acquired by foreign as well as native speakers of the language. We concede that competence is a tree that would naturally grow on native rather than foreign soil, but we insist that the tree can also grow on foreign soil that has acquired the properties of the native. It would seem that is why we can now discuss today British English side by side with American, Australian, Canadian or South African English. It would seem also why we must be able to speak of Nigerian English as a distinct dialect, the grammar of which is to be described in terms of the competence of Nigerians in the language.

The agency for promoting this competence in English in Nigeria is here taken to be education. It is only when there has developed in the country what can be referred to as an educated usage of English that there can emerge a Nigerian standard dialect of English; and it is only when there clearly exists a Nigerian educated English that the notion 'acceptability' can become demonstrable, describable and analyzable. But the tradition of using English and, indeed, the traditions of literacy and of formal education are as yet too young in Nigeria for a full development of a special educated brand of English usage. Undoubtedly the seed has been planted. There is already emerging, no matter at what inchoate state it may be, the notion of what is acceptable or what is educated. And surely it will grow to rich fruition in the future,[11] as long as the English language remains a second language in multilingual Nigeria and as long as it is backed by progressively improved and effective processes of teaching, learning and use in meaningful contexts.

From the lexical point of view the features of a Nigerian dialect of English are obvious to any observer of the Nigerian scene. This is not surprising since the area of vocabulary is where the contact of a language with another culture and geographical environment is recorded. Consequently, apart from words directly borrowed from Nigerian languages such as *oba, obi* and *obong* (from Yoruba, Ibo and Efik, respectively, each meaning a king or chieftain) there are abundant new words, such as *motor-park* or *lorry-park* (a station for lorries or buses), *mammy waggon* (a passenger lorry), *chewing stick* (a slice of a species of plant used by Nigerians as a tooth-brush), *market-woman* (woman trader), *acada woman* (female graduate or undergraduate), *go-slow* (a traffic jam), *pounded-yam* (a Nigerian food item, a kind of dough made out of a tropical tuber), *long-leg* (nepotism) and *been-to* (a person who has been abroad and has some foreign idiosyncracies). In addition, there are words that have referents different from those of British or American English words, such as *brother* (besides British or American meanings, a male person close to one, not necessarily a blood relation, and sometimes restricted to someone older than the speaker but not as old as his father), *sister* (a female counterpart of *brother,* as just described), and *father* (a male parent; also a relation, and sometimes any respected person as old as one's father). However, since the vocabulary of English is open-ended, it is not usually associated with linguistic acceptability. The notion of grammaticality associated with words is phonological and syntactical rather than lexical.

The levels of phonetics and phonology are the most sociologically interesting with respect to acceptability. No Nigerian standard pronunciation of English has emerged, and it may well be that rather than having only one standard there may be several standards built around the major indigenous languages of Nigeria. After all, pronunciation is that area of language use where linguistic interference from a bilingual's mother tongue is greatest. One might then naturally expect the emergence of several standards of pronunciation of English in Nigeria because of the existence of possibly hundreds of Nigerian languages. But several centripetal factors are also at work. First, almost all of the well-known languages of the country belong to the same Kwa family; hence, they all carry similar features of interference into their English. Secondly, most secondary schools and all post-secondary institutions are national in character. This means that pupils and students of various ethnic groups live together, learn English under the same institutional influences and thereby tend to acquire the same form of pronunciation. Thirdly, pronunciation is that area where effective teaching can be conducted over a large area to many people at the same time. Thus, for example, the use of radio, both in normal broadcasting and in special school broadcasts, has a unifying effect. This is particularly so as British Received Pronunciation forms the basis of all books, records and tapes made available for school teaching. Consequently, although there has not yet emerged one Nigerian standard,[12] there are two common characteristics of English spoken in the country. There is generally a lack of distinction between long and short vowels, and tones are used instead of stresses, giving the output a peculiar rhythmic and intonational pattern nearer to a syllable-timed language than a stress-timed one. However, there are two interesting aspects of public reaction to English pronunciation in Nigeria that touch upon acceptability. On the one hand, fluency is considered as a desirable element of English pronunciation, and lack of fluency is derided. On the other hand, the greater the resemblance of one's pronunciation to the Received Pronunciation model the more it is frowned upon as being hypercorrect. This second issue to an appreciable extent works against maximum success of practical phonetic classes at the institutions of higher learning, particularly the universities. In effect both non-fluent speech and hypercorrect British (Received Pronunciation) forms of English pronunciation are not encouraged generally in the country.

Educated usage, which is taken here as more or less what determines the standard form of a language or standard forms of the dialects of it, is most reflected in syntax rather than in lexis, phonology or phonetics. Thus of all the linguistic levels syntax is the one least affected by dialectal variations. Consequently the syntax of English in Nigeria is generally under the same concept of grammaticality (and degrees of it) as may be found in the World Standard English. Unlike in phonology, where there is a great difference between what is regarded as grammatical (say, British Received Pronunciation) and what is considered as acceptable (say, fluent speech marked by very little distinction between short and long vowels and resembling syllable-timed rather than stress-timed speech), there is very little gap between syntactical grammaticality and syntactical acceptability of English in Nigeria. The notion of syntactical grammaticality usually determines the syntactical acceptability of any expression. That, however, does not mean that the level of syntax is free from linguistic interference.

Indeed, there is considerable linguistic interference at the level of syntax. Unlike in phonology and phonetics, and more like what obtains in lexis, the centripetal factors earlier noted tend to produce the same common syntactic effects throughout the country. Consequently, the syntax of Nigerian English is marked by deviant uses of prepositions, such as the wrong use of *in* for *at, on* for *at*, and *to* for *from;* the omission of prepositions *(knock the door);* and the omission or insertion of the determiner (as in *got to post office*). Similarly, the syntax is characterized by peculiar use of tenses (particularly the frequent use of the present progressive instead of simple present, as in *we are learning English every day at school* and *we are hearing you, speak on*) and the deviant use of modals such as *will, can, shall* and *may,* in contrast with *would, could, should* and *might,* particularly in the expression of politeness (*cf.* Afolayan 1974).

With the rapid growth in education[13] and the consequent pressure on the forging of educated usage, we are now in Nigeria at a stage when we are aware of common errors and have the urge to eradicate them, and we even make efforts to that end. But as Charles Barber has aptly noted in respect to semantic change:

> A mistake by a single speaker will not have any lasting effect on the language, but often the mistake is committed by many speakers, because of some typical situation in which the word is commonly used, or perhaps because of something in the structure of the word itself, and then a semantic change is in process (Barber 1964: 11).

Nigerian common errors in using the World Standard English are bound to result in the development of a Nigerian Standard English and with it a full notion of linguistic acceptability of English in Nigeria.[14] In particular, common errors that have common sociological, psychological and linguistic sources are so bound. Such are the use of *good night* as a parting greeting at the end of a school day at about 2:00 p.m. or at the close of offices at about 3:00 p.m.; the use of *on* instead of *in,* in *sleep on bed* or *shoot him on the head;* and the use of the peculiarly Nigerian English expression *on seat.*[15]

NOTES

1. In effect the country is without any language spoken and used by the majority of her citizens. The sociolinguistic situation is made yet more complex by the fact that the

numerical strength of the effective users of English may indeed be weaker than that of each of the three leading indigenous languages of the country (Igbo, Hausa and Yoruba).

2. The post-independence political situation of the country led to a *coup d'etat* in January 1966 and a counter-*coup* in July, and it culminated in a civil war which began in July 1967 and ended in January 1970.
3. During the Civil War the slogan of the Federal Government of Nigeria was: 'To keep Nigeria one is a task that must be done.'
4. The languages used at the intital stage of primary education by the various states include the following: North-Western State, Hausa; North-Central State, Hausa; North-Eastern State, Hausa and Kanuri; Kano State, Hausa; Kwara State, Hausa, Igala and Yoruba; Benue-Plateau State, Hausa, Idoma and Tiv; Lagos State, Yoruba; Western State, Yoruba; Mid-Western State, Edo, Igbo, Ijo, Ishan, Isoko, Itsekiri, Ora, Urhobo and Yoruba; East Central State, Igbo; South-Eastern State, Efik; and Rivers State, Ijo and various languages that were earlier mistaken for dialects of Ijo (see Williamson 1968 and the text above).
5. As a result of largely political arguments clothed in a specious academic garb, a policy of not making a pass in English necessary for obtaining a certificate was embarked upon in 1964. The policy has proved such an academic failure that it is now being abandoned.
6. Full code-switching is marked by the use of a language other than the one the speaker has been using in a discourse to express a full sentence, a paragraph or even a longer stretch completing the discourse. Partial code-switching is marked by the interpolation of a word or words or any fragment of a sentence in another language into a discourse otherwise expressed in a different language. In each case, of course, the languages involved are English and any indigenous Nigerian language such as Efik, Edo, Igbo, Hausa, Kalabari or Yoruba.
7. See UNESCO Monographs on Fundamental Education 1953. Note that this claim is being tested out in educational research, the Six-Year Yoruba-Medium Primary Project, undertaken by the Institute of Education of the University of Ife, Ile-Ife. The experiment is in its sixth year, and the results so far are positive.
8. This alternative approach to educational language problems in being currently attempted by the Six-Year Yoruba-Medium Primary Project (note 7). Evaluation reports, formal and informal, of the Project so far have suggested that it may indeed be a more rewarding approach.
9. This figure has been suggested as a result of the experience of the Primary Project (see notes 7 and 8).
10. A son of the present writer has demonstrated this possibility. He went to London before he was three. There he attended a day nursery where he was the only non-British child and subsequently went to a primary school. Thus he learned his English entirely from native speakers of the language. He lived with his parents who, desirous of keeping him bilingual, spoke to him always in Yoruba, the only language (an indigenous Nigerian one) the child knew before going to Britain. At the age of seven the child returned to Nigeria, completed his elementary education in the University of Ife Staff School (an English-medium international school) and is now attending a Western State Government Secondary School. When he arrived in Britain, his mother tongue was obviously Yoruba. By the time he returned to Nigeria his primary language (mother tongue?) was English. But now, once again, his mother tongue is Yoruba.
11. There has been considerable debate in the country among teachers and scholars of English whether the Nigerian Standard English has arrived or not. Articles on the

subject have appeared in the *Journal of the Nigeria English Studies Association*. The two suggesting that the Nigerian Standard English has arrived (Walsh 1967 and Adekunle 1974) have not, in the opinion of the present writer, shown more than that such a dialect is actively in the making. The former attaches too much importance to common errors, and the latter, although reflecting a greater analytical study of the situation, fails to give adequate attention to the notion of 'educated usage' (what it is and who uses it, where and when). The present writer believes that the common features in Nigerian English today fall under three separate categories: the uneducated ones which are bound to be outside Nigerian Standard English; the educated but less likely candidates for final adoption; and the educated and likely candidates for final adoption. The validity of this suggestion may demand a fuller treatment but such cannot be attempted here and is, in any case, not centrally relevant to the topic at hand. It is sufficient to note that the major factor that distinguishes the last two categories is whether Nigerian speakers with at least secondary education can intuitively recognize a common error as such or not. If they do, the error is less likely for adoption as an item in Nigerian Standard English, unless there are very strong sociolinguistic or psycholinguistic pressures for its adoption. If, however, the error is generally regarded to be non-deviant, then it is a candidate for final adoption.

12. See Strevens (1965) for a description of the features of the kinds of English pronunciation common not only in Nigeria but also in West Africa, resulting from the various factors described here.
13. Secondary and post-secondary education (particularly at the university) can be regarded as the greatest contributor to the emergence of educated usage of English. There has been much growth in both levels of education recently. For example, prior to independence in 1960 there was only one institution giving university education (University College, Ibadan, in special relationship with the University of London) but now there are six full-fledged degree-granting universities (at Benin, Ibadan, Ife, Lagos, Nsukka and Zaria), each with a student population more than four times that of the previously existing single one. Yet the recently launched Third National Development Programme (1975–1980) aims at increasing the pace of development: four new universities are expected to be built and the existing ones greatly expanded.
14. It must be noted that both British and American dialects of English have very strong influences on the form of English used in Nigeria. Since Nigerian independence in particular American influence has been increasing, partly because of the United States' role in international affairs and partly because of Nigeria's increasing acceptance of American forms of education. The West African Examinations Council is bound to play some significant role in this process of establishing degrees of linguistic acceptability of English in Nigeria. All schools take the same examinations conducted by it. Besides, there is the great direct and indirect effect of the process of standardizing the setting and assessment of the examinations through examiners, largely drawn from the ranks of Nigerian teachers. The Nigeria English Studies Association, an academic society for teachers of English, with its journal and annual conferences, may also have a significant contribution to make.
15. Errors such as those involving the use of *good night* have sociolinguistic sources. The equivalent of *good night* in several Nigerian languages (*Okiakhwe* of Etsako, *Sai gobai* of Hausa, *Ba wa eria* of Kalabari, *O ki nha kho* of Uneme and *O daa ro* of Yoruba) literally means 'till next morning or day', and, although mostly used in the evening, can be used any other time of the day when people are parting for the day. In contrast, the deviant use of *on* for *in* (or vice versa), as in *sleep on bed, shoot him on the head* and

get in the train, have sociolinguistic, psycholinguistic and purely linguistic sources. Nigerians usually sleep on bed-sheets, not in them; they perceive the gunshot as affecting the surface of the head; and in their mother tongues a single word can be glossed as *in, on* or *at* (for example, Yoruba *ni*).

REFERENCES

Adekunle, M. A. (1974), 'The standard Nigerian English', *Journal of the Nigeria English Studies Association,* 6 (1).

Afolayan, A. (1974), 'Politeness in English', *Journal of the Nigeria English Studies Association,* 6 (1).

Barber, C. L. (1964), *Linguistic Change in Present-Day English.* Edinburgh and London, Oliver and Boyd.

Chomsky, N. (1965), *Aspects of the Theory of Syntax.* Cambridge, Mass., M.I.T. Press.

Lyons, J., and Wales, R. J., Eds. (1966), *Psycholinguistic Papers.* Edinburgh, Edinburgh University Press.

UNESCO Monographs on Fundamental Education (1953), *The Use of Vernacular Languages in Education,* Vol. 8. Paris, UNESCO.

Quirk, R. (1966), 'Acceptability in language', pp. 184–201 in R. Quirk, *Essays on the English Language: Medieval and Modern.* London, Longman.

Strevens, P. D. (1965), 'Pronunciation of English in West Africa', in P. D. Strevens, *Papers in Language and Language Teaching.* London, Oxford University Press.

Walsh, N. G. (1967), 'Distinguishing types and varieties of English in Nigeria', *Journal of the Nigeria English Studies Association,* 2 (2).

Williamson, K. (1968), 'Languages of the Niger Delta', *Nigeria,* 97, pp. 124–130.

DEREK BICKERTON

Some Problems of Acceptability and Grammaticality in Pidgins and Creoles

As was perceptively observed by Ardener (1971), pidgins (contact languages lacking native speakers) and creoles (languages claimed to have resulted from the nativization of pidgins) have long constituted a thorn in the side of general linguistic theories, offering data for which those theories could never provide adequate explanation. The field of acceptability is no exception to this state of affairs.

The problem of determining what are acceptable utterances in pidgins and creoles has, indeed, been compounded by the chequered career of pidgin-creole studies. Until quite recently, for instance, 'young linguists [were] advised not to waste their time on such peripheral subjects but to study 'real' languages if they wanted to get on in the academic world' (DeCamp 1971: 13). A major reason for academic disapproval was the belief that pidgins and creoles were not 'true languages' insofar as they lacked any coherent and uniform system of grammatical rules. In reaction to this, pioneers in the field (see especially Hall 1955) felt obliged to insist that pidgins and creoles were every bit as systematic and rule-bound as standard languages were then supposed to be. Thus, any data that showed the existence of variation in pidgins and creoles were minimized or simply ignored, and, in a number of cases, idealized descriptions were produced which bore only a limited relationship to what the majority of speakers actually uttered. Variation is, however, almost always present, and there are two processes to which creoles are prone which greatly increase its incidence. These are decreolization (the tendency to merge with the European language with which the creole is related – a tendency which seems to occur whenever the two are in contact) and repidginization (a process which may result when a creole language is used as a second or contact language by neighboring populations who have limited access to native-speaker models).

However, now that work by Labov, C.-J. Bailey, Carden, etc., has shown that standard languages themselves are full of variation the pidgin-creolist no longer has to prove that his field comes up to scratch in this respect. Rather than grooming his candidates for entrance to the Proper Languages Club, he can now begin to ask questions such as what we are to understand by 'acceptability' and 'grammaticality' in a pidgin or creole context, what reliance we can place on speaker intuitions and to what extent a valid grammar can be based on such intuitions.

But before we can begin to consider such questions, we may need to re-evaluate rather thoroughly the nature of pidgins and creoles. Hitherto, these have been treated as autonomous language systems which constitute, for all intents and purposes, steady states; in Bickerton (1974; 1975), however, massive evidence is produced to show that they can be more accurately conceptualized as stages (still none-too-well defined) in an ongoing process. This is not, of course, an original idea – the notion of a 'pidgin-creole cycle' was put forward by Hall (1962) – but its descriptive implications are likely to remain largely ungrasped as long as a static-synchronic paradigm reigns in general linguistics. The nature of the process is illustrated in Figure 1.

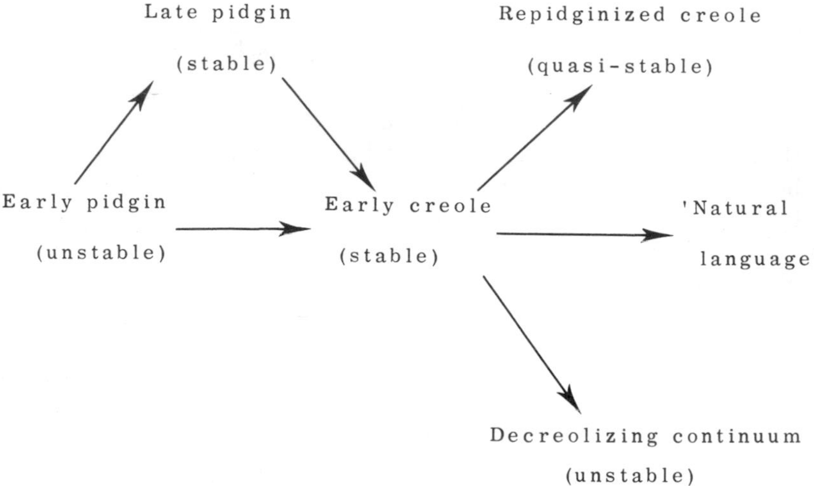

Figure 1. *The pidgin-creole cycle and the stability of its stages*

Thus we see that a pidgin may creolize early while still in an unstable condition (the case of Hawaii, and probably of most or all Caribbean creoles) or late, when it has been leveled and stabilized by several decades of use (the case of Tokpisin). Subsequently, it may continue on its course like any independent language (e.g., Sranan), repidginize through use as a contact vernacular on the fringe of its native area (e.g.,

Krio) or decreolize through prolonged contact with its related superordinate language (e.g., Jamaican Creole, Gullah, etc.). As indicated, these stages will differ considerably in their degree of linguistic stability, and these differences will have clear consequences for the status of acceptability judgments at each stage.

As regards the early stages of pidgin development, our researches in Hawaii have provided independent support for Silverstein's (1972) position that there is no such thing as 'competence in a pidgin', but that speakers, working from the grammar of their own native languages, add extension rules which generate superficially similar surface structures. To Silverstein's analysis of Chinook Jargon, I would add only two points; first, that surface outputs need not even be similar (Japanese speakers of Hawaiian Pidgin often have SOV surface order, Filipino speakers virtually never do), and, second, that at least some speakers in a pidgin situation may be capable of imitating the outputs of members of language groups other than their own. As one such speaker put it, 'If I am to talk to somebody else, I have to talk their way.' This speaker, of predominantly Hawaiian ancestry, reported herself as saying to an elderly Japanese lady, *mago dis said go, wasamada yu no lidi weichi yo?* 'Your granddaughter went that way, why don't you wait a little while?', instead of the more general Hawaiian pidgin *yu grandata go dis said, wasamada yu no weit lili bit?* Note the speaker's use of Japanese lexical items (*mago*, 'grandchild', *yo*, emphatic particle), of Japanese word order (sentence-final *go, weichi*, 'wait') and of Japanese phonological features such as paragogic vowels. The same speaker quite consciously rationalized this process:

> So we use the Hawaiian and Chinese altogether, in one sentence, see: And they ask me if that's a Hawaiian word, I said no, maybe that's a Japanese word we put in, to make a sentence with a Hawaiian word, and the Chinese the same way too . . . in order to make a sentence for them to understand you.'[1]

In this early-pidgin, macaronic stage, one could argue that nothing is grammatical but that anything is acceptable, provided that it works communicatively. Nothing can be grammatical because there is, as yet, no grammar distinct from the quite different grammars of the contributing languages. That speakers may permute those grammars as well as the different lexicons is shown by the example above, and it is not easy to see what constraints, if any, would govern that process.

However, this state of affairs must gradually yield, over time, to one which more closely approximates that of a 'normal' language community. Again, an anecdote may best illustrate conditions where a pidgin has stabilized.[2] A linguist doing fieldwork in the Solomon Islands was carrying writing materials into a new house when a young boy who knew him, but whose control of Solomon Islands pidgin was far from perfect, called out:

Masta em i pepa em i haus.

What he meant was, of course,

'The white man is carrying papers into his house'.

But what he actually said was something like

'The white man is paper he is house'.

Everyone in earshot spontaneously burst into roars of laughter and repeated the boy's solecism over and over with gleeful chuckles, because everyone knew that he should have said:

Masta em i karim pepa i go long haus.

Such a situation would be unthinkable if there were not stable norms of acceptability to which speakers could refer; in Hawaii, nobody laughs at anything anyone says, no matter how outlandish, and local standards of courtesy form only part of the explanation for this. We must assume, pending research in this area, that the relationship between grammaticality and acceptability does not differ significantly from that which holds in developed languages, and the same is probably even more true of a creole that has undergone neither repidginization nor decreolization. However, when we encounter these two latter phenomena, the picture again changes rather abruptly.

About repidginization, not much is yet known. Comments by Berry (1961) on variation in Krio lead one to suppose that it creates a wide spectrum of different lects and that, in consequence, speakers might differ considerably on what they regarded as acceptable. It would not seem likely, however, that this variation would ever approximate the near anarchy of the early pidgin stage, since in repidginization (as with the pidginization of African languages in territories adjoining their homeland) there exists a model (in this case, the developed creole) which is physically accessible and also (if 'natural-semantactic', as claimed in Bickerton 1974) easier to learn than one of the so-called 'natural languages'.[3] About decreolization, on the other hand, a good deal is now known – enough, at least, for one to be able to state that it poses problems of acceptability and grammaticality more acute, perhaps, than in any other field of language.

Let us begin with a typical example. On one occasion, a passage written in standard English was given to a class of twenty first-year undergraduates in the University of Guyana. All of the students were native Guyanese, and it should be emphasized that all were from working-class or lower-middle-class backgrounds and were in full-time employment (at the time in question – 1969 – all classes were held at night and the well-to-do sent their children overseas to college); they were therefore all in contact with some lect or lects of the local vernacular. They were asked to translate the passage into their idea of Guyanese Creole. We need go no further than the first three words, 'I was sitting . . .', translated in no less than thirteen different ways:

(1) *a woz sitin.*
(2) *ai de sidong.*
(3) *mi bin sidong.*
(4) *a de sitin.*
(5) *a bin sitin.*
(6) *a did sidong.*
(7) *ai biin sitin.*
(8) *mi bina sidong.*
(9) *ai bin sitin dong.*
(10) *a bina sidong.*
(11) *a woz sitin dong.*
(12) *a did sitin.*
(13) *mi bina sit.*

Are we to assume these students did not know their own language? The suggestion seems absurd, yet in what noncreole language could the same simple affirmative statement be made in even a fraction as many synonymous forms? And what could be done by the orthodox generative linguist who elicited these thirteen forms from his first thirteen informants? The answer to the last may be readily guessed: he can ignore the bulk of them, especially those that can be treated as 'English interference' (as if any Anglo-Creole didn't owe its very *existence* to 'English interference'!) and pick out either the commonest one or the one that looked least like English, listing one or two others as 'dialectal variants'.[4] He can thus produce a grammar that will look like what traditional grammars of languages are supposed to look like. He will, however (as I have shown at some length in Bickerton 1975), completely distort the real grammar of the community and produce an artefact that does not have observational, let alone descriptive, adequacy.

If we examine examples 1–13, we will note that, in addition to any lexical or phonological differences, there are representatives of no less than nine different verbal structures, viz. *woz* + *Ving, de* + V, *bin* + V, *de* + *Ving, bin* + *Ving, did* + V, *biin* + *Ving, bina* + V, and *did* + *Ving.* Far from being the performance errors of speakers 'ignorant of their own language', we find that all these structures occur, some with a high degree of frequency, in recordings of natural Guyanese speech:

(14)	*a woz workin az a kuk*	'I was working as a cook' (*cf.* 1,11)
(15)	*mi de a luk mi kau*	'I was there looking for my cow' (*cf.* 2)
(16)	*mi bin gatu wea lang buuts*	'I had to wear long boots' (*cf.* 3)
(17)	*a de tekin aut di pleits*	'I was taking the plates out' (*cf.* 4)
(18)	*a bin duin dat ting stedi*	'I was doing that continuously' (*cf.* 5,9)
(19)	*a did step pan yu lang taim*	'I would have trodden on you long ago' (*cf.* 6)
(20)	*we biin planin tu go tu yu*	'We were planning on going to you' (*cf.* 7)
(21)	*mi bina go fu Dewan*	'I was going for Dewan' (*cf.* 8, 10, 13)
(22)	*sambadi elsiz haus hi did goin tu ripeer*	'It was somebody else's house he was going to repair' (*cf.* 12)

In six out of the nine cases, there is identity of form and meaning between the translations and their equivalent recorded examples. As for the remaining three cases, there is one difference of form (15) and two differences of meaning (16, 19). Let us take the difference of form first: *de* + *a* + V, of which we have several attestations, is a not particularly common basilectal form: *de* + V does not occur at all in recorded material. However, there is an independently motivated phonological rule which assimilates adjacent low vowels across morpheme boundaries, and it is conceivable that, for some speakers, this rule might extend to mid-front vowels, giving *de* from *de a.* We may conclude that 2 is of rather dubious grammaticality. The meaning differences are a little more complex. Normally, the *bin* of 3 and the *did* of 6 both have a point-action or unrealised-condition meaning when they co-occur with non-stative verbs (as *did* does in 19) or a past-state meaning when they co-occur with statives (as *bin* does in 16); they cannot refer to a continuous action when they are found, as in 3, 6, 16 and 19, with the unmarked verb-stem. However, the primary meaning of *sidong* is not 'to sit down (action)' but 'to sit (state)', and it may be an eccentricity of English, rather than of Creole,[5] that the latter will take progressive aspect. Moreover, there is independent evidence that *sidong* belongs to a small group of Guyanese verbs (e.g., *de,* 'to be (locative)', *stanop,* 'to stand') which, like English *smell,* neutralize the stative-nonstative distinction. If this assumption is correct, then versions with *bin* + V and *bina* + V (the more normal form for progressives) would both be grammatical.

In this way we can account for nine of the thirteen versions, and the others (with one exception) can be accounted for by common lexical *(mi/ai, sidong/sit/sit dong)* or phonological *(ai/a)* alternation. The exception is 10, to my mind the most questionably grammatical of the versions; elsewhere (Bickerton 1973: 666) I have claimed that co-occurrence of *a* as subject pronoun and *a* as nonpunctual aspect marker is barred by a strict implicational rule. However, this claim has been questioned (Cooper MS); and, even if it can be supported, it could be claimed that it is merely a consequence of the low-vowel assimilation rule referred to above. If so, the rule that would block * *a a* sequences would not necessarily block *a bina* ones.

We must note that the translations do not, as might appear at first sight, freely permute variable elements. If this were so, we might expect to find forms such as **mi woz sidong* or **ai bina sitin dong;* but such structures were neither given by the students nor found in recordings of speech, and indeed a majority of speakers would unhesitatingly reject them. On the basis of these facts, it would appear that the favorite generative interpretation of such utterances – that only one or a few are fully grammatical, the others acceptable but ungrammatical – cannot be the correct one. Since we can relate most of the versions to the overall development of Guyanese grammar (see sections on *bin, bina, biin* and *did* in Chapters 2, 3 and 4 of Bickerton 1975), since we can reject out of hand several versions that the students did *not* provide, and since we can raise doubts about the grammaticality of one or two versions, it would seem more plausible to suggest that all or nearly all the versions given are grammatical ones. Certainly none would provoke laughter, although one or two might cause a superior smirk in some quarters.

This brings us to the issue of acceptability versus grammaticality. One would mount quite a strong argument to the effect that, while all the versions are grammatical, their acceptability varies widely with the informant concerned. Another experiment bears out this argument. On several occasions, pairs of sentences were presented to informants: in each case, one member of the pair would be an actually uttered sentence, the other, the same sentence with some small grammatical alteration. Informants rejected the 'actual' sentences and accepted the 'distorted' ones, or accepted both, or rejected both, just as often as they rejected the distorted, and accepted the actual, sentences. One could argue that the actual sentences were performance errors and the 'distortions' were sometimes accidentally right; this would not, however, account for the total absence of any consistent pattern. It would appear that the average informant in a creole continuum falls into one of two classes: either he is so overcome by the wealth of variation in his vernacular that he will literally refuse to reject any sentence entirely, no matter how unlikely on grammatical grounds, or he will give judgments based on his own productive range. As this is in every case narrower than the entire continuum – markedly so, in some cases – he will reject a number of sentences that another speaker might find quite grammatical. And, since productive ranges differ quite widely from person to person, contradictions of this kind will multiply almost infinitely.

It follows that the investigator of a creole continuum who relies on informant judgments will only succeed in locking himself into the following paradox: he will not be able to extract the system until he has resolved his informants' contradictions, but he will not be able to resolve those contradictions until he has extracted the system! The study of actual speech outputs is the only sword that will cut through this Gordian knot. Once that has been carried out, it becomes possible to systematize and interpret informant judgments. In the case we have just examined, it will be possible to state that the plethora of versions for 'I was sitting...' is in part due to uncertainties about the stativity of *sidong,* in part due to the regular replacement of *bin/bina* in the basilect, first by mesolectal *did* or *biin* and later by acrolectal[6] *woz... ing,* and that the possibilities of co-occurrence between these and the pronominal and lexical replacements are handled by implicational rules of varying strictness. It will be possible, also, to say in what kind of context and by what kind of speaker each version is likeliest to be uttered (indeed, when using informants, 'Who would be likeliest to say X?' is a much more profitable question than 'Is X acceptable or not in your dialect?'). But insofar as probably no speaker masters productively the entire continuum, I can see no way in which an investigator could arrive at the overall grammar of that continuum if he relied solely on the acceptability judgments of native speakers.

We see, then, that the question of grammaticality and acceptability in pidgins and creoles is a complex one, and one which varies according to the stage of development reached by particular examples of the classes. At two extremes, the situations seem almost polar opposites; we have suggested that in early pidgins, everything is acceptable and nothing is grammatical, while in the process of decreolization that produces creole continua, almost everything may be grammatical while, for given individuals, much less may be acceptable. Obviously, we still have a vast amount to learn about the precise status of the two concepts in pidgins and creoles.

Further studies in the area should, however, contribute insights into the whole issue of what, exactly, it means for an utterance to be labelled 'acceptable' or 'grammatical' in language X. In particular, we need to know more about the kind of norms on which such intuitive judgments are based. Hitherto, many linguists have behaved as if such norms lay firmly entrenched in the *noumena,* beyond the reach of intelligent scrutiny. However, the picture of pidgin-creole development sketched here indicates that there is a time, in that process, when norms do not exist (i.e., first generation Hawaiian plantation pidgin) and a later stage (i.e., contemporary Solomon Islands pidgin) where norms have become fairly established. The questions we need to start asking, even though it may be some time before we can come up with satisfactory answers, are: how and by whom and under what circumstances are such norms developed? Is their acceptance gradual or abrupt? Is the existence of a core group of native speakers, even though they be only a small minority, an essential prerequisite for such norms? It should be apparent that the way in which any 'new' community establishes norms in language must resemble very closely the way in which such a community establishes norms in the fields of values, attitudes and patterns of social interaction. To understand the process, therefore, can only serve to tie language in more closely with other, perhaps equally rule-governed but at present more diffuse-seeming, forms of human activity which must equally reflect the cognitive and perceptual faculties peculiar to the species and the modes in which those faculties interact with the species' environment; such understanding could therefore serve as a step, small, perhaps, but significant, towards a unified science of man.

ACKNOWLEDGMENT

The research on which this paper is based was supported in part by Grant No. GS39748 from the National Science Foundation, to whom grateful acknowledgment is hereby made.

NOTES

1. There is evidence that, in the macaronic process, a speaker may even forget what language he or she is drawing on. A few moments later, the same speaker, in explanation, said:

   > They said *mahea ko* – you see that's Chinese way of telling 'Where you going?' *Mahea* it mean 'where'. *Ko* is Chinese they pronouncing 'go'... 'Come' is *hele mai* in Hawaiian, but you going tell them *hele mai* they won't understand you. They going tell you *pi'i mai,* you see, that means 'come'. *Pi'i mai,* yes, that's Chinese; *mai* is a Hawaiian word.

In fact, all the words used here (*mahea,* 'where', *hele mai,* 'come', *mai,* 'towards speaker', *pi'i,* 'climb') are Hawaiian. There is considerable independent evidence that many, perhaps most, early Chinese immigrants to Hawaii acquired, not a pidgin English or even a macaronic pidgin, but Pidgin Hawaiian. A shift in the use of *pi'i* might then have been interpreted as Chinese by the speaker, whose knowledge of Hawaiian is limited.

2. For this anecdote I am indebted to Peter Lincoln.
3. For instance, there is strong evidence that the creole spoken by Guyanese of African descent in the first half of the nineteenth century was learned almost perfectly, without anything one could call 'repidginization', by the many thousands of indentured laborers from India who were brought into what was then British Guyana from 1837 on and that this learning took place despite the fact that contact between Africans and Indians was minimal (see Bickerton 1975, especially Ch. 1 and App. III).
4. That this is no straw-man travesty, but a literal account of what actually happens, can be seen by examining Bailey (1966, particularly the Introduction and pp. 138–140; for comment, see Bickerton 1975, pp. 11–12). It should be emphasized that the dialect continua in Jamaica and Guyana are little short of identical with respect to both their basilectal rules and subsequent decreolization processes.
5. A major reason for the failure of any linguist so far to provide a description of any Anglo-Creole which is even remotely adequate is the automatic assumption – ever-present, no matter how vehemently the linguist professes his faith in creole autonomy – that English is the norm against which the creole must be measured. If the reasoning of Bickerton (1974) is correct, and creole is in some sense more natural than English, then surely this relationship should be reversed. In a more recent paper (Bickerton MS) I have tried to show that, in at least one area of the grammar, creole is far closer to natural logic than English is, and it may well be that many of the problems that have long bedevilled English grammarians may be resolved by treating English syntax as a distortion of creole syntax, rather than vice versa.
6. The term 'basilect' was first used by Stewart (1965) to describe that variety of a dialect continuum which deviated most markedly from the standard language. The terms 'acrolect' and 'mesolect' were first used by Tsuzaki (1967), though they were also employed by the present author in his work in Guyana (1967–1971) while he was still unaware of Tsuzaki's use of them. In the sense in which they are used here, 'acrolect' refers to that variety of a dialect continuum which differs least from its related standard dialect, 'basilect' refers to that variety which differs most from the standard, while 'mesolect' includes any variety or varieties intermediate between acrolect and basilect. As all creole continua seem to be of 'chain' rather than 'parallel' formation, the terms are convenient and useful so long as one remembers that they refer to relative positions on a scale and not to reifications.

REFERENCES

Ardener, R. (1971), 'Introduction', in R. Ardener, Ed., *Social Anthropology and Linguistics.* London, Tavistock.

Bailey, B. L. (1966), *Jamaican Creole Syntax.* London, Cambridge University Press.

Berry, J. (1961), 'English loanwords and adaptations in Sierra Leone Krio', pp. 1–16, in R. B. Le Page, Ed., *Creole Language Studies.* London, Macmillan.

Bickerton, D. (1973), 'The nature of a creole continuum', *Language,* 49, pp. 640–669.

– (1974), 'Creolization, language universals, natural semantax and the brain', *Working Papers in Linguistics,* 6 (3), pp. 125–141. University of Hawaii.

– (1975), *Dynamics of a Creole System.* London, Cambridge University Press.

– (MS), 'Reference in natural semantax'. Mimeo.

Cooper, V. O. (MS), 'On the notion of decreolization and St. Kitts Creole personal pronouns'. Paper presented at the 1975 International Conference on Pidgins and Creoles, University of Hawaii.

DeCamp, D. (1971), 'The study of pidgin and creole languages', pp. 13–39, in D. Hymes, Ed., *Pidginization and Creolization of Languages.* London, Cambridge University Press.

Hall, R. A., Jr. (1955), *Hands off Pidgin English.* Sydney, Pacific Publications.

– (1962), 'The life-cycle of pidgin languages', *Lingua,* 11, pp. 151–156.

Silverstein, M. (1972), 'Chinook Jargon: Language contact and the problem of multilevel generative systems', *Language,* 48, pp. 378–406, 596–625.

Stewart, W. A. (1965), 'Urban Negro speech: Sociolinguistic factors affecting English teaching', pp. 10–18, in *Social Dialects and Language Learning.* Champaign, Ill., National Council of Teachers of English.

Tsuzaki, S. M. (1967), 'Hawaiian English-pidgin, creole or dialect?', *Pacific Speech,* 1 (2), pp. 25–28.

TEUN A. VAN DIJK 4

Acceptability in Context

1. THE PROBLEM

1.1 One of the crucial problems of current grammatical theories is their empirical foundations. What do grammars actually account for? Linguistic intuitions of native speakers, systematic language use, a set of socioculturally determined conventional norms or something else? It need hardly be recalled here that Chomsky's Saussurean distinction between 'competence' and 'performance' has met with growing criticism, both in psycholinguistics (*cf.* Bever 1970) and in sociolinguistics (Labov 1970). On the one hand, it has been stressed that linguistic intuitions are only a limited part of our linguistic abilities and that cognitive strategies play an important role in our verbal performances. On the other hand, a social basis in the form of a 'homogeneous speech community' has turned out to be a too-gross simplification, and the usual conception of grammatical 'rule' is presumably too idealized. Such and similar objections, based on serious empirical research, has blurred the handy methodological distinction between theoretical properties of utterances, viz. their *grammaticalness,* and their 'real' properties, determining their factual *acceptability.*

1.2 It is the aim of this paper to shed some light on this problem from the point of view of recent work in text or discourse grammars and in pragmatics and their empirical, especially cognitive, basis. In both research directions it has been shown that grammaticalness of sentences and acceptability of utterances, respectively, should be accounted for *relative* to the structure of verbal and non-verbal *context.* Nevertheless, it should be made clear whether the attempts toward the elaboration of some fragments of a text grammar can be empirically warranted (at least from a formal or theoretical point of view). Some familiar questions, concepts and criteria are expected in such an inquiry, e.g., with respect to the 'psychological reality' of discourses or discourse rules and categories or with respect to the existence of linguistic intuitions about the well-formedness or coherence of discourses or of a clear distinction between a text and a semi-text or non-text of a language.[1]

In the perspective of current work in psychology and psycholinguistics such a 'traditional' approach to the problem of the empirical basis of text or context (pragmatic) grammars must be made with care. For example, we have no *a priori* grounds for deciding whether some phenomenon should be accounted for in terms of a grammatical 'rule' or in terms of a cognitive 'process'. That deficiency seems to weaken the usual criticism of text grammar, viz. that sentences belong to competence/grammar and discourses to performance/cognitive or social theory, since such a distinction is no longer clear even for sentences. Thus, we witness a progressive merging of grammars and cognitive models, expecially in recent proposals in Artificial Intelligence.[2]

1.3 Our main point, thus, is to show that, even if a more sophisticated version of the distinction between grammaticalness and acceptability is maintained, such a distinction should be made explicit in the perspective of systematic (con-)textual analysis. In other words, if a grammar is the central, theoretical core of a theory of performance, it should contain a set of discourse rules and a pragmatic component in order to establish the required connection with models of cognitive strategies and social conventions.

2. THE PHILOSOPHY OF 'ACCEPTABILITY'

2.1 Since the notion of 'grammaticalness' has been given extensive attention, it seems useful to begin our discussion with a brief specification of some central features of the different notions of 'acceptability' in social, psychological and linguistic (meta-)theories. We want to know which explicit meaning can be assigned to such terms as 'accept', 'acceptance', 'acceptability' and their cognates.

2.2 A first problem in such a preliminary philosophical account is whether '(to) accept' should be described as an *act*. According to recent work in action logic,[3] an act is a bodily event, a 'doing' – or the absence of such a doing – caused by a conscious organism, a 'person', able to control his own doings, intending to perform such a doing and usually with the purpose to thereby cause other events to happen, to not happen or (not) to continue. This awkward sentence is an abbreviated informal definition of the results of much philosophical and logical work and neglects specific intricacies. Now, under this definition, at least one reading of the term 'accept' can be described as an act. When I accept a present or an invitation I usually perform a series of doings (e.g., moving my hand, nodding or saying something). These doings are intentional because I have to decide whether I shall accept something or *refuse* or *reject* it. The purpose of such an act may be the event/state of my becoming/being 'happy' with the thing I accepted, i.e., the realization of the purpose may be consistent with my wishes and/or those of somebody else or be consistent with some social convention. The accepted 'thing' may be an object that is concrete and transferable (i.e., in possession), an act or an interaction, with which the desired state or event can be brought about.

We use the verb *to accept,* however, in this reading only in order to denote an act which is not 'situationally evident', so to speak. If, say, somebody gives or sends us a book, it is natural to 'take' or 'receive' it. In an 'accepting' situation, however, there exists a serious possibility that the thing *offered* may be refused or rejected, as we saw above. In such situations we decide whether to accept or to refuse, and hence we have *reasons* or *grounds* for such acts. These reasons are based on our evaluation of the offered object with respect to the chance that its acceptance realizes or continues a desired state of affairs. Hence, the object must satisfy a number of specific *properties judged satisfactory* in that perspective. One of the additional conditions is finally that the one who accepts, the 'acceptor', not only has the freedom to decide whether to accept or not but also has the recognized ability or right to judge whether the desired properties are satisfied. This places the acceptor, perhaps only momentarily, in a dominating position with respect to the 'offerer'.

The logical form of the predicate 'to accept', thus, is at least a four place relation:

(1) *X accepts Y from A because of V*

or

(2) *X accepts Y, with properties W, from Z.*

A formulation closer to our normal usage of the term would be:

(3) *X accepts Y as U from Z.*

e.g., in such sentences as 'He accepted that book as a present from John', or 'The faculty has accepted that book as a doctoral dissertation', where the objects must satisfy certain criteria. In the formulae (1)–(3) *X* and *Z* are person variables, *Y* an object variable and *V, W* and *U* are property (or intentional object) variables. Other arguments, e.g., for time, place or circumstances, may be added: we may accept something in some possible world which we reject in another because our desires or their possible chances of realization may be different.

2.3 The above analysis, in philosophical jargon, of the act of accepting seems to bear also, at least partially, on our usual understanding of 'acceptability' in linguistics. Substituting the variables in (3) for the corresponding constants, we would get something like:

(4) A (native) speaker-hearer accepts an utterance from another speaker (e.g., a linguist) as a sentence of his language.

This is roughly the full form as it is usually understood, but a couple of difficulties arise. It is true that a native speaker, according to our definitions given above, must be assigned the abilities to judge whether the object satisfies certain properties and, if not, to reject or refuse the object. The properties in question are both grammatical properties and 'cognitive' properties like structural complexity, length, etc. However, it is well-known that the language user may well not be able to accept the utterance 'as a sentence' because he may not have the notion or concept of a sentence at all and certainly not the theoretical concept of a sentence. Thus, he may accept the utterance simply 'as a (good, normal) utterance of his language'. Acceptance, in such cases, may be *implicit* (tacit) or *explicit*. The explicit case is rare and only occurs in those situations where evaluation of utterances is required (in tests and in teaching the language). Acceptance (or rejection) in that case is the intentional act, based on motivated decisions, where the motivation may be intuitive but where the decision itself must be 'known'. As Bever (1970) has pointed out, such an act requires specific (linguistic) abilities.

The implicit case of acceptance is the 'normal' or natural one and occurs in the *course of a conversation*. It may be asked whether 'accepting' in such a case is an act or whether accepting is involved at all.

When hearing an utterance of his language during a conversation, a language user does not seem to *do* something which we may qualify as the act of acceptance. To be sure, he *does* listen or read, which are acts, because they are controllable doings: he may decide not to listen or to read. But, the act of acceptance is not simply performed by accomplishing the acts of listening or reading, since these acts are also conditions for rejection. Next, phonemes/morphemes will be identified and the syntactic structure analyzed with a set of rules and strategies together with a semantic 'parsing' that puts interpreted words or phrases in the appropriate 'logical' categories of a meaning representation, etc. This is (very, very) roughly what *happens,* and perhaps the language user also *does* these things, but they *occur to* his mind rather than his causing them intentionally to happen. They are not even 'mental acts' (whatever that may mean) but series of mental events, i.e., processes. If the process takes a normal course, i.e., if the syntactic structure corresponds to the rules present and the semantic interpretation makes sense, the utterance (as such) is *automatically accepted,* much in the same way as a computer may accept a sentence if it has the appropriate programs to process it. The mental processes going on are thus normally not thought about and may even be inaccessible. We only know that something is *wrong* when the input utterance does *not* satisfy the different rules, strategies and categories we have available (our 'tacit' language knowledge). In that case there are grounds to *reject* the sentence or part of it, a rejection which may be expressed or not. The expressions of rejection are often conventionalized and need not be treated here. Thus, whereas rejection is an act according to the definition, acceptance of a linguistic utterance is either simply a cover term for the complex mental processing or it is a 'negative' act like omissions or forbearances. However, as acts these doings must be intentional, which is hardly the case in sentence processing. So, we'll say that acceptance is an automatized mental act (or series of mental acts) because in certain circumstances it is controlled consciously, thought about and carried out. In this respect the act is like that of a *decision* (or even is a decision, whether the input utterance satisfies the rules and structures in the processors). Hence, the sole external evidence that a mental act of acceptance is carried out in a course of conversation is the absence of explicit rejections.

The acceptance of an utterance, moreover, is not merely based on syntactic and semantic rules/strategies but also on *pragmatic* rules, conditions and structures. In that case the utterance is accepted not (only) as an object but as a speech act. Instead of talking of an utterance-object (a token of an utterance type or a sentence type), we may analyze the speech act in the usual way and perhaps speak of morphophonological, syntactic and semantic (propositional, referential) 'acts', with the same proviso for 'acts' as made above. At these levels, the different acts may be said to be *appropriate* or not, depending on whether in most similar circumstances most language users would accept them, which is part of the definition of a convention (Lewis 1968). This pragmatic condition reminds us of the fact that the simple phrase 'acceptability of an utterance' (worse: 'of a sentence') not only can be intended as implying an 'act' by hearers/readers but should also imply some act of the speaker having produced the utterance. 'Producibility' seems too awkward, but we would need a term indicating the fact that an utterance also satisfies the rules and structures (and the intentions) of the speaker. Although we may ideally require that the producible is also acceptable, this may in fact often not be the case.

We shall now attempt to demonstrate that only relative or contextual grammaticalness reflects systematic processes of acceptance.

3. RELATIVE GRAMMATICALNESS

3.1 There are well-known cases of sentences which are grammatical but not acceptable. Let us here analyze some examples of the converse case: 'sentences' which are acceptable but not grammatical in the strict sense:

(5) A: Did you hit him?
B: No. He me.
(6) A: With what has the postman been murdered?
B: John thinks with a knife.
(7) A: Sorry, I couldn't make it in time.
B: Obviously.

As such, the utterances of speaker B can hardly be called grammatical by a grammar accounting for isolated sentences, although they are perfectly acceptable in the whole conversation. Hence cognitive strategies should be called on to help explain such cases of systematic (i.e., not *ad hoc*) acceptability. Strategies operating on the typically *incomplete* B-inputs alone, however, can not be of much help. In (5) there may be ambiguity between direct and indirect object *me,* in (6) the first interpretation would be that *with a knife* is an instrumental linked with the immediately preceding predicate *think* and in (7) the adverb may be sentence- or predicate-modifying. Hence, any serious cognitive model can account for the B-utterances only in relation to the A-utterances. Structural and substantial information from the preceding utterance is thus necessary for the interpretation, and hence the acceptability, of the following utterances of the conversation: in (5) *he* substitutes for *you* (referring to B) and *me* substitutes for *him,* where the verb/predicate remains identical and is deleted in surface structure, whereas in (6) and

(7) a whole proposition is deleted for which one additional category (instrumental, adverb) is provided. It should be stressed that whatever cognitive processes are involved, they must at least partially be based on (all-or-none) rules: e.g., *He I,* in (5) would be both ungrammatical and unacceptable. So it seems to make sense to speak of grammatical and ungrammatical incomplete sentences and that requires treatment of dialogue discourses like (5)–(7) in the grammar. The particular rules, e.g., of substitution and deletion, involved in these examples may well have proper cognitive correlates (avoiding repetition, perceiving/marking contrastive information, etc.).

3.2 The problem, then, is: what would such a grammar look like? First of all, it must be stressed that the phenomena discussed above regularly appear within the sentence:

(8) I hit him, and he me.
(9) Peter thought that the postman was murdered with an umbrella, but John thinks with a knife.

So, in any case, a grammar must capture the generalization that certain rules apply similarly in complex sentences and in sentence sequences. Given that a classical sentence grammar (syntactically, semantically or categorically based) can account for (8) and (9), the argument would be that the *same* rules (transformations) would account for the discourse phenomenon. This view is the standard criticism against text grammars, and it is correct – at least, as far as these cases are concerned. Of course, some adjustments must be made (for example, transformations would have to apply across 'independent' S-nodes, in which case, what sort of a node would the topmost be?) but they would (perhaps) be marginal. If this is correct, and if the grammar captures the generalization, it would no longer be a sentence grammar but a (weak) discourse grammar because it characterizes structures of discourses. More correctly, the difference would disappear; we would just have grammar, and that is the way it should be.

Thus, an adequate grammar accounts for the structure of (complex) sentences and of certain structures of sentence sequences (discourses) which are based on the same rules determining the structure of complex sentences. In classical terms this might imply, for example, that in such cases the deep structures of the sentence/sequence are identical but that their surface structures are different. One problem immediately arises here: *why* are these surface structures different; are they just structural variants, i.e., having the same meaning and pragmatic function?

Other questions arise at the same time: if the different structures are variants and if they are based on the same rules, may we freely make sentences out of sequences and sequences out of complex sentences? If so, sentence grammars and discourse grammars coincide. Of course, that assumes that classical sentence grammars provide all the semantic constraints determining complex sentences (which they don't).[4]

3.3 Although it may be demonstrated that important differences (especially pragmatic) hold in general between complex sentence expressions and sequences, we shall take some clear cases where a sequence is not easily reduced to a complex sentence with the same meaning:

(10) (a) John! Can you hear me? Shall I help you?
(b) *John, can you hear me and shall I help you?
(11) (a) Can you tell me the time? I have no watch.
(b) *Can you tell me the time and I have no watch.
(c) Did you tell him the time because he had no watch.
(12) (a) I promise to be there in time. Will you also be there?
(b) *I promise to be there in time and will you also be there?
(13) (a) Yesterday I had a funny dream. I was president and . . .
(b) *Yesterday I had a funny dream and I was president . . .
(14) (a) Peter is drunk. He always is when he visits Amsterdam.
(b) ?Peter is drunk and he always is when he visits Amsterdam.
(15) (a) Perhaps Harry is ill. He was not at the meeting.
(b) *Perhaps Harry is ill because he was not at the meeting.

In all these cases the (b)-sentences are ungrammatical, awkward or mean something different from the (a)-sentences. Apparently, utterances manifesting different speech acts (like request and statement in (11)), having different (meta-)levels of communication as in (10), sentences under the scope of some 'world-creating' noun (predicate) as in (13), generalizations (14) and motivations/conclusions can not simply be expressed in one sentence.

Although we cannot, in this brief paper, give a serious analysis of the examples, we may note that the ungrammaticalness of the (b)-sentences is essentially for pragmatic reasons. Thus, in (11) the meaning of the second sentence is not directly connected with the meaning of the first sentence. Rather the proposition underlying the second sentence is a *condition* for the appropriateness of the speech act of a request or question, i.e., a question is appropriate only if I do not yet know the answer or have no means to supply the answer myself (by looking at my watch). More generally, we might suppose that a sequence of sentences is a one-many mapping from speech acts: one speech act may be accomplished by the utterance of one or more sentences, but several speech acts cannot be accomplished by uttering one sentence except perhaps in cases of indirect speech acts, see Searle (1973) and Franck (1974). The theoretical problems are intricate here. An alternative proposal may be that sentences and speech acts are related by a one-one mapping: each sentence-utterance accomplishes one speech act. Yet, at least at one level of description (see below), it might be useful to let a whole sequence-utterance be one speech act, e.g., a statement. Thus the sequence

(16) I am cold. Could you please close the window?

manifests a statement and a request, but *as a whole* seems to function as a request, where the statement specifies one of the conditions, viz. the motivation, of the request. If this observation is correct, mappings from pragmatic structures may have discourses or fragments of discourses as their scope and not only sentences. Notice also that a one-sentence version of (16), viz.

(17) I am cold, so could you please close the window?

has very peculiar properties. The connecting *so*, here, does not have semantic character, i.e., relating facts or propositions by causal, logical or conceptual implication, but has pragmatic character: it relates the fact expressed in the first sentence with the action (viz. the request) of appropriately uttering the second sentence, not with the 'content' of that second sentence, at least not directly. This is perhaps a reason why the written version of (17) is not well-formed because *so* should introduce a new, independent sentence. Our intuitions about sentence boundaries seem to be very unreliable indeed as an empirical base for a (sentence) grammar.

3.4 The conclusions which may be drawn from the preceding (admittedly still highly informal) remarks seem to be the following: (a) a grammar accounting for isolated sentences underpredicts their (un-)acceptability – as utterances – in a discourse; (b) acceptability of sentences in a discourse is not only based on cognitive interpretative processes but on rules which may also hold for complex sentences; (c) theoretical notions like 'sequence', 'discourse' or 'text' are necessary because not every discourse can be reduced to a complex sentence (nor the converse, *cf. if*-clauses); (d) whatever the semantic equivalence of sentences with sequences, their surface differences are based on underlying pragmatic differences. Finally, it may be noticed without further examples that sentences which as such are both grammatical and acceptable may become unacceptable in the discourse, e.g., because of presupposition violations. That is, a sentence can be interpreted only, and hence accepted, relative to the set of interpretations of previous sentences (a set which may be empty, see below). In formal semantic terms, not to be spelled out here, this means that a sentence can be interpreted only in those model structures related with the model structures of the previous sentences. That is, instead of sentence models we have discourse or *text models* (Ballmer 1972).

Thus, the general conclusion is that acceptability is in principle better 'modelled' by a grammar accounting for the structure of sequences.

4. PRAGMATIC ACCEPTABILITY

4.1 Sentences are not only interpreted/accepted with respect to previous sentences (indeed, the previous sentence set may be empty as we saw) but also to *pragmatic context*. Neither the precise structure of the pragmatic context nor the rules and constraints relating it with the structure of the utterance can be discussed here.[5] We shall assume a pragmatic context to be defined primarily in terms of sets of propositions and rules characterizing the internal structure of speaker and hearer: their knowledge, beliefs, wishes, etc. Semantic models are in this way 'contextualized' with respect to speaker and hearer and some other properties of the (fragment of the) possible world in which they are communicating.

A first generalization which comes to mind is to reduce all 'textual' rules to 'contextual' rules. That is, we let constraints from preceding sentences be equivalent to constraints from 'previous' propositions in the epistemic sets of speaker and hearer, changing linearly with the production of subsequent sentences. Elsewhere (van Dijk 1974a), we have given some arguments against such a reduction of a discourse grammar to a pragmatic sentence grammar: the pragmatic component must be added to a proper discourse grammar. Above, for example, we hinted already at the fact that pragmatic mappings may have whole discourses as their scope.

Although it cannot be denied that sentences change the pragmatic context (e.g., the knowledge of the hearer), the constraints in an uttered discourse cannot be fully explained on the basis of an (ordered?) set of propositions alone, e.g., a *presupposition base*. On the other hand, such a pragmatic base is necessary, e.g., for the interpretation of pronouns that have no antecedents and are being used deictically. Similarly, previous sentences as such are not enough to provide the necessary information for the interpretation of following sentences; entailments, meaning postulates, etc., based on previous sentences must be supplied by the set of pragmatic presuppositions and corresponding inference rules. What is also needed is the preceding *verbal* (surface) structure of previous sentences. Assuming that a passive sentence has an abstract underlying proposition with a structure like its active counterpart, we would not be able to explain why the following discourse is ungrammatical:

(18) A: Was he hit by you?
B: *No. He me.

Other arguments against the reduction hypothesis relate to the use of connectives, adverbs, predicates, etc. *(thus, consequently, conclude),* presupposing previous sentences/utterances, not merely propositions (which might have entered the epistemic set of the hearer in a different way). Hence, a discourse may have its proper underlying theoretical unit (a 'text') even when, in performance, production and perception are controlled by linear cognitive processes moving from sentence/clause to sentence/clause.

4.2 Utterances, as we saw, are acceptable if their underlying discourses satisfy the rules of relative grammaticalness and interpretability. At the same time an utterance is acceptable in a conversation only if it is a speech act which is also *appropriate relative to* other (speech) acts of the conversation or interaction. The various appropriateness conditions are those given in recent philosophical and linguistic work and need not be specified here for the different speech acts. Thus it seems difficult to have one discourse-utterance manifesting both a request and an order because the preparatory conditions for these acts are inconsistent. Similarly, a request for an object can not precede or co-occur with the act of taking the object by force. Thus, just as a sentence can not be said to be grammatical/acceptable in isolation, so a speech act can not be said to be acceptable in isolation: two speech acts which as such are both appropriate may be incoherent or inconsistent or may have conflicting contextual pre-conditions. The same holds for the function of speech acts in interaction, though this is not an object for linguistics proper but for sociolinguistics or sociology.

4.3 An additional argument must be given for the hypothesis that a discourse apparently manifesting more than one speech act has nevertheless, as a whole, the function of one speech act. Consider the following dialogue:

(19) A: May I borrow your car? I'll bring it back at five.
B: O.K.

The affirmative answer of speaker B may be given only after a question-request and is usually pointless (or optional) after a promise. Therefore, it seems as if A's discourse should be interpreted as a request or as a request act where the promise act is 'auxiliary' or subordinated to the request. If the latter observation is correct, it would seem sensible to assign a *hierarchical structure* to a speech act sequence of a conversation, much in the same way as our other actions, though linearly (or concurrently) ordered in time. We light our pipe as an auxiliary to the act of smoking and strike a match in order to light the pipe, etc. Hence the acceptability of a word, phrase, sentence, discourse and their respective utterances and speech acts themselves is relative not only to linearly preceding elements but to a hierarchical structure. This means that discourses, at the pragmatic level, too, cannot possibly be satisfactorily described in terms of a sentence grammar merely generating sequences of which only the sentences have hierarchical structure.

5. MACRO-STRUCTURES

5.1 Returning to the structure of the discourse, we have one result, viz. that grammaticalness of sentences is *linearly relative* to preceding sentences or propositions in text and pragmatic context, and one hypothesis, viz. that sentences are *hierarchically relative* to the semantic representation of the discourse, as it is syntactically expressed in complex sentences. Consider, e.g., the following discourse:

(20) Mary has met a bright guy from Harvard. He is red-haired and wears horn-rimmed spectacles.

Here, the second sentence is semantically modifying the object of the first sentence. Similarly, further specification may be given of the particular meeting of the pair.

In this perspective, a third hypothesis may be formulated: underlying the linear and hierarchical structure of the sequence of sentences, there seems to be evidence for the presence of a more global level of semantic representation, which has been called the *macro-structure* of the discourse. A macro-structure is a theoretical construct, consisting of a hierarchical structure of propositions. Predicates or propositions from this macro-structure abstractly represent sets of sentences or propositions at the micro-level (sequence) level of the discourse. Thus a structure like (PAST) (MEET) [Mary, (CLEVER) (MAN)] may underlie, intuitively, a long description of the meeting and of the man Mary met. Such macro-structures may be directly expressed in the discourse, e.g., in the first sentence of (20), where they may announce or resume the *global meaning* of the whole discourse. This is a first piece of linguistic (semantic) evidence.

Secondly, a sentence in a discourse may have the necessary syntactic and semantic relations with previous sentences, but this constraint is not sufficient to define one *globally coherent* discourse. That is, each sentence might provide a further associative proliferation of *any* of the concepts in the preceding sentences. However, it is an empirical fact that in general such discourses are not acceptable. The linear expansion must be structured under macro-constraints. That is, each sentence must be functionally dependent on at least one macro-category, e.g., AGENT or ACTION, or PLACE, etc. Thus, each semantic representation of a sentence in a discourse is conceptually associated with a macro-concept. Again, this is a property of the discourse itself and not (merely) a fact of cognitive processing.

Thirdly, (types of) discourses are acceptable only if their macro-structure satisfies a number of further constraints. Both theoretical and empirical research on narrative discourse, for example, have resulted in the establishment of a macro-syntax, for which terms such as 'introduction', 'complication', 'resolution' and 'conclusion' have been used.[6] Similar categories were known already in ancient rhetoric.

5.2 Other arguments in favor of a macro-structural component in a discourse grammar may be provided. However, there are a number of difficulties which must not be overlooked and which require particular care with the formulation of such an hypothesis:

(1) Although perhaps empirical (cognitive) evidence for macro-structures can be assessed – see below – the arguments in favor of an account in the grammar are weak.

(2) Whatever the grammatical evidence for such structures, a serious grammar for macro-structures requires explicit categories, rules of derivation and interpretation, which have not yet been provided.

(3) Even if a formal language for their description would be provided

we would not yet have the rules mapping macro-structures into sentential representations of the sentences of the discourse – and hence a relation with surface structures – which is essential for any grammar.

These and similar critical arguments against a macro-structure hypothesis have been mentioned in the literature,[7] and they are justified. If a solution to these problems can be provided at all, it would at least take the following arguments into account:

(1) No strict distinction can be made between a justification for grammatical rules and categories, on the one hand, and cognitive processes and categories, on the other hand.

(2) A formal language for macro-structures has the same format as any adequate language accounting for 'meaning'-structures.

(3) If a solution for argument (3) above can be found this would provide sufficient ground for having a macro-structure theory in the grammar.

(4) Besides purely formal problems, the hypothesis requires much more empirical (descriptive) warrants: hardly any systematic and explicit discourse descriptions have been given in linguistic research.

Another problem upon which the hypothesis depends is the precise formulation of the aims and tasks of a (linguistic) semantics. If such a semantics would have to assign 'meaning-structures' to utterance-types, then there are no *a priori* reasons why such meanings would not also have the 'holistic' nature postulated in a macro-structure hypothesis. Along the usual Frege-Tarski line, both linguistic and formal semantics are required to construct an interpretation of an expression on the interpretation of its parts. It is not so easy to decide whether our hypothesis is inconsistent with this requirement: a macro-representation of a discourse is also based on the interpretation of its parts, viz. its sentences. Typically 'semantic' categories like Agent, Object, Event or Action, etc., do not necessarily dominate 'words' or concepts, but surely also propositions, as is already the case in classical transformational grammars where S-nodes are recursive. Similarly, those categories may dominate *sets of propositions.* Intuitively, as we mentioned earlier, the Agent of the discourse may be identified by a set of propositions, and the same holds for an Event. The formal problem is, however, that we do not simply need a set of sentences to identify, e.g., the Agent, but parts of the sentences of that set. That is, we must 'extract' from each sentence precisely the information relevant for the identification and construction of some macro-category. This may all be very plausible, e.g., in the perspective of cognitive processes, but it is pretty vague. What we need are the rules to do the operations described.

5.3 What is the moral of these general remarks for the grammaticalness-acceptability discussion? Clearly, what we want is that the grammar predicts that certain utterances are unacceptable because of a violation of macro-constraints. Let us give a concrete example to illustrate this point. Consider the following discourses:

(21) A: Did you hear about the bank robbery?
B: No, what happened?
A: Yesterday morning I was at our bank round the corner. Suddenly, one of the clients took a gun out of his pocket. He shot a couple of times in the air and then aimed at the cashier. He said that he wanted all the cash she had in her desk. She was very frightened and gave it to him. Then he ran away. The police have not yet caught him.

(22) Suddenly, one of the clients took a gun out of his pocket. She was very frightened and gave it to him. The police have not yet caught him. Yesterday morning I was at our bank round the corner (. . .)

(23) Yesterday morning I was at our bank round the corner. The bank is a terrible building. The buildings in this part of town are horrible. But I like living here. The town has no industry. My brother works in a factory. His boss is a terrible guy. He was born in New York in 1909. At that time you could still live in the city (. . .)

Intuitively, we find (21) an acceptable conversation (apart from some stylistic aspects and elements of spoken language, neglected here) and A's narrative acceptable. In (22), however, the order of the sentences of that narrative has been changed, which clearly makes the discourse not only ungrammatical at the semantic level, i.e., incoherent, but also unacceptable: the linear referential relations are mixed up. Discourse (23) does satisfy the constraints for linear coherence: each sentence has a semantic link with a previous sentence. Still, we would hardly consider it acceptable: there is no 'point', 'line' or 'theme' in it, and we would probably qualify it as pathological. In other words, there is no macro-model in which in each sentence can be interpreted: the relations between the (micro-)models in which the sentences are interpreted exist but are fully arbitrary. Discourse (23) would at most be a collection of the topics talked about during an informal conversation. In case the grammar would be able to formulate the macro-constraints, it would be able to predict the differences in acceptability of (21) and (23).

Notice, also, that macro-structures may have direct 'linguistic' relevance: in (21) A's question is about a bank robbery, and the narrative he gives in his reply is about the robbery. But the term 'robbery' itself does not appear in the narrative and yet B knows that the proposition of A's question and the meaning of the narrative have the same referent, viz. some event which may be characterized as (YESTERDAY) (ROB) [SOMEBODY, (OUR) (BANK)]. Hence, macro-structures may be directly expressed in surface structure. A macro-semantics should specify the specific relations between such a sentence and the global and specific meaning of the discourse. That such relations exist may also be concluded from the fact that a sentence like 'The bank was *not* robbed' would be inconsistent with the narrative discourse, even if it is not strictly inconsistent with any sentence of it. The inconsistency, then, can only be explained between the sentence and the underlying macro-proposition of the discourse. In other terms, the whole ordered sequence of sentences of the discourse *entails* 'The bank was robbed'. Even if a macro-structural component in the grammar is superfluous, the semantics should provide the rules specifying why this sort of entailment may be true or false. Similarly, at the empirical level, the grammar should account for the fact that native speakers can make such conclusions, identify the equivalence relation in a conversation like (21), and detect inconsistencies between sentences and whole discourses. These are only a few of our semantic abilities.

The conclusion from these arguments and examples seems to be that the phenomena involved are directly relevant to a theory of grammar and that therefore it seems warranted to look for a solution of the puzzles mentioned in section 5.2.

6. DISCOURSE AND COGNITION

6.1 Since only some of the formal problems involved in pragmatically based discourse grammars can be solved at the moment, it is important to investigate the empirical foundations of such a grammar. More specifically, we want to know which cognitive structures and processes are involved in the production, interpretation, storage, retrieval, recall, recognition, etc., of such complex verbal utterances as complex sentences and discourses. Are these cognitive processes fundamentally different from those operating on simple sentences? Is it possible to make a distinction between perceptual, interpretative and productive strategies on the one hand and rule-based operations on the other hand?

6.2 Independently from work on discourse in linguistics, such and similar questions have recently attracted the attention of psycholinguists and cognitive psychologists. Since the early explorations by Bartlett (1932) on memorization of stories, a number of interesting experiments have been carried out on discourse material. Because no explicit grammar or cognitive model for the processing of such material was available, most of the experiments were based on intuitive analytic categories and procedures. Some of the major findings and assumptions of this work will be briefly given here. It is clear that such results can be considered as arguments in favor of a text grammar, in particular of the macro-structure hypothesis, *only* if it is agreed that an adequate grammar must provide the 'closest possible fit' to the systematic phenomena of verbal behavior.

6.3 It is well-known that early experimental psychology of language behavior very often made use of nonsense material to test learning, recall, etc. Together with a general reaction against behavioristic approaches to natural language, mainly initiated by Chomsky and Miller around 1960, the nonsense and word-list material was gradually replaced by sentences. In this research one of the major goals was to find psychological evidence for particular grammatical rules (transformations), e.g., by testing reaction times. The hypotheses involved there, however, turned out to be overly optimistic: there is no direct relation between particular rules and regularities in test behavior. Bever (1970), in his article referred to earlier, demonstrated that much of our verbal behavior is based on cognitive strategies which need not run parallel to the rules and their operations as provided in the grammar.

At the same time the interest in learning the recall tests shifted to semantics. It was pointed out that surface structure of sentences – or syntactic structure in general – is not learned and only fragmentarily recalled or recognized: information processing is based on underlying semantic structures. The memory models involved, hence, became 'semantic' or 'conceptual', constructed out of propositions (with their case structure represented in a tree graph, for example) or networks (for discourse representation, see, e.g., Kintsch 1974).

6.4 It is against this background that recent research on discourse must be viewed. Even if discourse material was used, this was often not to test learning or recall for complex material as such or for the rules or constraints underlying it, but to get insight about 'contextual cues' in learning sentences. In other discourse experiments the tradition goes back to Bartlett's work. Having a story reproduced several times (often a very long time apart) after presentation, he found that the exact words, phrases and sentences were not recalled in the later trials, and that in the long run only some 'outline' of the story, perhaps together with some striking detail, was recalled. New detail may reappear if consistent with, or inferable from, that outline. The main hypothesis, then, is that recall is essentially *constructive,* i.e., in perception and storage a basic structure, a *schema,* is formed upon which detail of the original input or new (added) detail can later be recalled. The core of our processing of complex structures like discourses is obviously such a scheme. It was further found that elements in the discourse which could not easily be understood were transformed (by reduction or further explication) to more explicit or better-known structures (rationalization). Finally, it was found that the inference and rationalization procedures, the construction of schemata, and the recall or addition of detail were strongly dependent on personal interests, attitudes and feelings, and on social conventions. Similar conclusions were drawn from experiments with serial reproduction of discourses by various subjects after each other.

Paul (1959) replicated some of Bartlett's experiments in a more sophisticated way and arrived at similar conclusions. In general, discourses which are relatively 'explicit' are better recalled than their 'obscure' counterparts, where coherence must be established by the subject through inferential steps not presented in the text itself. However, this facilitation is more marked for unfamiliar material: we have no difficulty in supplying inferences in discourses about topics we know rather well. In repeated serial reproduction the more familiar and the more explicated texts remain coherent, even when 'skeletonized', which may not be the case for relatively difficult, obscure or unfamiliar material. One of the explanations is that schemata can be constructed more easily when related to schemata already present in memory. Other differences in task behavior are based on differences in cognitive style of the subjects: some subjects look for the global meaning (forgetting detail, and hence importing new detail in recall) whereas others are interested in specific details, being less able to construct a more generally coherent pattern. But, as was already demonstrated by Cofer (1941), recall of ('logical') ideas is always better than verbatim recall.

Further detail in this direction was supplied by Gomulicki (1956), who showed that the recall of elements of a passage is directly proportional to 'its contribution to the total meaning of the passage'. Apparently, during interpretation, special mnemonic processes operate such that relatively 'important' concepts are abstracted from the material. Thus, in a narrative, Agent and Action are more important than descriptive elements. More generally, our recall for events and actions is better than that for states, scenes or object properties. Such phenomena may be explained – Gomulicki did not provide such explanations – by the fact that events and actions are better 'organized', i.e., temporally and causally ordered, than, e.g., scenes.

Similar results about the abstraction of important concepts from discourse material were obtained by Lee (1965), who showed in particular that the organization of paragraphs and the presence of summaries, conclusions and title facilitate this abstraction process. The importance of titles in the interpretation of discourses was also demonstrated by Dooling and Lachman (1971) on material which was intentionally vague and ambiguous. Earlier, Pompi and Lachman (1967) and Lachman and Dooling (1968) had postulated the construction of 'surrogate structures', which need not directly depend on the words of the passage themselves, but which are a combination of theme, image, schema, abstract and summary. During encoding and reproduction such abstract categories serve as 'cores' around which individual concepts/words, phrases and sentences are interpreted or produced. The assumption that reading and (re-)production of discourse are not only based on properties of isolated sentences has been demonstrated also in several contributions to the volume edited by Carroll and Freedle (1972), e.g., by Crothers, who identified the 'theme' with higher order nodes, and by Frederiksen, who showed that problem solving is based on 'superordinate (semantic) processing'.

One of the more concrete results in the investigation of the relations between grammar rules and memory processes was Slobin's (1968) finding that recall of passive sentences in discourse – and their storage as passives – depends on the degree of focus or importance of the (logical) subject of such sentences in the discourse: if that subject is unimportant or not specified at all, the sentences may be stored as (truncated) passives of which the subject is the 'logical subject' of the passage. This result is one of the examples where original coding hypotheses (complexity of grammatical rules entails complexity in storage and retrieval) had to be modified.

Bower (1974), finally, made a distinction between micro-structure and macro-structure of a discourse and showed that interference of interpolated details does not improve recall of macro-structures but causes confusion in the recall of micro-structural elements. Macro-structures in this account are not well-defined and seem to be constructed of 'major categories' representing key events in the discourse.

6.5 Although the survey of some selected papers on the cognitive processing of discourse given in the previous section is very fragmentary and oversimplified, the main results seem to be consistent with our hypotheses.[8] However, a great number of problems have not yet had sufficient theoretical and empirical attention. For our discussion it remains to be demonstrated that the processes of abstraction (*cf.* Bransford and Franks 1972) and the formation of schemata or macro-structures are not merely cognitive strategies for the organization, storage and retrieval of complex information, but that such strategies presuppose the existence of grammatical rules. The inference processes involved seem to be based not only on inductive world knowledge but also on our knowledge of conceptual meaning structures, meaning rules and postulates of natural language. The structure of a macro-structure is thus determined by general semantic rules, identical with those for propositional structures: in interpreting a discourse we select the elements which may be the Agent, the Action(s), the Object or the Circumstances of the global meaning. Strategies and rules, just as for sentences, may not run parallel: the first Agent introduced in a story will as a hypothesis be taken as the discourse-Agent, but this strategy may be falsified by further information. Similarly, a conclusion or result of an argument or narrative may be given initially in the discourse, but the rules of macro-syntax/semantics will nevertheless assign the correct interpretation to such a discourse. Reordering of global segments of a discourse seems to follow the same rules as those for sentences. The interesting advantage of this hypothesis of the parallelism of structures and rules at the micro- and macro-levels is that we need only one set of rules and strategies to process both. The big problem remaining, however, is the formulation of the grammatical rules (and the cognitive processes underlying them) of *macro-interpretation,* taking concepts, concept clusters and propositions at the sequence level to concepts, concept clusters and propositions at the macro-level by abstraction, reduction ('semantic pruning') and generalization.

Although our – still not sufficiently explicit – hypothesis seems to have some 'holistic' properties characterizing much work in Gestalt theory, the underlying methodology is rather 'associationistic' according to the criteria set out by Anderson and Bower (1973). Macro-structures are not mystical 'emergent' properties of a discourse but are constructed on the basis of semantic properties of words and sentences. If a formal model of this construction can be provided we would have an explicit warrant for our main assumptions in this paper, viz. that the factual acceptability of sentences depends on their function in the discourse as a whole and that the acceptability of discourses is based on the presence of a macro-structure defining its 'unity' and on the pragmatic function in the conversation. At this point the hypotheses put forward have their direct bearing on social psychology and sociology, since they specify the cognitive foundations of our representation of reality and the organization of interaction.

NOTES

1. For further references on discourse and text grammars, see van Dijk (1976c) and Petöfi and Rieser, Eds. (1973), and the bibliography by Dressler and Schmidt (1973).
2. See Schank and Colby, Eds. (1973) and a survey in Anderson and Bower (1973), Chap. 4.
3. We may refer to the exploratory work by von Wright (1967) and further elaboration in Brennenstuhl (1974) among many other studies on action in philosophy and logic.
4. For a discussion on the logical constraints of connection see van Dijk (1974c, 1976a), referring to recent work in relevance or conditional logics and their semantics.
5. We think of several directions of research here: philosophical by Austin, Searle, Grice and Schiffer, logical by Montague, Cresswell and Ballmer, linguistic by Bartsch, Kummer, Wunderlich, Karttunen, Sadock, Kasher, etc. For references, see van Dijk (1976b).
6. For an action theoretical explication of this assumption see van Dijk (1974b) in which further references on narrative research are given.
7. A collection of reviews on text grammatical work has been published by the Projectgruppe Textlinguistik (1974).
8. For further detail, see van Dijk (1975), in which a more precise theoretical analysis of the discourse experiments is given, as well as their consequences for a theory of text grammar. See also van Dijk and Kintsch (in press) for further references.

REFERENCES

Anderson, R., and Bower, H. (1973), *Human Associative Memory*. Washington, Winston.

Ballmer, T. (1972), 'A pilot study in text grammar.' TU, Berlin. Mimeo.

Bartlett, F. C. (1932), *Remembering*. London, Cambridge University Press.

Bever, T. G. (1970), 'The cognitive basis for linguistic structures', in J. R. Hayes, Ed. *Cognition and the Development of Language*. New York, Wiley.

Bower, H. (1974), 'Selective facilitation and interference in retention of prose', *Journal of Educational Psychology*, 66, pp. 1–8.

Bransford, D., and Franks, J. (1972), 'The abstraction of linguistic ideas: A review', *Cognition*, 1 (2/3), pp. 211–249.

Brennenstuhl, W. (1974), *'Vorbereitungen zur Entwicklung einer Sprachadäquaten Handlungslogik'*. Ph. D. Diss., TU, Berlin.

Carroll, J. B., and Freedle, R. O., Eds. (1972), *Language Comprehension and the Acquisition of Knowledge*. Washington, Winston.

Cofer, N. (1941), 'A comparison of logical and verbatim learning of prose passages of different lengths', *American Journal of Psychology*, 54, pp. 1–20.

Crothers, E. J. (1972), 'Memory structure and the recall of discourse', pp. 247–283 in: J. B. Carroll and R. O. Freedle, Eds., *Language Comprehension and the Acquisition of Knowledge*. Washington, Winston.

Dijk, T. A. van (1972), *Some Aspects of Text Grammars*. The Hague, Mouton.

– (1974a), 'A note on the partial equivalence of text grammars and context grammars'. University of Amsterdam. Mimeo.

– (1974b), 'Philosophy of action and theory of narrative'. University of Amsterdam. Mimeo. [Abridged as 'Action, action description, narrative', *New Literary History*, Spring 1975].

– (1974c), 'Relevance' in grammar and logic', Paper contributed to the International Congress on Relevance Logics, St. Louis, Mo., U.S.A., September.

– (1975), 'Recalling and summarizing complex discourse'. University of Amsterdam. Mimeo.

– (1976a), 'Connectives in text grammar and text logic', in Teun A. van Dijk and János S. Petöfi, Eds., *Grammars and Descriptions*. Berlin, New York, De Gruyter.

– (1976b), 'Pragmatics, presuppositions and context grammars', in S. J. Schmidt, Ed., *Pragmatik II/ Pragmatics*. Munich, Fink.

– (1976c), *Text and Context*. London; Longman.

Dijk, T. A. van and Kintsch, W. (in press), 'Cognitive psychology and discourse', *Trends in Text Linguistics*. New York, Berlin, De Gruyter.

Dooling, J. L. and Lachman, R. (1971), 'Effects of comprehension on retention of prose', *Journal of Experimental Psychology* 88: 216–222.

Dressler, W. and Schmidt, S. J. (1973), *Textlinguistik. Kommentierte Bibliographie*. Munich, Fink.

Franck, D. (1974), 'Indirekte Sprechakte'. University of Düsseldorf, Dept. of Linguistics. Mimeo.

Frederiksen, H. (1972), 'Effects on task induced cognitive operations on comprehension and memory processes', pp. 211–245. In J. B. Carroll and R. O. Freedle, Eds., *Language Comprehension and the Acquisition of Knowledge*. Washington, Winston.

Gomulicki, B. R. (1956), 'Recall as an abstractive process', *Acta Psychologica*, 12, pp. 77–94.

Kintsch, W. (1974), 'Memory representation of text'. Paper presented at the Loyola Symposium, April 30.

Labov, W. (1970), 'The study of language in its social context', *Studium Generale*, 23, pp. 30–87. [Also in W. Labov, 1972 *Sociolinguistic Patterns*, U. of Pennsylvania Press].

Lachman, R., and Dooling, D. J. (1968), 'Connected discourse and random strings: Effects of number of inputs on recognition and recall', *Journal of Experimental Psychology*, 77, pp. 517–522.

Lee, W. (1965), 'Supra-paragraph prose structures: Its specification, perception and effects of learning', *Psychological Reports*, 17, pp. 135–144.

Lewis, D. (1968), *Convention*. Cambridge, Mass., Harvard University Press.

Paul, I. H. (1959), 'Studies in remembering: The reproduction of connected and extended verbal material', *Psychological Issues*, Monograph Series.

Petöfi, S., and Rieser, H., Eds. (1973), *Studies in Text Grammars*. Dordrecht, Reidel.

Pompi, K. F., and Lachman, R. (1967), 'Surrogate processes in the short-term retention of connected discourse', *Journal of Experimental Psychology*, 75, pp. 143–150.

Projektgruppe Textlinguistik [University of Konstanz] (1974), *Probleme und Perspektiven der neueren Textgrammatischen Forschung*. Hamburg, Buske Verlag.

Schank, R., and Colby, K. M., Eds. (1973), *Computer Models of Thought and Language.* San Francisco, Freeman.

Searle, J. R. (1973), 'Indirect speech acts'. UC, Berkeley. Mimeo.

Slobin, D. (1968), 'Recall of full and truncated passive sentences in connected discourse', *Journal of Verbal Learning and Verbal Behavior,* 7, pp. 876–888.

Wright, G. H. von (1967), 'The logic of action: A sketch', pp. 121–146 in N. Rescher, Ed., *The Logic of Decision and Action.* Pittsburgh University Press.

ROBERT D. EAGLESON 5

Sociolinguistic Reflections on Acceptability

Although the interest in grammaticality which has sprung up with the advent of transformational-generative theory may have led to a broadening of perspectives, it would still be largely true to claim that most investigations into acceptability in the past have arisen in response to debate and in an endeavor to combat prescriptions intuitively felt to be erroneous. Despite the establishment of descriptivism as the proper mode in professional circles for the study of languages and despite the efforts of linguists on the popular front, it is still possible to find prescriptivist attitudes being expressed in the world at large. So keenly felt can objections be to given linguistic forms that some will even go to the trouble of getting their protests in print. Evidence of this can regularly be found in the correspondence columns of newspapers. Here is an example from a recent spate of letters which appeared in a major daily newspaper in Australia.

(*The Sydney Morning Herald,*
December 18, 1974, page 6)

> Sir, Rex Sutton (Letters, December 10) is certainly justified in (feeling like) throwing up on hearing 'at this point of time.' If my memory serves me correctly it was a very prominent former politician who started it all too. I fear he may have lived to regret it.
>
> But what about some of the other expressions one hears, consistently, on television, on radio, in the street and in the office. First of all there is the ubiquitous 'you know' from the semi-literate and 'between you and I' (even one of Sydney's wealthiest accountants used this beauty). 'On behalf of my wife and myself,' or 'my staff and myself' and so on (mostly politicians) and 'he gave it to you and I' are others that cause contractions in the region of the solar plexus.
>
> Rex Sutton may regard his pet aversion as the daddy of them all but, for mine, the big daddy is 'this is right,' kicked off in the 1960's by pseudo-intellectuals, taken up by university lecturers and senior

> public servants and now the centre-piece of many an over-the-backfence suburban washday conversation.
>
> George Blackman

A little earlier there had been criticisms of spellings, outbursts against pronunciation changes (for example, /et/ in place of /ɛt/) and onslaughts on the misuse of words.

No matter how biased the observations in these folk outbursts might be and no matter how much we want to decry the false attitudes to language which they reveal, nevertheless they do offer, albeit indirectly, information on changes taking place in the linguistic practice of the community. They also provide strong indications of shifts in acceptability in the community, for usually the berated form has already acquired a certain frequency in use. Protests rarely come until a form has a body of users and is offering a challenge to established practice. The critics may be ridiculous in their condemnations, but they are useful as grassroot witnesses to changes in process.

Pertinent at this point are the human originators and early propagators of these changes. Are they likely to belong to certain social classes rather than others? Once started, do alterations in practice and modifications in acceptability spread more quickly among speakers of a particular socioeconomic status? Interestingly, these questions seem rarely to have been asked in the environment of acceptability studies in the past. Facts and findings about usage have been released, but invariably the investigators have restricted themselves to exploring the practice and/or attitudes of the more educated members of the community. Leonard (1932), for example, selected as his judges or informants 30 linguists, 130 teachers of English, 30 editors, 22 authors and 19 businessmen. The Mittins *et al.* (1970) study of attitudes samples 457 persons, of whom 397 were lecturers or teachers of English or teacher-trainees; the remainder were drawn from managerial or professional occupations. It is not a criticism of these and other investigators that they so restricted themselves because it is amongst educators and writers in particular that questions of usage can be burning issues. Sociological differences, however, deserve closer attention.[1]

Evidence that in usage as elsewhere social factors could be interacting with linguistic practice has not proved so simple to collect through traditional procedures of investigation. While one can with greater ease gather data on the general characteristics of nonstandard dialects in the community and provide ample information on the occurrence of double negation, subject re-duplication, distinctive verb forms, etc. (see Eagleson, in press), it is less easy to collect detailed evidence on those specific items of usage over which there has been some debate in the community at large and which all sections of the community use to some extent. Many an informant will engage in conversation freely, but this leaves the occurrence of a particular form very much to chance. Although the more educated informants will usually cooperate, it has been my experience that most of those with a lower economic and educational standing are diffident about and generally resistant to taking part in any type of test situation and in particular submitting to a lengthy set of operational tasks. Of those who do cooperate, some, through nervousness or unfamiliarity, are so erratic in fulfilling the requirements of the tests that their responses to any test item cannot be considered reliable and have to be discarded. As a result, we have so far collected only a small number of results from informants with a lower socioeconomic status that will throw light on the sociolinguistic aspects of acceptability. The following comparisons and observations are offered with obvious reservations and with these limitations in mind.

The twenty-seven informants whose results are being considered here ranged between 25 and 60 years of age. None of them had received more than two years of secondary schooling. Their occupations either currently or previously (for those who are now housewives) include factory operators, nursing aides, shop assistants, domestic duties, tradesmen and machinists. They are all native-born speakers of Australian English and are labelled Group A in the following tables. For comparison I put alongside their results those coming from a group of twenty graduate secondary school teachers who were tested in the same year (1974) (Group B in the tables below). The test procedures were modelled on those developed by Quirk with Svartvik (1966) and with Greenbaum (1970).

We might start with the co-occurrence of *got* with *have* in such structures as *He's got to take the dog for a walk*. When the informants were asked to convert this sentence into a question, they responded in the following ways:

	Group A	*Group B*
have + N + got to	19(70%)	8(40%)
do + N + have to	5(19%)	11(55%)
have + N + to	0	1(5%)
other	3(11%)	0

When they were required to convert *Has the car got to be serviced?* into a statement, the following results were obtained:

	Group A	*Group B*
have + got to	14(52%)	7(35%)
have to	6(22%)	13(65%)
do + have to	7(26%)	0

Although we might be impressed by the suppression of obligational *get* in the interrogative even among members of group A, it is nonetheless true that far less suppression occurs with them than with the teachers in Group B. It would seem that there are sections in the community which are less susceptible to the prohibitions of the classroom and the purists and are more likely to persist with questioned practices.

We might next consider the treatment of the interrogative when the main verb is *have* – that is, *have* in its non-auxiliary role, roughly equivalent in sense to 'possess', 'own'. The informants were required to convert *The old man has a winter coat* into a question. In all, three different types of structure emerged:

	Group A	*Group B*
have + N	15(55%)	16(80%)
do + N + have	9(34%)	3(15%)
have + N + got	3(11%)	1(5%)

The significance of these figures emerges when we compare them with the informants' handling of the negative with *have*. The operation of negation on *The doctor has an old black Bentley* yielded the following results:

	Group A	*Group B*
have + neg	6(22%)	6(30%)
do + neg + have	18(67%)	12(60%)
have + neg + got	3(11%)	2(10%).

In negation the structure incorporating *do* is in the ascendancy. In the interrogative, however, *have*-inversion still dominates, but – and this is very much to the point in hand – it is being challenged by the *do*-construction among the group with lower status. If there is a general trend towards the use of the *do*-construction in all situations as seems to be indicated by this evidence, then equally clearly the trend is more advanced in one section of the community than another.

To take a more straightforward item we might consider the spelling of *all right* which was investigated through a selection test. Here 78 percent of Group A produced the spelling *alright*. The corresponding figure for Group B was 20 percent. The shift towards the single word spelling is obviously more favored by people far less concerned with and involved in writing, although the percentage for teachers is also noteworthy.

Even though we recognize that we had only a small number of informants, the data seem sufficient to indicate that in areas of disputed usage lower status groups will be divided, just as other groups are, but they will be more likely to adopt despised usages or change to new usages.

Some verification of the claims just made, although again with a small sample, came from a parallel testing of 17 students in a secondary school in a disadvantaged area in Sydney. The parents of all the students involved were working class, and thus there is a link between these students and the informants of Group A. Obligational *get* was preserved 47% of the time during the operation from statement to question, and 53% of the time from question to statement. With *have* as a main verb, only 24% opted for the *do*-construction in the question, while 76% held to *have*-inversion. In negation, however, 71% use the pattern with *do,* while only 11% use *have* + *not* and 17% *have* + *not* + *got.* As far as *all right* is concerned, the majority (53%) adopted the single word spelling *alright.*[2] Again the group is divided in matters of usage. There is also no exact correlation with either of the previous groups, but there are definite similarities between the practices of these students and those of Group A, who come from the same social background as the students.

What is most important is the fact that when tested in 1974 these students were in the final year in the secondary system and would soon sit for a major public examination. Despite this length of schooling and current involvement in it, they still used linguistic forms which would not be countenanced by most teachers. This might indicate not only the strength of the influences of the outside community but also the prevalence of those forms in the community.

As further support of our general thesis, we might also take into account the results of a pilot comparative study of arts and science students at the University of Sydney in 1971. In fact it was some of these results which prompted the investigations reported above. The 40 students – 20 in science and 20 in arts – were in the third year of their undergraduate course and hence to a certain extent removed from the influence of formal lessons in English received at school, although those in the Faculty of Arts were all taking a course in English language. The test procedures were the same, although there were some differences in the test material.

With obligational *get* we found only 8 (40%) of the arts students retaining *got* in the question, and even fewer – 6 or 30% – in the statement. Twelve (60%) of the science students, however, retained it when they changed a statement into a question and 10 (50%) when they worked in the reverse direction.

When asked to convert *You have a match* into a question, the university students produced the following range of forms:

	Science	*Arts*
have + N	11(55%)	13(65%)
do + N + have	9(45%)	3(15%)
have + N + got	0	2(10%)
have + N + (got)[3]	0	2(10%)

The operation of the negative on *I have a black Bentley* produced:[4]

	Science	*Arts*
have + neg	2(10%)	2(10%)
do + neg + have	15(75%)	12(60%)
have + neg + got	3(15%)	3(15%)
have + neg + (got)[3]	0	2(10%)
have + no + N	0	1(5%)

Finally, 50% of the science students turned in the spelling of *alright,* while only 30% of the arts students adopted this form.

Two observations may be made about this last set of figures. If the samples are at all representative, then science students have marked differences in usage from arts students. Moreover, the science students show tendencies similar to those of lower-status groups. But of them, too, it could be said that they are less subject to conservative pressures.

In support of this last observation, it is interesting to look at the attitudes expressed on other structures by the two groups of students. Take, for instance, *like* used as a conjunction. Students with an arts background were far less ready to accept it than those with a science background. Only 50% of the arts group were prepared to give a clearcut judgment in favor of the test sentence, *It looked like it would rain* (another 35% were doubtful and 15% opposed). With the science students on the other hand we have 90% in favor and only 2 out of 20 (or 10%) against.[5]

We have almost the same situation with that good old hobby horse, the split infinitive. The science students are either completely happy with it or unaware of it: their figures 18 for, 1 doubtful and 1 against. The arts students responded with 10, 8 and 2, respectively. With *who* in place of *whom* (e.g., Who do you want?), the results of one group are the complete reverse of the other. The Science students responded 12–3–5;

the arts students 5–3–12. The divergence in professed attitudes between the two groups is striking.[6]

Even though the sizes of the samples are small and we are therefore not in a position to make too much of the results, nevertheless certain observations would seem to be in order, especially in view of the fact that the results of the three sets of experiments show similar tendencies. Certainly we have evidence that division in usage occurs at various levels in the community. It is not necessarily the case that one socioeconomic group will be settled in its practice, while in others there will be a degree of variation. While it is no doubt valid to concentrate one's investigations on the usage of the cultivated, as Leonard (1932) tried to do, only a limited view of the total situation results, and one can remain unaware of all the forces which may be predisposing either the whole or part of the community to prefer one form or structure.

Again, in areas of debate the proportions favoring one form and not another may vary from social group to social group in the community. To treat all informants together without any discrimination could give a false or less valuable picture. If we were, for example, to treat groups A and B as a unit and to conflate their results, we would establish that the majority of the population, namely 53 percent, had adopted the single word spelling *alright,* but this would be misleading. As our tests with the university students show, there will be occasions when we should give consideration to quite fine distinctions among our informants. Not only is it useful to know what the current state is with respect to a given item of usage, but it is also valuable to uncover tendencies and the pressures likely to vary the present situation. In this process of widening the scope of acceptability studies, which seems to me to be essential, we will simultaneously be producing useful sociolinguistic data.[7]

Tantalizing by-questions arise from such facts as these. Are changes, no matter what their origin, promoted more rapidly among lower socioeconomic groups with limited education? How many changes in linguistic practice actually begin among these groups and spread to others? Moreover, it has been proposed by historians of the language (*cf.*, e.g., Baugh, 1960: 189) that a factor contributing to the extensive changes which took place in English in the period immediately after the Norman Conquest was the relegation of English to a large extent to be the speech of the uninfluential, lower classes with the consequent removal of conservative influences usually exerted by the educated classes. Is the evidence just advanced a modern confirmation of the validity of such claims? Do the less educated still exert a powerful influence on the direction taken by the users of the language? How legitimate is Blackman in singling out the semiliterate in his letter above? We cannot even presume to answer these questions yet, but the investigations reported here do point up a fascinating area that calls for more extensive exploration within the context of acceptability.

ACKNOWLEDGMENT

This research was supported by a grant from the University of Sydney.

NOTES

1. Attention to these differences can be found in the work of such scholars as Labov (1972) and Gunnel Tottie (1971).
2. The full results for the secondary students are:

(a) *Obligational get*

(1) Question		(2) Statement	
have + N + got to	8 (47%)	have + got to	9 (53%)
do + N + have to	7 (41%)	have + to	7 (41%)
other	2 (12%)	other	1 (6%)

(b) *Have*

(1) Question		(2) Statement	
have + N	13 (76%)	have + neg	2 (12%)
do + N + have	4 (24%)	do + neg + have	12 (70%)
		have + not + got	3 (18%)

(c) *All right*

all right	8 (47%)
alright	9 (53%)

3. *Got* occurs in brackets in the informants' responses.
4. The test sentence for the negative was originally used by Quirk and Svartvik (1966) for the same type of investigation. Their informants reacted in the following manner:

have + neg	53%
do + neg + have	32.5%
have + not + got	9%
have + no + N	5.5%

These figures contrast markedly with the Australian ones and point to a difference between British and Australian practice. Again there could be social factors operating here.

5. There is another side to this story which should be noticed. Only one student – and he was from the arts group – changed the structure at the point *like* in the operation test, substituting in its place *as though.* The remaining 19 arts students retained it, revealing once more that practice and attitude can be out of step.

6. On the whole, attempts at giving judgment tests to informants with lower socioeconomic status turned out to be fruitless, and consequently no results are presented here. The concepts involved in a judgment test seemed not to be clearly grasped by such informants.
7. Age and sex differences might also be introduced as well as other social parameters into our investigations.

REFERENCES

Baugh, A. C. (1960), *A History of the English Language*. London, Routledge and Kegan Paul.

Eagleson, R. D. (in press), 'The evidence for social dialects in Australian English', *International Journal for the Sociology of Language*.

Greenbaum, S., and Quirk, R. (1970), *Elicitation Experiments in English*. London, Longman.

Labov, W. (1972a), *Language in the Inner City*. Philadelphia, University of Pennsylvania.

– (1972b), *Sociolinguistic Patterns*. Philadelphia, University of Pennsylvania.

Leonard, A. A. (1932), *Current English Usage*. Chicago, National Council of Teachers of English.

Mittins, W. H., Salu, M., Edminson, M. and Coyne, S. (1972), *Attitudes to English Usage*. London, Oxford University Press.

Quirk, R., and Svartvik, J. (1966), *Investigating Linguistic Acceptability*. The Hague, Mouton.

Tottie, G. (1971), *Have To: A Study of Usage and Acceptability in Present-Day British English*. Stockholm University.

ROBIN LAKOFF

6

You say what you are: Acceptability and Gender-related Language

Her voice was ever soft
Gentle and low, an excellent thing in woman.
W. Shakespeare, *King Lear* 5.3, 272–3

Within the model of transformational generative grammar, questions of grammaticality at first were the ones deemed interesting, important and, indeed, answerable; to the extent that the question of acceptability was raised at all, it was felt to reflect 'performance' rather than 'competence' and therefore to be out of the range of interest of linguistic theory proper. Today, when our model is much more sophisticated and we are very much more demanding of our theory, we tend to be a bit bemused at our insensitivity to the data, a mere decade – nay, seven or eight years – ago; but there was good reason for it, and it is lucky for us today that we in the past were so blind to the facts.

Grammaticality implies an either/or (*/non*) distinction; assuming (an untenable assumption in reality, but the enterprising linguist should be able to believe six impossible things before breakfast) that one can divide all the sentences of a language according to such a criterion makes for a tolerably workable theory. Binary distinctions such as this are relatively simple to make, and there will likely be widespread agreement among linguists as to the assignment of asterisks; indeed, such a theory virtually entails such agreement, since questions of personal idiosyncrasy and imaginativeness are thereby ignored. In those far-off days, too, it will be recalled, binariness of various sorts of features was a feature of transformational theory: phonological distinctive features, syntactic selectional restrictions and semantic markers all were binary. It was tempting to believe that linguistic markers, like other animals, came in pairs, and it was therefore natural to assume that grammaticality was an either-or question.

Syntactic rules were formulated on this basis. Either a derivation was subject to a particular rule or it was not. If a phrase-marker underwent a rule in accordance with its structural description and the conditions on the rule, the resultant derivation would prove grammatical; otherwise an asterisk would be assigned, and that was that. The validity of a particular formulation of a rule was checked this way, too: if sentences were, by this automatic procedure, assigned stars when the native speaker would declare them grammatical, or not assigned stars when he would not, the assumption was that something was the matter with the formulation of the rule; a better one had to be found. The least, in fact, that one could expect of a theory (one that was observationally adequate) was that it would allow all and only the sentences of a language to be generated – another way of saying what I said above.

Assuming, again, that this evaluation procedure approximated the facts of language, it was a simple, streamlined and elegant procedure. It is obvious that only under such an assumption could rules of the type that were being written at that time have been written at all. Of course, we see with our 20–20 hindsight that this very fact – that binary grammaticality judgments necessitated as well as permitted the rules of classical transformational grammar – casts doubt on the entire set of assumptions we call classical transformational grammar; but at the time, this seemed to us the way things ought to be in a well-ordered universe, and we were still capable of believing, with our endearing childlike faith, that the linguistic universe was well-ordered.

It is further true that a new theory can arise only out of an old theory; it was out of transformational grammar with all its faults that we have constructed our present-day theory with its unnumbered virtues. The change in emphasis from grammaticality to acceptability was forced upon us, around 1967 or 1968, by our recognition of a whole new range of data and our consequent search for more sophisticated explanations for the occurrence and nonoccurrence of sentences. Where grammaticality judgments were determinable by purely linguistic criteria, acceptability judgments invaded the realms of psychology and sociology, greatly increasing the range of facts one had to look at, as well as the range of possible explanations. But we found we could no longer honestly restrict the concept of explanation to purely linguistic determinants; and inexorably at the same time we found that our judgments were no longer predicated on a binary system of grammaticality, but had to make use of a hierarchy of acceptability.

The necessity for this became clear to me when I was looking (1969) at the use of *some* and *any* in English. When Klima (1964) had examined the data, he had attempted to make grammaticality judgments about the use of these forms, to assign asterisks to sentences on the basis of purely linguistic data. (He managed to sneak psychological assumptions into his set of criteria by the use of his [+affect] marker, but he never openly acknowledged that this was the purpose, or the effect, of adopting his apparently linguistic and apparently binary marker.) When I started looking at sentences containing *some* and *any,* however, I found it impossible to declare many of them purely 'in' or purely 'out'; one could declare a sentence 'good if one made the following assumptions about the state of the speaker's mind' or 'generally out, but acceptable in case the speaker is in a particular and peculiar social situation'. And of course, social, psychological and linguistic situations intersect and interact with one another, so that immediately it was clear we were dealing with a delicately shaded and rather interminable hierarchy of acceptability.

What also became clear with some more thought was that the hierarchical fuzziness was the norm, the clear grammatical judgment rather the exception, an artificial construct useful for the facilitation of theory development rather than an accurate perception of how speakers spoke in the real world. Even those sentences that had previously been adjudged unexceptionably grammatical could now be seen for what they were – good *if* one were uttering the sentence in a particular social-psychological environment; and in fact, many of the sentences so insouciantly described as fully grammatical were now, in the clear light of day, seen to be rather bizarre, like Gleitman's well-known

(1) I wrote my grandmother a letter yesterday and six men can fit in the back seat of a Ford.

That is one obvious case of a sentence that is fully grammatical, that is, linguistically unexceptionable; and yet, if we are judging acceptability – that is, the probability of such a sentence being uttered, or the number of conceivable real-world circumstances or the normality of the real-world circumstances in which this sentence is apt to be used – we find a different judgment pertains, and we must rank this sentence low on an acceptability hierarchy.

On the other hand there are sentences which, taken out of context, are bizarre; some even violate selectional restrictions, such as Morgan's (1973) celebrated example:

(2) I think with a fork. [Morgan's (106)]

As Morgan notes, 'fragments' such as (2) are intelligible when interpreted from the point of view of a larger context, discourse or social; sentence (2), for instance, is fully intelligible if uttered as a reply to (3):

(3) How does Nixon eat his tapioca? [Morgan's (105)]

Sentences like (2) would have been asterisked in any classical transformational discussion, as it violates certain selectional restrictions. Yet sentences such as this are frequent in ordinary speech and hence would rank high on any rational acceptability hierarchy. So there are sentences that are ungrammatical but of relatively high acceptability *in context*. Thus, given the correct set of social, situational and linguistic contexts, both (1) and (2) might be considered good sentences of English. The difference between the two in this regard is that, while one can imagine a reasonably high number of contexts – and 'plausible' contexts, too – in which (2) might be uttered, the same cannot be done for (1). So, defining acceptability in this way, the 'ungrammatical' (2) is a 'better' or more acceptable sentence than the 'grammatical' (1).

Another way to view the grammaticality/acceptability distinction is to say that grammaticality is a special case of acceptability. A sentence is grammatical if it is acceptable according to purely linguistic criteria. Grammaticality is acceptability shorn of social and psychological differentiations. Then it seems fairly apparent that grammaticality is a very highly specialized and not terribly useful concept, outside the realm of strictly autonomous syntax. As soon as we concur that autonomous syntax is not a viable level of analysis (as various works written in the last ten years have, I feel, conclusively proved), we see that a separate notion of grammaticality is neither necessary nor possible within a coherent linguistic theory. But if we discard grammaticality as a criterion, how are we to talk about cases of the kind discussed above, where, apparently, grammaticality and acceptability do not coincide? Here we must speak of normal extra-linguistic context. Although a sentence is judged by its appropriateness in its social, psychological and linguistic contexts, we may assume that some of these contexts outrank others in determining whether a sentence is acceptable. Thus, (1) would have to be judged acceptable in terms of linguistic context, unacceptable in psychological context (that is, a participant in a discourse would be hard put to figure out what the two parts of the conjunct had to do with each other, and hence the conjunct as a whole is psychologically invalid). But (2) is unacceptable in terms of pure syntactic grammaticality (selectional restrictions between verb and adverbial phrase are violated) but psychologically viable (since participants are capable of figuring out from prior linguistic context what has to be supplied to make the sentence in this particular form intelligible). Further, we may say that in certain social situations – e.g., informal discourse – (2) is acceptable. But in others, though the participants have the psychological ability to make sense of the utterance, they are unwilling or unable to use it, and so we must confine the acceptability of (2) to certain social contexts. These examples serve to show that psychological acceptability outranks purely linguistic acceptability.

In any case it is clear that using acceptability rather than grammaticality judgments forces us into a much more complex theory of syntax and one with many more variables, but one which, used correctly, makes for more accurate predictions – which is, after all, what a linguistic theory should do. It is a far more problematic theory, however; and the assignment of particular points on the hierarchy to particular sentences is not the hardest issue to be solved if one is to make good use of the notion of hierarchical acceptability. What I want to do for the remainder of this paper is examine one particularly vexing problem: the applicability of the concept of acceptability to one dialect of American English, and the question of when a judgment of acceptability ceases to be a linguistic judgment and becomes a political statement.

In earlier work (1975) I talked about differences between men's language, or rather the standard language, and 'women's' language. I catalogued a number of features that seem to characterize women's language, in those segments of the American populace that, consciously or otherwise, make that distinction. (It is useful to bear in mind, here and in succeeding discussion, that a speaker's disavowal of the use of, or even the knowledge of, women's language does not mean she does not or cannot use or understand it. In socially and psychologically charged issues such as whether or not one speaks women's language, one's judgments as to one's own speech patterns may easily be false; what one says is by no means identical to what one wishes one says or fears one says. This fact colors *all* intuitive observation, as Labov has correctly noted; but it colors the most strongly those observations where the observer has something to gain or lose by his (or her) decision. And although some women will find it necessary to believe that they *always* use women's language, and others that they *never* do, it is probably true that all of us use some of it some of the time, whether we want to or not, whether we hear outselves doing it or not.)

Let me recapitulate briefly what I consider characteristic of women's language:

1. Special vocabulary – in particular, women seem to discriminate linguistically among colors with more precision than do men.

2. Use of adjectives that principally express the speaker's feelings toward the subject under discussion: *charming, adorable, divine* and the like.

3. Use of empty intensifiers like *so, such.*

4. Greater adherence to standard 'correct' forms, avoidance of slang and neologisms, both lexically and grammatically. For example, psy-

chological studies of kindergarten-age and nursery-school children indicate that, even at this age, little girls are guardians of 'correct' grammar: they 'drop their *g*s' in participial endings *(runnin', talkin')* much less than boys, use fewer substandard forms *(ain't, snuck),* less double negation *(I didn't do nothin'),* use fewer 'bad' words and in general articulate more precisely. These traits become a part of traditional adult women's language.

5. Use of lexical, grammatical or phonological devices to suggest hesitancy or deference. Examples:

a. Prefacing declarative utterances with *I guess,* questions with *I wonder,* etc. In this way the speaker mitigates the force of her speech act, creating an impression of hesitancy to impose her opinions on other participants in a discourse and thereby giving an impression of politeness, or deference. Of course things are not necessarily what they seem, and the politeness, or deference, may be conventional rather than real. But confusion may easily arise, and the speaker's character be judged by her superficial style – marking her as indecisive, inarticulate and fuzzy-minded. On the other hand, if, in traditional American culture, a female speaker habitually fails to employ these devices, she is categorized as aggressive and unfeminine. Until recently, most speakers have opted for the first of these uncomfortable options.

b. Silences or interjections like *ah, um* . . .

c. Use of questions where a declarative would be more appropriate (i.e., where the speaker is in possession of the necessary information, if anyone is). In such cases, the question is not a request that the addressee supply *information* but rather that he supply *reassurance* that the speaker's speech-act is acceptable to him.

d. Lower vocal volume, sometimes a mere whisper.

6. Greater use of euphemism for topics that are considered to be taboo or unladylike, as well as greater tact in avoiding sensitive topics in the presence of people they are sensitive to. For this reason (also a part of non-linguistic behavior, of course) women have typically been considered the arbiters of etiquette as well as the mainstays of conservatism. This latter role is also illustrated in point 4. Otto Jespersen was perhaps the first to discuss the role of women in linguistic conservatism. More recently Labov has made the opposite claim: that women are linguistically more innovative than men. As with most cases of conflicting claims, both are probably partially valid, and each especially valid in the writer's contemporary society. It is also true that a group might be conservative in one aspect of language use, radical in another. Thus, if the behavioral role of a particular group were facilitated by an emergent

linguistic form, the group to whose advantage it would be to adopt this form might well do so more quickly than other social groups and in this regard appear especially innovative. But in other aspects of language use, the same group might elect to be more conservative. For example (as discussed by Edwin Newman [1974] among many others) a relatively recent trend in American speech favors the use of speech-act hedges like *like, y'know, I mean* . . . (For some discussion of the role of these hedges in American English, see my review of Newman [to appear].) Now as I noted above, for reasons consonant with their traditional social role, women have a tendency to use hedges more profusely than do men. It might therefore be to their advantage to adopt these hedges more quickly and more profusely than men do. But they might still stoutly resist other changes, e.g., the use of *like* for *as.* Labov, I believe, was talking about phonological innovation. Often, nonstandard phonological forms sound 'cute', or nonserious, and mark the speech-act in which they occur as amusing, social rather than informative. For example, we can think of the shift to Black English among middle-class white academics when they are feeling linguistically playful or the use of baby-talk by one speaker to show that he isn't really in sympathy with someone else's complaints. The more serious the occasion, the more pompously conservative the style, and bombast seems in our culture to be more available to men than to women. Thus it would be to a woman's advantage to use phonological forms that made her sound 'cute' and nonserious – for the same reason that it is to her advantage to have in her lexicon adjectives like *charming, divine* and *adorable.* In other times, women might be assumed to be more innovative because they were less educated, were less in touch with a formal norm. And where women are seen as the arbiters of respectability, it is to be expected that they will resist any change that can be viewed as a lowering of standards, linguistic or moral.

7. Greater variation in pitch and intonation. This difference might be viewed in either of two ways: as a means of achieving indirectness or as a way of expressing emotion. By making use of pitch and intonation variation, one can express thoughts and feelings nonverbally which it might be difficult or uncomfortable to put into words. But if one has no intention of explicitly talking about one's feelings, more emotional warmth is conveyed by a speech style that allows these variations than one that does not. So to judge what such a trait connotes for an individual's speech-style, one must first examine the rest of her (or his) style.

Then we may say that three basic trends characterize women's language as a deviation from the standard:

1. Nondirectness: e.g., 5, 6, 7
2. Emotional expression: e.g., 2, 3, 6 and 7
3. Conservatism: e.g., 4 and 6

Point (1) does not figure in this summary, and indeed it is rather misleading to categorize 'special vocabulary' as idiosyncratic to women's language. The deeper point to be made here is that every subculture has its own vocabulary and that vocabulary will involve terms that are of specific use to the particular culture in question. Whorf, of course, was the first to raise this issue when he pointed out that Eskimo has six words for 'snow' where English has just one – presumably because snow is much more important in the Eskimos' lives than it is in ours, and minute differences in the quality and quantity of snow are for them of crucial importance, as they are not for us. So they need precise words to make these crucial distinctions, as we do not. As I have said elsewhere, this is undoubtedly the reason for the more precise color-discrimination vocabulary among women because it has traditionally been considered important for a woman to possess this sort of expertise, for fashion and interior decoration have both been women's work. Of course, men have their own special highly developed vocabularies, e.g., in regard to automobiles and sports, to which women traditionally have not been privy.

What we find, then, in looking at those traits that distinguish women's language from neutral language is that we can define them in terms that cover more purely linguistic behavior. In fact, the only distinctions it seems reasonable to assert between the two forms of English, rather than arising directly out of differences in the learning of a linguistically relevant grammatical system, appear to stem from differences in what is socially and psychologically expected of women in terms of explicit behavior, both linguistic and nonlinguistic. Where women's speech differs syntactically from the standard it does not differ in containing more, fewer or differently stated rules. I know of no syntactic rule present in one group's grammar and entirely absent from the other: that is, I know of no case where a sentence utterable by one group would be totally impossible in all contexts for the other. In this sense we are not even dealing with differences in the linguistic conditions for the applicability of rules, or their order, as is true of dialect differences in quantifier-crossing as discussed by Carden and others. It is not out of the question that this *might* be so, and in other languages it would not be overly surprising if it were so. How would it look? It might mirror Carden's cases. Thus, suppose that all English-speaking men, when they encountered (4):

(4) All of the boys don't like some of the girls,

interpreted it as (5):

(5) None of the boys like certain girls: namely, Mary, Alice, Nancy . . .

Whereas, faced with the same sentence, all English-speaking women interpreted it as (6):

(6) Only some of the boys – Fred, John, Max . . . – like some of the girls.

But, as I say, I know of no such cases. Rather, even where syntactic rules such as question-formation are involved, the difference between the dialects lies in the fact that in one a sentence is usable in more social or psychological situations than in the other. So we cannot define the two dialects in terms of purely linguistic autonomous-syntactic distinctions. Additional reason for this belief is the fact that even if a woman will not or cannot use certain forms that are not parts of traditional women's language, she can certainly understand them and, if she is of a certain personality type, when she encounters them in other people's speech, can correct them, i.e., indicate what forms in *her* dialect are equivalent to the ones she has heard.

All this suggests that linguistic deviation from the norm is but one form of social deviation from the norm. But here we must raise another, and more troubling, question: what do we mean when we talk about the norm? Whose norm? And to what extent, when we talk about norms and standards and deviations, are we invoking value judgments? Psychological writers in particular often claim piously that they intend no reproof when they speak of abnormality or aberration; but actually one typically finds the implicit claim that the standard is better, and if you know what's good form you'll adhere to it. Of course, this then constitutes a self-fulfilling prophecy. The same has been true too often in the past in linguistic dialectology, which tended to be prescriptive and, more or less overtly, looked with disapproval at 'substandard' forms. But in the case of women's language the question becomes a bit more complex: if a woman in our society speaks traditional women's language, and more generally behaves like a traditional woman, is she conforming to our cultural norm? Or deviating from it? And if we must be prescriptive, what shall we punish as deviant? More positively, for what kinds of behavior shall a woman in our society be rewarded? What, returning to the theme of this essay, constitutes 'acceptability' for a woman in this culture – linguistically and behaviorally?

In fact it is less the bare notion of acceptability that causes difficulty than the fact that it is made into a prescription. In the same way we can talk about expectation being a two-edged concept. We *expect* women to talk a certain way, which is only partly damaging; but we also expect it of women that they will behave a certain way, and thereby we impose a value judgment, either that it's good for a woman to talk traditional women's language because it fits the stereotype, which is by definition good because it does not force us to readjust our perception of reality; or it's bad for women to speak women's language because it deviates from the norm, and the norm for society as a whole is viewed as a good thing to adhere to, and any deviation is to be criticized. And both linguistically and otherwise, when we say that a certain form of behavior is 'acceptable' for a woman, we tend to be prescribing – both for the woman, that she act this way to indicate she 'knows her place,' and for a man, that he *not* act this way, to show he knows *his*. This kind of prescriptivism is constraining and destructive. We should be able to think about acceptability in regard to linguistic gender distinctions without recourse to value judgments, just as linguists several generations ago pointed out that description did not imply prescription, that talking about a norm did not imply that deviation from that norm was censurable. I recall that Paul Goodman – no doubt in good company – made this mistake some years back in an article in the *New York Review of Books,* in which he criticized Chomsky's linguistic work on the grounds that – by distinguishing sentences that were grammatical from those which were not – he was squashing linguistic creativity and innovation. But the distinction between description and prescription is still blurrier, even among linguists, than we might like, particularly in areas where we have been brought up to make value judgments before we learned to be disinterested academic observers. The question of gender-related roles is one of these highly charged areas, and it therefore behooves us in discussing acceptability as a factor in understanding women's language to bear in mind that there is a danger that we will confuse linguistic norms with social values.

There are other confusions to be avoided. The notion of acceptability, I have said above, implies a standard against which a speech act may be judged. It has also been pointed out that, in talking about acceptability as opposed to grammaticality, that standard is grounded in social and psychological context: an act of speech or behavior is judged acceptable in a specific context. Now, it would seem at first glance that men and women, being these days participants in the same activities, similarly educated, at least superficially raised alike, would share this set of contexts. A male and a female, participating in a specific kind of behavior, linguistic or otherwise, would perceive the context in which the behavior was to take place similarly. But if acceptability implies appropriateness within a particular social-psychological setting, and as we have suggested men's and women's languages differ somewhat in terms of what is acceptable, then we are faced with a paradox.

We must, rather, assume, I think, that a given context is interpreted one way by a male speaker, another by a female. Actually, it will be recalled we are dealing with a complex hierarchy of acceptability, and it is in principle not at all unlikely that different speakers will arrange their worlds in quite different ways. It is not as though every male speaker of English defines Contexts A-L, let us say, as 'situations requiring directness' and M-Z as 'requiring nondirectness', while all women interpret situations A-P in the former way, Q-Z in the latter. We would prefer to say - continuing for the sake of clarity to look at the division of social contexts in this extremely simplistic way for the moment – that women would tend to interpret situations as requiring nondirectness until further down in the alphabet than men typically would. But all sorts of variations are conceivable. That is, what I mean by saying that traditionally women's language has tended toward nondirectness is that women will interpret a greater number of social contexts as being appropriate for nondirect expression than will men; and perhaps as well, that women will, in a situation in which both men and women would tend toward nondirectness, tend toward greater nondirectness. But this implies that a woman's social/psychological context is often, or perhaps always, different from that of a man. Whether innately, or through early education, a woman learns to perceive social situations, and interpret psychological events, one way, a man, another. Hence a setting that would evoke one set of linguistic responses in a man would be expected to evoke another in a woman.

If this is true, it seems reasonable to say that, if we want to even out the differences in linguistic behavior between men and women (a goal the utility not to say feasibility of which is in my mind very much open to question), linguistic behavior cannot be changed directly but only through somehow educating men and women so that they typically perceive the same situation in the same way. Of course, many questions are being begged here: it is also apparent that no two individuals, in all likelihood, perceive a single social or psychological setting precisely identically. But we are talking here about somewhat grosser differentiations; the problem is, how much grosser? Since we have been talking in terms of a complex, highly individualized hierarchy, at what point do we draw the line and stop speaking about individual idiosyncrasies and start recognizing broader sex-linked distinctions? Since it will, predictably, never be so that 100 percent of the men react in one way to a situation, 100 percent of the women a different way, at what point do we decide we are dealing with 'women's language'?

We tend to consider women's language as the aberration from the norm, the standard. To do so raises more problems.

First, there is the implication that to be a woman is to be a deviant. This has traditionally been true – people have looked at men's behavior as the norm, as rational, and men's language likewise. Hence it has been typical – to the extent that such a topic has even been considered worthy of discussion – to talk about women's language. Men's language is language and need not be further specified. But this is the case also as we would expect for other aspects of human behavior. Until recently no one has lifted an eyebrow at questions like, 'Was will das Weib?' suggesting that a woman was a thing apart, something *we* could analyze. But the question 'Was will der Mann?' would have been unthinkable. But if men's behavior is the standard, so normal that it is not even worth investigating in its own right, then a woman cannot expect equality with men. She simply is not parallel to a man, and thus cannot expect to be treated similarly.

Moreover, there is another danger in looking at women's language as having special and idiosyncratic standards for acceptability. What is a woman to do? If she adopts the frame of reference of a man – supposing she can – she will be ostracized by traditional society for not conforming to what is acceptable for a woman. If, on the other hand, she does adopt women's behavior, she will be treated nonseriously because her behavior is not commensurate with the standard, the behavior expected of men.

There is one corner of the real world where, interestingly, the distinction between men's and women's language seems to be blurred: the same set of social and psychological conditions, or very nearly so, are operative in determining the acceptability of utterances both of men and of women. This occurs in academia. The traits I listed earlier as characteristic of women's speech are frequent in academic men's speech, and academic women's speech tends at the same time to use these devices less than does the speech of traditional women. This is not, I think, to imply that academics are sexless or that academic men and women find themselves in social settings that cause them to perceive their roles differently less often than does the general populace. Rather, I think that this difference indicates that male and female professionals, in academia, regardless of gender, perceive their roles as similar and hence tend to have similar perceptions of the social and psychological settings in which they find themselves. It is interesting that the distinction is not erased in favor of the masculine form, but rather there is a neutralization toward the center. What is of interest in this is that in society generally, when there is pressure to blur sex distinctions in roles, usually women seek to adopt men's prerogatives, seldom the reverse. But in academia some of women's prerogatives – nondirectness and expression of emotions – are adopted by men. I have suggested elsewhere that these traits have less to do with anything inherent in the female character than they do with being at the periphery of power, or opting out of power. Academics, the British upper class men, and women all share this situation, for various reasons and in different ways, and hence, to a rather surprising extent, share their language.

My conclusions then are clear:

1. There is a women's language in American English, if by that we mean that in a particular context, women and men may not express the same thing in the same way.
2. This difference is not traceable to the purely linguistic grammar: the distinctions are not statable in terms of syntactically conditioned rules, nor are they statable as *either/or* pairs. The differences involve hierarchical acceptability – some sentences are better for women to say in some circumstances.
3. Acceptability in language is directly related to social and psychological perceptions; a sentence is defined as acceptable if it is fitting in the setting in which it is used. Grammaticality, then, is a special case of acceptability, in which only the linguistic aspects of the social-psychological setting are taken into account.
4. Therefore it seems likely that men and women learn to view similar social and psychological contexts differently and hence will find it appropriate to utter different sentences in the same setting.
5. Women's language differs from the standard in being more nondirect, more capable of expressing emotion and more conservative.
6. There is a danger in opposing 'women's language' to 'the standard', as there is of opposing any group's behavior to a hypothetical 'standard'; and it is by no means clear what is best for women or for society: to perpetuate the dual standards of acceptability or seek to merge them.

REFERENCES

Klima, E. (1964), 'Negation in English', in J. A. Fodor and J. J. Katz, Eds., *The Structure of Language: Readings in the Philosophy of Language*. Englewood Cliffs, N.J., Prentice-Hall.

Lakoff, R. (1969), 'Some reasons why there can't be any *some-any* rule', *Language,* 55, pp. 608–615.
– (1975) *Language and Woman's Place.* New York, Harper and Row.
– (forthcoming), 'Review of E. Newman, *Strictly Speaking', Centrum.*
Morgan, J. L. (1973), 'Sentence fragments and the notion, "Sentence"', in B. Kachru *et al.,* Eds., *Issues in Linguistics in Honor of Henry and Renee Kahane.* Urbana, Ill., University of Illinois Press.
Newman, E. (1974), *Strictly Speaking.* New York, Bobbs-Merill.

W. J. M. LEVELT / J. A. W. M. VAN GENT
A. F. J. HAANS / A. J. A. MEIJERS

7

Grammaticality, Paraphrase and Imagery

1. INTRODUCTION

The concept of grammaticality is a crucial one in generative linguistics since Chomsky (1957) chose it to be the very basis for defining a natural language. The fundamental aim of linguistic analysis was said to be to separate the grammatical sequences from the ungrammatical ones and to study the structure of the grammatical ones. It is, therefore, not surprising to see that this central linguistic notion became the subject of much study and controversy. A major part of the discussions centered around the following points: (a) semigrammaticality, (b) reliability and validity of grammaticality judgments, (c) the psychological status of linguistic (e.g., grammaticality) intuitions.

(a) Though the principal distinction is that between grammatical and ungrammatical, there may be different degrees of ungrammaticality. Various authors have developed theories on degrees of ungrammaticality (Chomsky 1964; Katz 1964; Ziff 1964; Lakoff 1971). They are all based on the consideration that given a grammar, ungrammaticality can be varied as a function of the seriousness and number of rule violations. These theories are based on the principle that absolute grammaticality exists and that only strings outside the language show degrees of (un-) grammaticality. It should be noted that other linguists never used a notion of absolute grammaticality. Harris' transformation theory, especially his operator grammar (1970), is based on the principle that transformations preserve the order of grammaticality; e.g., if two passives have a certain order of grammaticality, this order should be preserved for the corresponding actives. This is a major test case for the correct formulation of transformation rules. In this way there is no linguistic need for the notion of absolute grammaticality. Levelt (1974c) studied the question to what degree linguists would be handicapped (i.e., linguistic theory would become untestable) if the notion of absolute grammaticality were replaced by this 'preservation-of-order' principle. It turns out that very little of interest is lost, whereas some unexpected gains are made. Moreover, the logical definition of a language as a set of strings no longer requires the notion of absolute grammaticality. Fuzzy set theory (Zadeh 1971) makes it possible to meaningfully discuss *degrees* of set-membership. It would be very advantageous if linguistic theory construction could do without the notion of absolute grammaticality, especially in view of the following point.

(b) The reliability of absolute grammaticality judgments turns out to be very low. Various recent experiments (Levelt 1972; Greenbaum 1973; Snow 1974) testify to this. In the early years of the transformational grammar this was not an important issue, since the 'clear cases', i.e., the highly uncontroversial cases of grammaticality and ungrammaticality, were sufficient for constructing and testing linguistic theory. It was expected that, in its turn, the theory constructed in such a way would decide on the 'unclear cases'. This hope has vanished: more and more subtle theory is now being constructed on less and less clear cases. In such a situation one would expect linguistics to turn to appropriate behavioral methods of data gathering and (statistical) analysis. Nothing of the sort occurs, however. Levelt (1972) showed that various procedures that are used for obtaining grammaticality judgments lead to systematic biases and distortions. We know of no linguistic studies, except Greenbaum's, where grammaticality judgments are put to statistical test in order to accept or reject certain linguistic hypotheses. Levelt (1974c) gives examples of testing various linguistic theories by means of experimentally obtained linguistic judgments.

The validity of grammaticality judgments has been studied by several authors (*cf.* Maclay and Sleator 1960; Quirk and Svartvik 1966), especially in order to relate the notion to other linguistic intuitions, such as meaningfulness, or to psychological variables like comprehensibility. In the present paper another psychological variable, imagery, will be related to grammaticality.

(c) The theoretical scope of Chomsky's transformational grammar was greatly expanded when it was taken to be a description of the language user's linguistic competence, not merely a formal system characterizing a certain linguistic set. Linguistic intuitions became the royal way into an understanding of the competence which underlies all linguistic performance. However, if such a linguistic competence exists at all, i.e., some relatively autonomous mental capacity for language, linguistic intuitions seem to be the least obvious data on which to base the study of its structure. They are very derived and rather artificial psycholinguistic phenomena which develop late in language acquisition

(Gleitman *et al.* 1972) and are very dependent on explicit teaching and instruction. They cannot be compared with primary language use such as speaking and listening. The empirical domain of Chomskian linguistics is linguistic intuitions. The relation between these intuitions and man's capacity for language, however, is highly obscure. An extensive discussion of these issues can be found in Levelt (1974c).

It is this latter point that we want to take up in the present article. Our question will be a psychological one: Where do grammaticality intuitions come from? It makes no sense to assume *a priori* that the domain of linguistic intuition is a relatively closed one, as many linguists appear to do. Such intuitions are highly dependent on our knowledge of the world and on the structure of our inferential capacities. So the general question should be: what sort of process underlies the formation of a grammaticality judgment? The only way to approach this question is to ignore all *a priori* linguistic restrictions and to regard it as a problem in human information processing.

At the same time it should be obvious that answering this question will require much experimentation. At present, however, this is still a virginal area. We know of one remarkable study where a process analysis is made of grammaticality judgments: Moore (1972) studied this behavior *vis-à-vis* sentences where subject, verb or object was the locus of ungrammaticality. Reaction time analysis showed a definite order of focusing the different parts of the sentence in forming the judgment.

Moore did not go into the question of how judgment of the focused part took place. One could think of various factors playing a role here. It is one possibly important factor which we want to take up in this paper: imagery. Analysis of this factor may, as we shall see, show some light on the processing of sociolinguistic cues in speech perception.

2. THE USE OF IMAGERY

If one asks an informant how he performs the judgment task, a usual answer is something like: 'I try to imagine a situation in which the phrase or sentence can be said.' The informant seems to 'use' imagery in answering the grammaticality or acceptability question: he tries to find a cognitive, preferably visual, context in which the sentence could make sense. But what exactly does it mean to 'use imagery'?

A decade of imagery research has not solved this problem. It is especially still controversial whether humans have two separate representational systems for verbal and nonverbal information, respectively.

If one believes this to be the case (Paivio 1971, 1974), 'using imagery' is addressing the non-verbal representational system during information processing. The facilitative effect of using imagery in interpreting words, phrases or sentences could then partly be ascribed to the fact that two representational systems, instead of one, are involved in the comprehension or judgment task. If one assumes the existence of only one general representational system (Anderson and Bower 1973), 'using imagery' reduces to an attractive triviality: instructing the subject to use imagery in some comprehension or memory task would only encourage him to spontaneously generate 'expansion' of the verbal material. He would, in a more extensive way, 'scan' the meanings (i.e., representations) of the different elements in the material, which means retrieving various connected memory structures, etc. This would increase the probability of finding the connections that are crucial for the experimental task. The facilitative effect of 'using imagery' should be a-specific, according to this theory: it is not the image that intervenes and causes the solution, but the experience of an image is an epiphenomenon which is caused by enhanced memory activity. Anderson and Bower present rather convincing experimental evidence for their position, but it is not necessary here to prejudge this theoretical controversy. There is full agreement that the instruction to 'use imagery' is facilitative for a large variety of comprehension and memory tasks. This facilitative effect can, moreover, be obtained by using concrete (or 'high imagery') material. Abstract (or 'low imagery') material is harder to use in verbal tasks, leading to more errors and longer reaction times. It is, therefore, clear that the judgment process itself is different in the two cases.

3. GENERAL HYPOTHESES

In this paper we want to consider whether this difference in process also leads to differences in grammaticality judgments. In line with the general findings we would, more specifically, expect the following results:

(1) Grammaticality is higher for high imagery (or concrete) verbal material than for low imagery (or abstract) material.

(2) Grammaticality judgments are faster for high imagery (H.I.) material than for low imagery (L.I.) material.

We assumed that, in making a grammaticality judgment, the subject tries to find a context in which the sentence or phrase makes sense, i.e., a possible interpretation of the sentence. If this is the crucial part of the process, we would expect the same pattern of reaction times in paraphrase production as in grammaticality judgments:

(3) Paraphrasing will be quicker for H.I. than for L.I. material.

4. THE EXPERIMENT

Material and pre-experiment. In this experiment we used Dutch compounds as material to be judged. We took care that these compound constructions were not standard lexical items in Dutch, since in that case the judgment task could be performed by straight reference to the internal lexicon without further inference. In all other cases, using compounds is a productive process, in the same sense as creating sentences. However, we were interested in varying this productivity for the following reason. Certain types of lexical compounds are much more frequent than others. Frequent types are noun/noun (NN) and verb /noun (VN) compounds, whereas noun/adjective (NA) and adjective /noun (AN) compounds are rather infrequent. It is quite likely that a certain type of lexical compound is relatively frequent if the number of possible semantic relations between the two constituent elements is relatively high. This is certainly true for NN compounds where we have a large diversity of possible semantic connections. Lees (1960), who treats compounds as surface structures which are transformationally derived from deep structures, observes the following underlying grammatical relations to be mirrored in NN compounds, examples in parentheses referring to different sub-types:

subject/predicate *(girlfriend)*
subject/middle object *(doctor's office, arrowhead, armchair)*
subject/verb *(snake bite, gunshot, farm production, investment bank)*
subject/object *(windmill, milk bar, fingerprint, grocery store)*
verb/object *(bull fighting, birth control, book review, bartender, disc jockey)*
subject/prepositional object *(ashtray, airmail, bulldog, egghead, snowball, date line, aircraft)*
verb/prepositional object *(reception desk, color photography)*
object/prepositional object *(tearoom, football, apple sauce, mud pie, apple cake, iron age).*

Underlying relations for VN compounds are, according to Lees:

subject/verb *(wading bird, dance team)*
verb/object *(call girl, pickpocket, chewing gum)*
verb/prepositional object *(bakehouse, playing cards).*

These productive forms are contrasted with AN compounds, which only express subject/predicate relations *(madman, red skin).* Lees does not treat NA constructions, since his object of study is nominalizations. One could think of 'as-as' relations *(blood red, stone dead),* adjective + prepositional phrase relations *(top heavy),* etc. (see Quirk *et al.,* 1972, 1028).

According to Dutch frequency counts, VN constructions are about 6 times as frequent as AN constructions (which are more frequent than NA compounds); NN compounds are 4 times as frequent as VN constructions. This order corresponds well with the order of transformational productivity.

We would expect that for non-lexical compounds (i.e., compounds which are not standard items in the dictionary), those that allow for a large variety of semantic relations (NN and to a lesser degree VN) will allow for quicker processing, i.e., smaller reaction times for paraphrase and grammaticality judgments. Psychologically, this is for exactly the same reason as the facilitative effect of imagery: more 'expansions' of the verbal material are generated since the compound type allows for a higher diversity of semantic relations. An additional hypothesis, therefore is

(4) Lexically productive types of compounds (NN, VN) are, with respect to less productive types (NA, AN), judged and paraphrased faster and rated more grammatical.

A corollary to this last hypothesis is that ambiguous types of compounds (i.e., compounds like *'gold light'* which can be conceived of either as NN or as NA) will more probably be interpreted, and therefore paraphrased, as the more productive form (in this case NN). Also, they will behave like the more productive form with respect to reaction times and grammaticality judgments.

In order to compose the experimental material a preliminary list of 24 supposedly high-imagery and 24 low-imagery compounds were constructed for each category (NN, VN, NA, AN), as well as 9 ambiguous compounds for the 4 possible ambiguous types NN/NA, VN/AN, NN/AN, and NN/VN. This set of 228 compounds was, in different random orders, presented to 24 subjects for imagery ratings. Twenty-four of these compounds occurred twice in the list, in order that there should be a check on the subjects' rating consistency. All 24 subjects turned out to be sufficiently consistent: rank correlations ranged from .52 to .99, with an average of .83. We followed an adaptation of the original Paivio (1971) instructions which ask the subject to rate how easily the material leads to mental images of things or events. The subjects were asked to rate their judgment for each compound on a seven-point scale (from 1 for 'low imaginable' to 7 for 'high imaginable'). These rating were averaged over subjects, and on the basis of these data we selected the 15 highest- and 15 lowest-rated compounds for each type (NN, VN, NA and AN). The eight average imagery values are given in the first and fifth row of Table 1. Also the four highest and four lowest valued compounds in the ambiguous categories were determined. Since the latter involved leaving out one compound for each ambiguous type we did not obtain clear-cut imagery dichotomies for the ambiguous compound types. Table 2 presents average imagery values for these types.

The compounds obtained in this way formed the experimental material for the main experiment. Summing up, the stimulus material consisted of 15 H.I. and 15 L.I. compounds for each compound type, plus 8 for each of the 4 ambiguous types, i.e., 4 (15 + 15) + 4 (8) = 152 stimuli.

5. PROCEDURE AND SUBJECTS

Since we wanted to release both grammaticality judgment and paraphrases for each compound, each of our 10 subjects participated in two sessions. In one session they did the paraphrase task and in the other the grammaticality judgments. The two sessions were separated by at least one day. Five subjects had the paraphrase session first, and the other five the grammaticality session. Subjects were men and women, of slightly post-college level education and ranging in age from 20 to 40. Each subject was treated individually.

(1) *The paraphrase task.* The subject was seated in front of a memory drum by means of which the 152 compounds could be presented one by one. Each subject received a different random order. The list was preceded by 8 trial stimuli to accustom the subject to the task.

At a signal of the experimenter a new stimulus appeared in the window of the memory drum, which simultaneously started an electric timer. As soon as the subject had his paraphrase available he pressed a button, which stopped the timer, and gave his paraphrase. The latter was noted down by the experimenter, who then proceeded to present the next stimulus, etc. The paraphrase-instruction was presented to the subject in written form, and his comprehension was carefully checked during the eight-trial stimuli. The instruction stressed that the subject should describe the meaning or interpretation of the compound.

(2) *The grammaticality task.* The stimulus presentation was the same as for the paraphrase task. The subject was instructed to push the button as soon as he had made up his mind about the grammaticality rating. At or directly after pushing the button, the subject orally expressed this rating, which could be any number from 1 (highly grammatical) to 7 (highly ungrammatical). This numbering was continuously available to the subject on top of the memory drum. (In the further data analysis this numbering will be inversed, i.e., 7 for highly grammatical; this in order to make the grammaticality values compatible with the imagery values). The instruction given to the subject asked him to rate whether the stimulus could be a Dutch compound word, i.e., was 'good Dutch'. So, the term 'grammaticality' was not used, since it seems wrong to ask a naive subject to use an ill-defined linguistic technical term.

6. RESULTS AND ANALYSIS

Average results for the different conditions and tasks are presented in Table 1. Three separate analyses of variance were computed on the raw data: one for the grammaticality ratings, one for the grammaticality rating times and one for the paraphrase reaction times. Apart from the main factors high/low imagery, type of compound (NN, VN, NA, AN;

Table 1. *Average values for imagery (1–7), grammaticality (1–7), rating time (sec.) and paraphrase time (sec.)*

Type of compound	NN	VN	AN	NA
High imagery				
Imagery value	5.448	5.811	5.112	5.526
Grammaticality	5.440	5.767	4.649	5.340
Grammaticality rating time	1.863	1.773	2.031	1.883
Paraphrase reaction time	2.685	2.211	2.553	2.351
Low imagery				
Imagery value	2.426	2.411	2.162	2.126
Grammaticality	3.233	3.467	2.913	2.706
Grammaticality rating time	2.190	2.030	2.200	2.317
Paraphrase reaction time	4.288	3.897	4.228	4.109

the ambiguous compounds were analyzed separately) and subjects, another factor was carried into the analysis, namely, first vs. second session. It could be the case that prior presentation of the experimental material in the paraphrase task affects the grammaticality ratings of a subject in the second session, and inversely. However, no significant effect of this variable was found, so that we will ignore it in the following. We will now discuss each of the three analyses in turn.

6.1 Grammaticality ratings

Our first hypothesis predicted higher grammaticality for high imagery (H.I.) compounds than for L.I. compounds. This is what we found. The average grammaticality scale value for H.I. compounds turns out to be 5.299, for L.I. compounds 3.180. The difference is highly significant ($p < 0.00004$). The other significant result relates to compound type: different compounds have different grammaticality ($p<0.01$): the productive types are more grammatical than the less productive types: 4.337 for NN, 4.627 for VN versus 3.781 for NA and 4.023 for AN. This is in accordance with hypothesis 4.

6.2 Grammaticality rating times

The second hypothesis predicted quicker grammaticality judgments for H.I. compounds than for L.I. compounds. Average ratings times are 1.888 sec. and 2.184 sec., respectively. The difference of 296 msec. is significant ($p < 0.02$) and in accordance with the prediction. We did not find a significant compound type effect.

6.3 Paraphrase reaction times

From the third hypothesis we expected shorter paraphrase reaction times for H.I. compounds than for L.I. compounds. The average reaction times are 2.450 sec. and 4.130 sec., respectively. The difference (1.680 msec.) is highly significant ($p < 0.0004$), in support of the hypothesis. Again, there is no significant effect of compound type, contrary to the prediction in hypothesis 4.

6.4 *Ambiguous compounds*

The results for the ambiguous compounds are given in Table 2. In a corollary to hypothesis 4, we supposed that these constructions would behave like the more productive form with respect to reaction times and grammaticality judgments. In spite of several ways of analyzing the data we could not find any trace of such an effect. This is mainly due to the lack of compound-type effects for the non-ambiguous material. Hypothesis 4 is only supported for grammaticality ratings, not for reaction times. The effect of lexical productivity seems to be quite small. We will return to this in the discussion.

Table 2. *Average values for imagery, grammaticality, rating time and paraphrase time for ambiguous compounds*

Type of compound	NN/AN	NN/VN	NN/NA	VN/AN
Imagery value	3.770	4.359	4.778	3.843
Grammaticality	4.537	4.975	4.225	4.750
Grammaticality rating time	i.970	1.994	1.947	2.022
Paraphrase reaction time	3.387	2.830	2.761	3.135

The other prediction was that ambiguous compounds would be more probably paraphrased in terms of the more productive form. To check this, we analyzed all paraphrased protocols, but again with largely negative results: for NN/NA compounds we found 56% NN interpretations; for VN/AN there were 51% VN interpretations; for NN/AN we had 45% NN-type paraphrases; and for NN/VN compounds, there were 41% NN responses. In fact, within each type some compounds were judged one way by all subjects and other compounds just the other way. Many compounds gave very idiosyncratic reactions. In this light the number of different items per type (8) is certainly too small to draw conclusions either one way or the other.

7. DISCUSSION

The results of the present experiment are strongly supportive of our main hypotheses (1, 2, and 3), namely, that high imagery compounds are more grammatical and more quickly judged than low imagery compounds and that paraphrasing is quicker for H.I. than for L.I. material. Shortly, we will try to interpret these findings in terms of a process model for judging grammaticality. But let us first consider the additional hypothesis 4 for which the data gave little support. We did find that grammaticality is higher for lexically productive types of compounds than for less productive types, but neither grammaticality rating times nor paraphrase times were quicker for the productive types. Moreover, the data for ambiguous compounds did not show the expected tendency of a preference for the more productive interpretation of the compounds. In retrospect, it seems to us that the main reason for this lack of support is that it is naive to suppose that a productive compound type (such as NN) consists of productive compounds. A compound type was called productive if it allows for a large variety of semantic relations. This does not mean, however, that each compound itself allows for a large variety of semantic interpretations, but only that there exists a large divergence of compound interpretations within the type. Actually, it seems to be the case that for each compound there is a strong bias towards one particular interpretation, irrespective of the type of the compound and irrespective of ambiguity. *Hangman* will always be interpreted as 'the man hangs X', whereas *pin-up girl* is uniquely taken as 'X pins up the girl'; in our data we found similar strong biases for compounds of ambiguous types, as we mentioned earlier. Therefore, productivity does not seem to be a property of individual compounds. Differences in reaction times between compounds may be related to other linguistic properties.

One noteworthy candidate is the 'transparency' of the compound, i.e., the distance between surface form and semantic interpretation. For example, compare *madman* (the man is mad) to *redskin* (the skin is red → the red skin belongs to a man → the man belongs to a certain ethnic category). The latter one may take longer paraphrase and judgment reaction times. This transparency variable seems to be an interesting topic for further experimentation on grammaticality.

Let us now turn to the main results relating to the imagery variable. Theoretically we had supposed that the judgment process involves a search for a possible interpretation of the compound and that this search is quicker for H.I. than for L.I. material. In its turn the latter can be explained either by the existence of a dual verbal/nonverbal representational system (Paivio) or by a larger 'expansion potential' of high imagery material (Anderson and Bower). Since in both cases interpretation search is an integral part of the judgment process, one would expect a similar imagery-effect for paraphrase reaction times (hypothesis 3),

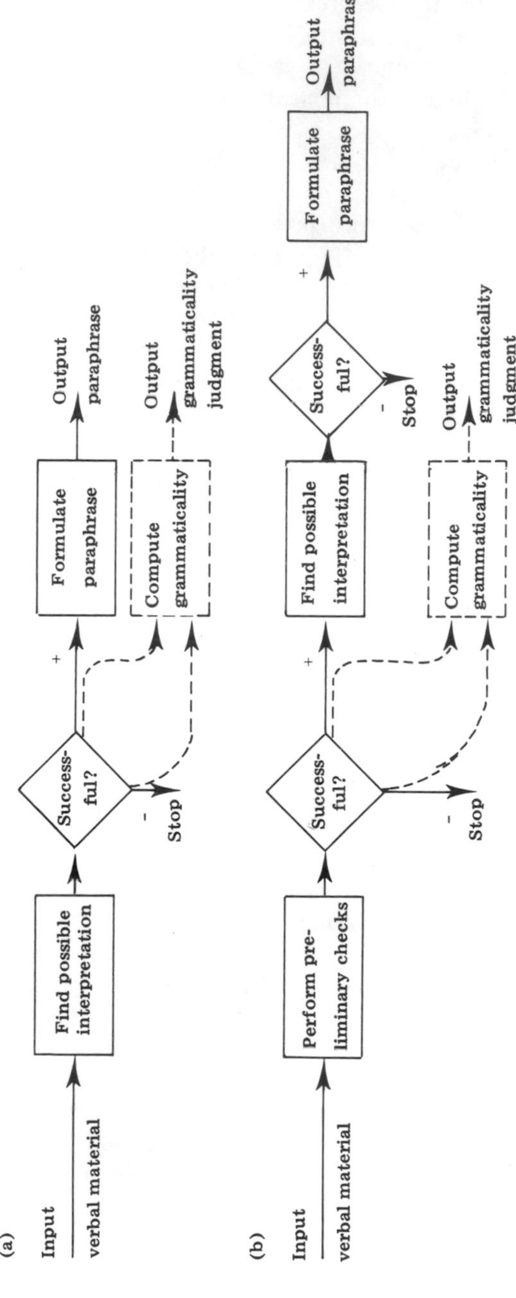

Figure 1. *Two models for grammaticality judgment and paraphrasing*

and this is what we found. However, further qualification is necessary in view of the reaction time data. Figure la represents the grammaticality / paraphrase model. If imagery only affects the interpretation search, paraphrase and grammaticality reaction times would be affected to the same degree. But we found a mean reaction time difference for grammaticality judgments of 296 msec., as compared to 1680 msec. for paraphrase reaction times. This leaves nearly 1400 msec. unexplained for the paraphrasing process.

We are left with two ways of accounting for this additional difference. The first is to suppose that imagery not only affects the interpretation search but also the later stage of paraphrase formulation. But neither in the Paivio model nor in the Anderson and Bower model is this particularly likely. For Paivio, paraphrase formulation takes place in the verbal system, which is not affected by imagery. For Anderson and Bower, no further inference is required as soon as the interpretation is available, and the 'expansion potential' interpretation of imagery would not work. We will shortly return to this.

The second is to suppose that no full interpretation is needed in order to give a grammaticality judgment. The subject may perform some preliminary checks on the material before starting his memory search (Figure 1b). If these checks involve some 'trial expansions' in the sense of Anderson and Bower, they will also be sensitive to imagery. These checks would then explain the 296 msec. difference in our results, whereas the interpretation search would account for the additional 1400 msec.

In order to experimentally exclude the first alternative, one could choose a task in which no *paraphrase formulation* is required. Instead of compounds one could use sentences and have the subject judge the truth or falsity of the sentence by means of two reaction keys. If the effect of imagery on reaction time reduces to the amount found in the grammaticality task, the conclusion should be that there is an additional imagery effect on paraphrase formulation, If, however, the verification task and the paraphrase task show a substantial difference in the effect of imagery (and this we expect), we can maintain the present supposition that the grammaticality judgment does not require substantial interpretation but can be based on some set of pre-tests.

If this latter model is correct, the major problem is to analyze the nature of these preliminary checks. It is well known that similar tests are performed in normal listening situations. There are not only phonetic checks which are essential for adaptation to a speaker's voice quality, but we also perform preliminary tests in the interpretive domain. Norman

(1972) gives as an example the speaker's question 'What is Charles Dickens' phone number?' The typical reaction is not intensive memory search followed by 'I don't know', but something like 'That's a stupid question'. Especially worth mentioning in this context are sociolinguistic checks, which probably also precede interpretation in a similar fashion. They are sometimes of a phonetic or phonological nature (e.g., in determining a person's dialect), but they may also involve some more interpretive activity. A nice example of the latter is the way in which the Javanese listener is able to quickly infer the speaker's social status. The presence of some words, affixes and turns of phrase are sufficient to immediately derive the status relationship (see Geertz 1968). In all these cases no full understanding is required for the completion of the tests. On the other hand, the results of such checks may have important consequences for the further interpretive process. The interpretations of an utterance will often be dependent on the inferred status relationship, and similarly the interpretative process may be stopped, i.e., communication may break down, if acceptability checks yield negative results.

In conclusion, the imagery data strongly suggest that no full interpretation is required to decide on the acceptability of a linguistic construction. The nature of the tests subjects do perform in order to cope with the grammaticality task stays largely in the dark. But we found that this testing process and its outcome is affected by imagery in the same way as other verbal associative and inferential processes.

REFERENCES

Anderson, J. R., and Bower, G. H. (1973), *Human Associative Memory*. Washington, Winston.

Chomsky, N. (1957), *Syntactic Structures*. The Hague, Mouton.

– (1964), 'Degrees of grammaticalness', in J. A. Fodor and J. J. Katz, Eds., *The Structure of Language: Readings in the Philosophy of Language*. Englewood Cliffs, Prentice Hall.

Geertz, C. (1968), 'Linguistic etiquette', in J. A. Fishman, Ed., *Readings in the Sociology of Language*. The Hague, Mouton.

Gleitman, L. R., Gleitman, H. and Shipley, E. F. (1972), 'The emergence of the child as grammarian', *Cognition*, 1, pp. 137–164.

Greenbaum, S. (1973), 'Informant elicitation of data on syntactic variation', *Lingua*, 31, pp. 201–212.

Harris, Z. (1970), *Papers in Structural and Transformational Linguistics*. Dordrecht, Reidel.

Katz, J. J. (1964), 'Semi-sentences', in J. A. Fodor and J. J. Katz, Eds., *The Structure of Language: Readings in the Philosophy of Language*. Englewood-Cliffs, Prentice Hall.

Lakoff, G. (1971), 'Presuppositions and relative well-formedness', in D. D. Steinberg and

L. A. Jakobovits, Eds., *Semantics*. London, Cambridge University Press.

Lees, R. B. (1960), *The Grammar of English Nominalizations,* Supplement to the *International Journal of American Linguistics,* 26.

Levelt, W. J. M. (1972), 'Some psychological aspects of linguistic data', *Linguistische Berichte,* 17, pp. 18–30.

– (1974), *Formal Grammars in Linguistics and Psycholinguistics*. The Hague, Mouton.
(a) Vol. 1. *An Introduction to the Theory of Formal Languages and Automata*
(b) Vol. 2. *Applications in Linguistic Theory*
(c) Vol. 3. *Psycholinguistic Applications*

Maclay, H., and Sleator, M. O. (1960), 'Responses to language: Judgments of grammaticalness', *International Journal of Applied Linguistics,* 26, pp. 275–282.

Moore, T. E. (1972), 'Speeded recognition of ungrammaticality', *Journal of Verbal Learning and Verbal Behavior,* 11, pp. 550–560.

Norman, D. A. (1972), 'Memory, knowledge and the answering of questions'. Paper for Loyola Symposium on Cognitive Psychology, Chicago.

Paivio. A. (1971), *Imagery and verbal processes*. New York, Holt, Rinehart and Winston.

– (1975), 'Imagery and long-term memory' in R. A. Kennedy and A. L. Wilkes, Eds., *Studies in Long Term Memory*. New York, Wiley.

Quirk, R., and Svartvik, J. (1966), *Investigating Linguistic Acceptability*. The Hague, Mouton.

Quirk, R., Greenbaum, S., Leech, G., and Svartvik, J. (1972), *A Grammar of Contemporary English*. London, Longman.

Snow, C. (1974), 'Linguists as behavioral scientists: Towards a methodology for testing linguistic intuitions', in A. Kraak, Ed., *Linguistic Science in the Netherlands '72/'73*. Assen, Van Gorkum.

Zadeh, L. A. (1971), 'Toward a theory of fuzzy systems', in R. E. Kalman and N. Declaris, Eds., *Aspects of Network and System Theory*. New York, Holt, Rinehart and Winston.

Ziff, P. (1964), 'On understanding "understanding utterances"', in J. A. Fodor and J. J. Katz, Eds., *The Structure of Language: Readings in the Philosophy of Language*. Englewood-Cliffs, Prentice Hall.

RAVEN I. McDAVID, Jr. and RAYMOND K. O'CAIN 8

Prejudice and Pride: Linguistic Acceptability in South Carolina

Those who have examined human speech have frequently commented on the differences between what people think they ought to say and what they actually say.[1] However these differences are phrased, they exist; and no amount of theoretical prestidigitation can remove them from our attention. It is for this reason that there have been numerous surveys of actual usage and of attitudes toward usage (Mencken 1963: 512–521; Creswell 1974). These surveys reveal that the Platonic ideals enunciated by the guardians of linguistic chastity are seldom justified by the usage of those who should be the best models for the generality; even the *American Heritage Dictionary* (1969) is more relaxed in its editorial comments than would seem warranted by its highly publicized Usage Panel – an apparent attempt to create an American analogue to the Immortals of the French Academy.

A realization of these differences between what people say and what they think they ought to say guided Hans Kurath in his design of the methodology for the *Linguistic Atlas of the United States and Canada.* Though careful to incorporate the best from traditional European dialect geography, Kurath unhesitatingly introduced modifications where American conditions required them; indeed, he transformed dialect geography by insisting that a systematic investigation of the speech of the *folk,* those least affected by standardizing forces, was insufficient. In every community a second informant should be interviewed, a representative of a contrasting cultural level, using what Kurath called *popular* or *common* speech. Such informants were more intensely subject to standardizing influences, education in particular, and were generally younger as well. Kurath's methodology also specified that in about one-fifth of the communities investigated, a speaker of the local prestige dialect be interviewed. Such *cultivated* informants might be alumni of reputable colleges and universities in their region, though for about half those on the Atlantic Seaboard, community opinion of their family rank more than compensated for any lack of formal higher education.[2]

Included as an essential adjunct to the phonetic record of the *Linguistic Atlas of New England* (Kurath *et al.* 1939–1943) and subsequent regional atlases were the observations of the field workers concerning the currency and social status of linguistic forms, whether phonological, lexical or grammatical. In addition to recording the forms obtained by questioning, the field workers were instructed to pay particular attention to recording variants from the informant's unguarded conversation – a task simplified for contemporary field workers by the tape recorder. The field workers were also instructed to denote forms (1) offered as spontaneous corrections, (2) accompanied by indications of doubt, (3) evoking expressions of amusement, (4) elicited only after repeated questioning, (5) offered hesitatingly, (6) repeated at the request of the field worker, (7) pronounced by the informant after being suggested – only as a last resort – by the field worker, or (8) offered by another local resident who happened to be present during the interview. Though such observations serve chiefly to indicate the attitude of the informant toward a particular form, they are a fruitful source of indications about the status of forms, perhaps that a topic and its terminology are unfamiliar or even taboo.

The explicit statements of informants about the currency or status of forms were denoted by the field workers as (9) heard, i.e., current, but not actually used by the informant himself, (10) old-fashioned or obsolete or replaced in the speech of the informant by a newer form and (11) modern, recently introduced, used only by younger persons or adopted only later by the informant.[3] Furthermore, not only do a number of the logical combinations of the designations (1) – (11) appear in the field records, but sometimes detailed elaborations of them as well. All forms recorded outside the context of a direct reply to some elicitation frame are labelled on the LANE maps, and significant elaborations by the informants are reproduced, sometimes verbatim, sometimes in summary, in separate commentaries to the maps.

It should surprise no one that the judgments of the LANE informants were sometimes in sharp contrast to actual usage, whether of informants themselves or of social groups or regions. Yet to date no investigator has attempted to correlate the LANE informants' judgments with the status of the forms actually used[4] in their communities, even though LANE is the only American survey for which the full phonetic record is available.[5] Regrettably, the most egregious disregard of Linguistic Atlas materials, published and unpublished, has been on the part of scholars in the emerging discipline of sociolinguistics; their judgments on language and society would seem to demand an examination of this evidence, at least as a starting point (*cf.* McDavid and O'Cain, forthcoming).[6]

It is for this reason that the two authors have decided to examine a small part of the evidence from the *Linguistic Atlas of the Middle and South Atlantic States*. The sociolinguistic judgments of the 32 cultivated informants interviewed in South Carolina will be compared not only with the actual status among the cultivated of the forms they judged but also with the actual status and the ascribed status of the same forms among the 112 uncultivated informants interviewed in South Carolina. The authors have limited themselves to South Carolina for several reasons, perhaps advantageous to the validity of their findings: (1) each is a native speaker of one of the varieties of cultivated English indigenous to South Carolina;[7] that they learned their respective varieties a generation apart adds breadth to their common perspective; (2) each has had extensive field experience with the varieties of English spoken in South Carolina;[8] that these experiences were nearly a generation apart likewise enhances their common perspective; (3) as South Carolinians they can speak there more confidently of social class than they might in other regions; (4) social class distinctions are relatively sharper and more persistent in South Carolina than in many other regions; and (5) in the South Carolina field records[9] there are more sociolinguistic judgments[10] on the part of informants than in almost any other state, and there are likewise more forms recorded from free conversation.

The copiousness of both the forms recorded from free conversation and the sociolinguistic judgments required several arbitrary limitations. Comparison of the usage and judgments of the informants on an individual basis would admit fewer comparisons, for not every informant judged the same forms (*cf.* McDavid 1974). We chose to examine the usage of South Carolinians as a group in just those cases where there is quantitative, and even some qualitative, convergence of sociolinguistic judgment; as a further limitation, we shall define the specific items singled out for detailed comparisons in terms of the number of judgments obtained from cultivated informants. The forms judged by the cultivated are those which do not have unequivocal status as Standard English but are, at least potentially, socially marked – broadly speaking, they are disputable usages in the opinion of those who define Standard English, not by their usage alone, but by their attitudes as well.

To survey the judgments of informants and the actual usage to which they correspond in South Carolina, then, the first step was to systematically search the field book of each cultivated informant for forms about which judgments were made. Such forms and the judgment given were

Table 1. *Judgments and items per category per informant*

	Lexicon		Phonology		Grammar	
Informant	Judgments	Items	Judgments	Items	Judgments	Items
3c	29	28	10	10	8	8
5c	17	17	9	8	3	3
6c	30	28	3	3	3	2
7c	20	20	0	0	0	0
7d	12	11	7	7	0	0
9c	13	13	10	10	6	5
9d	14	12	2	2	0	0
10b	6	6	1	1	0	0
10c	10	10	2	2	0	0
11g	34	33	9	7	1	1
2N11	32	27	11	10	4	4
11h	28	26	19	18	5	5
11i	33	30	24	21	15	13
11j	161	116	59	42	28	14
14b	37	31	6	6	4	4
18c	50	36	20	19	6	4
19d	1	1	3	3	0	0
20d	9	8	1	1	0	0
22b	15	13	4	4	2	2
22c	20	19	11	10	1	1
23e	19	16	3	2	0	0
24d	6	6	1	1	0	0
25c	13	12	2	2	0	0
26b	18	18	3	3	0	0
30c	48	42	13	10	5	4
36d	6	6	12	8	0	0
38c	8	6	5	5	0	0
38d	35	33	22	20	6	5
42b	22	19	9	9	0	0
42c	52	44	9	8	6	6
42d	13	13	13	12	4	4
42e	25	23	4	3	6	4

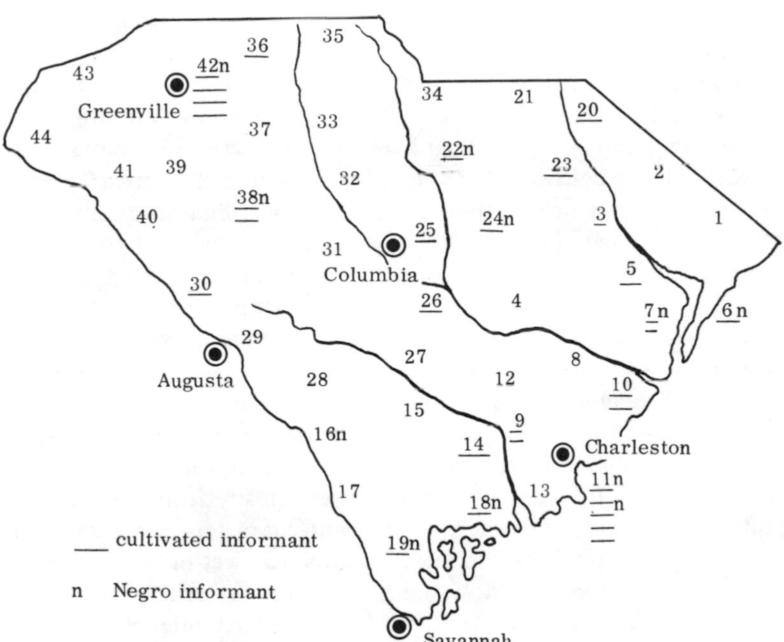

Map 1. *LAMSAS communities in South Carolina*

copied on index cards and filed by their linguistic categories: (1) lexical, (2) phonological, or (3) grammatical. Excluded from (1) were judgments about the meaning of terms, e.g., that a *piazza* is larger than a *porch* or *stoop*; included in (3) were both morphological and syntactic items. In a number of instances more than one card was filed for an informant for a single item in the Atlas work sheets (questionnaire), e.g., for the stressed vowel of *yellow* an informant might judge /ɪ/ as old-fashioned and /æ/ as modern. However, combined judgments, particularly common with forms characterized as heard, were treated as single judgments.

Table 1 displays the number of judgments and items judged in each of the three categories for each cultivated informant. Map 1 shows, designated by their LAMSAS serial numbers, the locations of the communities investigated in South Carolina. Underscorings denote the location and number of cultivated informants; numbers followed by *n* denote communities where Negro informants were interviewed.

Nearly all the cultivated judgments fall into the categories (9) heard, (10) old-fashioned or (11) modern, from above, and are often further specified as typical of a particular social group or region. Less frequently, terms may be characterized as jocular, correct or incorrect, informal, restricted to use in very limited contexts, etc. Several informants seem to favor certain designations for forms they do not use themselves, e.g., 18c favors poor white, and 42c favors rural; no informant seemed especially prone to designate usages as exclusively Negro; and though a large majority of the forms were associated with Negro usage by at least one informant, only infrequently is it the consensus of the cultivated that a usage is Negro. In a number of instances, mostly from among informants living along the coast, an informant characterizes a form as not being the dominant form among the cultivated, yet in the next breath declares that he uses it anyhow, e.g., /ɛt/ as the preterite of *eat*.

It is evident that some cultivated informants have offered many more judgments than others; in some cases the paucity of judgments is related to the incompleteness of the field record; on the other hand, some informants are more inclined to offer their opinions – it comes as no surprise to the authors that the greatest number of judgments comes from a Charlestonian, and that all the Charlestonians are relatively willing to offer opinions, for the self-assurance of Charleston is a well-advertised fact.[11] Notice, too, that as the number of judgments increases, the size of the gap between judgments and items generally increases; as informants become more interested in the language, they become increasingly discriminating, though judgment should be reserved on the question of accuracy.

After the figures for Table 1 were compiled, the cards were sorted according to the order of the appearance of each item in the LAMSAS work sheets. The number of cultivated judgments for each item was tallied and an arbitrary cut-off point was taken for each category. Not included in the following treatment of the individual items were lexical items for which fewer than 7 judgments were obtained, phonological items with fewer than 5 judgments and grammatical items with fewer than 4 judgments; left for consideration were 19 lexical items, 18 phonological items, and 8 grammatical items.

In the treatment of individual items there is a summary tabulation of the number of informants using each of the principal variants of an item. There is also a second tabulation, the number of informants attesting that there is some *restriction* (*cf.* Creswell 1974) on one or more of the variants; this figure is preceded by *r*.

Whereas the unmarked forms indicate the natural, even conversational, usage of the informants, the restricted forms are those not only explicitly judged by informants but also those whose naturalness is subject to question. Restrictions include the entire range of observations (1)–(11) above noted by the field workers. Suggested forms were not tabulated as unrestricted unless explicitly accepted as natural by the informants. For this reason, the number of restrictions will usually exceed the first judgment per item tally for the cultivated informants. This original tally may be still further increased by a number of inferential judgments; for example, if an informant characterized *groundnuts* as his natural usage during childhood, it is inferred that *peanuts* is a modern or newer term, even though not so characterized explicitly. Accordingly, there is not always an exact correspondence between the judgments cited in the tables of usage and the summaries of the items analyzed.

For the purpose of comparing judgments to actual usage the informants were divided into four groups: the cultivated informants, the Negro informants exclusive of the cultivated Negro informant, who is in a group by himself, and, taken together, the users of folk speech and common or popular speech. While no judgments indicated that the two latter groups need be separated, the numerous judgments that can be interpreted as 'not used in cultivated English' or 'not predominant in cultivated English' point to a cultivated-uncultivated dichotomy;[12] and, naturally, the comparison of cultivated usage and cultivated judgment is of interest. The separation of the ten Negro folk informants is occasioned by the frequent opinion that a usage is characteristic of them, but their tabulations can be considered jointly with those of the other uncultivated informants as well. Likewise the usage of the lone cultivated Negro informant, a member of Charleston's Negro elite, is tallied separately.

In the following summaries of usage and judgments (the latter marked *r*), the principal variants of each item are listed, and the number of occurrences of each is given. The usage of the folk and middle class are in the column headed I,II, and the columns headed N, 2N11, and III designate, respectively, the usage of the Negro folk informants, the cultivated Negro informant and the cultivated white informants. The lexical items are presented first, followed in order by the phonological and grammatical items. Within each category, the order of items corresponds to the order in the LAMSAS work sheets; numbers in parentheses refer to the pages in the work sheets.

LEXICON[13]

(2) *afternoon*

	I,II[14]	N	2N11	III
afternoon	60 r13	5	1	19 r4
evening	77 r2	6	1	10 r6
no response	3	2		4

The cultivated informants judged *evening* as heard (1), heard frequently (2)[15] or old (2); *afternoon* was judged new (2) or correct (1) and heard (1). The collective judgment that *afternoon* is (slowly) replacing *evening* as the term for the part of the day after midday is borne out by the facts of usage.[16] Though mixed usage is frequent, it is somewhat more prevalent in the middle class, for exclusive use of *evening* is usually characteristic of the oldest, least-cultivated informants, and exclusive use of *afternoon* is indicative of greater cultivation and youth. Finally, the judgments of the uncultivated are most often that *afternoon* is new or correct.

(3) *sunrise*

	I,II	N	2N11	III
sunup	61 r9	3 rl	1	8 r7
no response	14	4		13

The judgment of the cultivated is that *sunup* is a heard term; though it does occur in cultivated speech, only one cultivated informant did not offer *sunrise* as well. Though *sunup* is used by over half the uncultivated, only a third of the total use it exclusively, i.e., reject *sunrise*. The judgments of the uncultivated are evenly divided as to which term is predominant.

(7) *living room*

	I,II	N	2N11	III
living room	55 r8	2 r2	1	18 r4
parlor	55 r12	5	r1	17 r13
sitting room	53 r2	9		15 r6
front room	15 r2	2	r1	1 r3
drawing room	3		1	4 r4
hall	6 r6			1 r3
company room	5 r2			r1

The judgments of the cultivated indicate that *living room* is new (4) or natural (2); all the other terms are generally judged old in about half the cases and heard or less frequent in the other half. The uncultured judge *parlor* and the variants of *hall* as old-fashioned somewhat more decisively, in about two-thirds of the cases; they judge *living room* as a modern term unanimously. The three leading variants are not only of the same frequency, but there is no apparent geographical distribution of the terms; only rarely does each of the three fail to show up in any particular community, and there is no social distribution worthy of comment.

(8) *andirons*

	I,II	N	2N11	III
andirons	36 r9	5		18 r4
fire dogs	57 r13	2		9 r11
fire irons	5 r1			
dog irons	22 r3	6	r1	7 r3
dogs	8 r3			3 r2
irons	5	1		
no response	5	1		2

The cultured judge the prevailing folk term *fire dogs* as heard (7) or old (2); like judgments are given for the other folk terms. *Andirons* is considered new (3) or probably correct and appears to be the established usage among the cultivated, for alternate terms are almost always described as heard or old. *Andirons* does appear to be at least moderately well established in the cities, and when it does appear among the uncultured is almost always paired with other terms. The uncultured generally characterize *andirons* as a new term.

(9) *kitchen*

	I,II	N	2N11	III
cook house, ~shed, ~room	18 r7	1 r1		3 r7
stove room	9 r2	r2		r3

All the variants of universally used *kitchen* were characterized as heard by the cultivated, though with the additional specification rural (3) or poor white (1) at times. The only striking contrast with the judgment of the folk was that *kitchen* was called old (2) or paired with a variant that was considered new (3).

(10) *porch*

	I,II	N	2N11	III
porch	75 r11	7 r2	r1	26 r6
piazza	72 r25	10	1	20 r7
no response	2			

The cultivated, in about equal numbers, consider *porch* modern, *piazza* old-fashioned or *piazza* the usual term. The uncultivated almost unanimously characterize *porch* as modern and *piazza* as old-fashioned.[17]

(17) *frying pan*

	I,II	N	2N11	III
spider	73 r14	8 r3		14 r11
skillet	56 r11	7 r1	1	17 r6

Though *frying pan* is universal, *spider* is an older term that still enjoys wider currency than *skillet*. The cultivated usually consider *spider* old-fashioned (8); opinion is divided on *skillet,* which is somewhat more common in the usage of the cultivated and in urban areas, though the two terms are both found in nearly every community. The uncultured who offer judgments characterize *frying pan* as modern, or more often, pair it with a term they consider older.

(19.6) *paper bag*

	I,II	N	2N11	III
poke	13 r20	r1		1 r8
no response				5

Paper bag is universal, and the cultivated informants judged *poke* for the most part as heard but also old-fashioned (1) or not characteristic of their area (2). *Poke* is a Midland term (Kurath 1949: Fig. 70) and both the uses of *poke* and the cultivated judgments are from informants in communities above or near the fall line[18] in most cases. The folk[19] judge *poke* largely as a heard term, though occasionally as old.

(19.7) *crocus sack*

	I,II	N	2N11	III
burlap	24 r5	2	1	8 r5
gunny	5 r5		1	1 r4
guano	23 r5	3 rl		3 rl
tow	13 r3	1		2 r2
jute	12 r3			2 rl
no response				5

The consensus of the cultivated is that *gunny sack* is heard but uncommon and that *burlap sack* is new (2) or proper (1). *Crocus sack,* or less commonly *croker sack,* is all but universal, a fact the cultivated recognize (5). *Crocus sack* is judged most often as new (4) by the uncultured; less often the same opinion is given of the other variants, except for *jute sack, burlap sack, gunny sack,* and *guano sack* which are heard or rarer terms in the judgment of the folk. *Guano sack* is in a majority of cases the usage of the older, less cultivated informant in the communities in which it appears, generally those below the fall line, or if above the fall line, usually in communities nearer North Carolina. *Burlap sack,* the preferred variant of the cultured, is concentrated in the tidewater though also found above the fall line; among the uncultured, *burlap sack* is rare in the usage of the oldest, least cultured informants.[20]

(24) *kerosene*

	I,II	N	2N11	III
kerosene oil	25	3		8
coal oil	13 r23	rl		5 r7
lamp oil	9 r4	3	1	rl
oil	8 rl	1		5
no response	3	3		

The cultivated judged *coal oil* as heard (3) or as a rare or occasional term, and *lamp oil* was judged old. The folk judges reported *coal oil* as heard in a large majority of the cases, as not local (3) – specifically,

Northern (2) – and old, Negro or new (1 each). *Lamp oil* was reported as heard (3) or old. *Kerosene* is in general usage, and *kerosene oil,* though less usual, is evenly distributed geographically. *Coal oil* is generally found above the fall line along the upper reaches of the Savannah River or in communities relatively near the North Carolina border. In the low country, *coal oil* is associated with cultivated speakers in coastal communities.

(27.2) *vest*

	I,II	N	2N11	III
waistcoat	15 r23	1 r1		9 r14
jacket	23 r8	r2		3
no response	3	2		1

Waistcoat is characterized as a heard (9) or old (3) term by the cultivated. The folk are evenly divided between heard and old for *waistcoat,* but a large majority consider *jacket* old. *Vest* is predominant everywhere, and *jacket* is usually found above the fall line – when it appears below the fall line it is found only well away from the coast. *Waistcoat* is most often found in the low country – excluding the Pee Dee – where it is associated with the cultured and with the least cultured, but not with the middle class; above the fall line *waistcoat* is associated with the cultured or middle class and less among the least cultivated.

(27.3) *trousers*

	I,II	N	2N11	III
breeches	65 r17	6 r5	r1	15 r9
no response	3			1

Pants and *trousers* are virtually universal, and when judged are considered new or natural as a rule; frequently one or both occur with *jeans* or *breeches,* which are judged older. The cultured judge *breeches* generally as heard (6) or jocular (2). About half the folk judges considered *breeches* old, with the remainder about equally divided between jocular, frequent and rare.

(45) *doughnut*

	I,II	N	2N11	III
doughnut	52 r27	7 r1	1	16 r8
no response	18	2		6

The cultured informants judged *doughnut* as rare (3), not native (3) or new. Half the folk who offered opinions characterized *doughnut* as rare, and the remainder were about evenly divided between not native (6) and new (4). Though typical of cultivated usage, and found in every community, in nearly half the communities – mostly near or below the fall line – at least one informant failed to affirm *doughnut* as either familiar or natural.

(48) *food*

	I,II	N	2N11	III
vittles	35 r21	5 r2	1	8 r10
no response	5	3		5

The consensus of the cultivated is that *vittles* is a heard (5) term, sometimes further detailed as Negro usage (2), old (2) or jocular. The Negro folk informants characterize *vittles* as old or rural. The white folk consider *vittles* as Negro usage (5), heard (6), not correct (4), old (3) or rural (3). *Vittles* is rather evenly distributed geographically in South Carolina; socially it is most typical of the least cultivated informants and everywhere competes with the general *food* and the only slightly more common *rations*. Only occasionally judged, *rations* has a geographical distribution like that of *vittles,* and in the up country has a similar social distribution as well. In the low country, however, *rations* is more likely to be found in the speech of somewhat more cultivated informants, though it is significantly absent in the speech of Charleston.

(54) *peanut*

	I,II	N	2N11	III
peanut	r9			r8
pinder	66 r19	4 r2	1	11 r6
goober	35 r12	2 r1	r1	6 r4
groundpea	11 r6	3		
groundnut	22 r7	4		13 r3
no response	5	2		8

Peanut is usually characterized as new (5) by the cultivated; the other variants are judged heard or old as a rule, though *pinder* is sometimes judged natural (3). The majority of the uncultured judge *peanut* as new or rare, *groundnut* and *pinder* as old, and *goober* and *groundpea* as heard. Though *peanut* is almost universal, it has strong competition. *Goober,* except along the coast, is not common below the fall line, especially in the Pee Dee (*cf.* Kurath and McDavid 1961: Map 118); *pinder* is common everywhere. *Groundnut* is concentrated along the coast and is rare above the fall line; *groundpea* is common only above the fall line, with several scattered instances near the coast.

(79) *casket*

	I,II	N	2N11	III
casket	43 r21	2 r4	1	11 r6
box	20 r12	4 r1		7 r6
pinto	r4	2 r2		1
no response	12	2		6

Casket is judged by the cultivated most often as new (4), but genteelism and fancier also suggest newness. *Box* is equally judged as Negro and old-fashioned, and *coffin,* the general term, is once judged old. The folk informants nearly unanimously judge *casket* as new and *coffin* as the older term; like the cultivated informants, they are equally divided in their opinions on *box* as old or a Negroism. And unlike the cultivated, they report *pinto* as a Negroism, reported by 2N11 as old. *Casket* is found in all but a few scattered communities, with no apparent social distribution. *Box* is widespread in the low country, though not concentrated, and notably rare in Charleston; *box* is more common in the up country than in the Pee Dee, but with no appreciable frequency.

(93) *Merry Christmas*

	I,II	N	2N11	III
Christmas gift, ~ treat	57 r20	4 r2	r1	6 r8
no response	11	4		12

Christmas gift (occasionally *Christmas treat*) is most often reported as heard (4) by the cultivated; other judgments are Negroism (2), old (2) and jocular. The uncultured are about evenly divided in their judgments of *Christmas gift* as old, heard or formerly heard from Negroes. Only occasionally is *Christmas gift* not paired with *Merry Christmas* (19), and the reverse is true about as often (18).

(98) *lug*

	I,II	N	2N11	III
tote	25 r10			4 r8
no response	8			9

Tote is reported by the cultivated as a heard (4) term; it also has other judgments which can be summarized as informal (3). The judgments of the uncultured are heard (3), frequent (3), Negroism (2) and informal (2). *Tote* is found all along the North Carolina border and along the coast.

(100) *address* (the letter)[21]

	I,II	N	2N11	III
back	47 r28	5	1	1 r8
no response	21	5		15

The cultured informants consider *back* a Negroism (5) or a heard term (2). Three-quarters of the folk judgments are equally divided between Negroism, heard and old; the remaining quarter is evenly divided between *back* as laughable and *address* as a new term. *Back* is the exclusive term of 11 informants, mostly below the fall line; socially they are the least cultivated informants in their communities as a rule; *back* is the sole term of two of the Negro folk informants.

PHONOLOGY[22]

(8.2) *hearth*

	I,II	N	2N11	III
/æ/	12 r10	2		r3
/ɜ/	29 r19	3 r2	1	4 r9
/a/	r1	1		
no response	1			1

Cultivated informants report that /ɜ/ is old (4), heard and humorous (2), new or affected (2) or simply heard; /æ/ is considered a Negroism (2) or heard. The uncultivated informants characterize /ɜ/ principally as heard (10) and, in equal but smaller proportions, as old, new or correct. Likewise in even proportions they characterize /æ/ as heard or old. While /ɑ ~ ɑ̈/ is regular, notably in cultivated speech, /ɜ/ is also widespread below the fall line, including the cultivated speech of the coast; it is also found above the fall line in communities near the North Carolina border. /æ/ is considerably less common and is found principally in the low country above the tidewater.

(8.7) *soot*

	I,II	N	2N11	III
/ʌ/	36 r7	9	1	11 r6
[ɤ]	40 r3	3		9
/ʊ/	12			8
/u/	3 r2		r1	2 r3
[ʉ]	7			
no response				2

Cultivated informants are divided between heard and usual on /ʌ/ though on /u/ they agree that it is not general. The folk judgments are inconclusive, though they are not inclined to accept /ʌ/. [ɤ], a diaphone of /ʌ/, is common except near the coast, and it does not occur in cultivated coastal speech. /ʌ/, which is common in coastal cultivated speech, is rare above the fall line. Most instances of /ʊ/ and /u/ occur in cultivated or urban speech.

(17) *vase*

	I,II	N	2N11	III
/vɑz ~ vɔz/	r3			r5
/vez/	r1	1		6 r2
/væz/	r1			1 r1
no response	29	3		5

The cultivated consider /vɑz ~ vɔz/ affected, or judge it a heard form. /vez/ is a heard form; /væz/ is affirmed as natural, and still another informant says there are many pronunciations of *vase*, Strikingly, the standard /ves/ is almost universal in folk speech; of the few variants, all found along the coast, only one is not from a cultivated speaker.

(24) *kerosene*

	I,II	N	2N11	III
/æ/	47 r3	5		10 r5
/a/				r1
/ɪ/	1	1		1
no response	3	3		

All the cultivated judgments of the pronunciation of *kerosene* were from low-country informants, usually that /æ/ was a heard form (3) or a Negroism or in uneducated speech. /a/ was also cited as heard, but no examples occurred in actual usage. /æ/ is found in cultivated speech in all areas of the state and notably in the principal cities; it is more common below the fall line, where all three example of /ɪ/ were recorded as well.

(26) *apron*

	I,II	N	2N11	III
/epən/	30	8		4 r5
no response	5			2

Judgments about the status of /epən/ – always that it was old-fashioned – were recorded only from cultivated informants of the lower coastal region (Charleston and Beaufort[18, 19]). Two of these pronunciations in cultivated speech were recorded in the upper coastal region (Georgetown[6, 7]), and the other two were from near the coast. /epən/ is found in all areas of South Carolina, though somewhat more often below the fall line; in about one-third of the communities it represents the usage of the least cultivated informant.

(30) *creek*

	I,II	N	2N11	III
/ɪ/	13 r3	5 r1	r1	2 r10
no response	6			4

In the up country, the two cultivated informants who judged *creek* associated /ɪ/ with Charleston or Negroes. The opinion of the low-country judges was that /ɪ/ was heard (5) or old. The two cultivated uses of /ɪ/ were from rural area around Charleston; the only use of /ɪ/ outside the immediate coastal region was from a low-country Negro informant.

(35) *tusks*

	I,II	N	2N11	III
/tʌʃɨz/	60 r8	8 r2	r1	5 r6
no response	5	1		7

One cultivated informant found /tʌʃɨz/ humorous; the remainder judged it heard, additionally qualified as Negro (1) or old (1). For most uncultivated judges /tʌs(ks)/ has prestige, for they consider it new or correct or consider /tʌʃɪ/z/ as old-fashioned or as a heard form. /tʌs(ks)/ is the dominant form in cultivated speech and is also the exclusive form of about one-quarter of the uncultivated, most of whom are from below the fall line. Only a small minority use both forms. Aside from cultivated usage, no striking social distribution of the two forms is apparent in the usage of whites, though /tʌʃɪz/ prevails among the Negro folk speakers.

(45.6) *yeast*

	I,II	N	2N11	III
/ist/	68 r4	7		7 r6
/jist/	33	3	1	23
no response	5	2		4

One cultivated judge reports /jist/ is correct; another feels both pronunciations are natural; the remainder are equally divided between old and heard for /ist/. The folk judgments follow the same pattern as those of the cultivated. /jist/ prevails among the cultivated; its exclusive use by the uncultured is evenly distributed geographically, but socially is more characteristic of better-educated informants.

(45.7) *yolk*

	I,II	N	2N11	III
/jɛlk/	13 r2	3		2 r4
/jɜlk/	9			9 r2
/jok/	34			12
/jolk/	15 r2		1	6
no response	27	5		5

For the cultured judges /jolk/ is correct (1) and other forms are evenly divided between heard and old. The uncultured judges agree that /jolk/ is correct, or of /jɛlk/ that it is heard or natural. /jo(l)k/, the majority form in cultivated speech, is current in all areas. It competes with /jɛlk/ in the upper Savannah River watershed, and in fall line communities, where it prevails in cultivated speech; along the coast it is largely found in the speech of the least cultured. /jɜlk/ though in cultivated speech along and above the fall line, is not very common in those areas; in the low country it is concentrated in and above – inland

and coastwise – Charleston. The least common forms, [ʌ ~ ɪ ~ ɐ ~ γ ~ ɷ ~ ʙ ~ ʊ ~ ɒ] are also concentrated near the coast, generally in the speech of the uncultivated.

(45.8) *yellow*[23]

	I,II	N	2N11	III
[æ]	41 r16	8		8 r7
[a ~ ɑ]	11 r1			
[σ ~ ɒ ~ ɔ]	9 r3			3
[ɐ ~ ʌ]	21	4		4
[ɪ ~ ɨ]	23 r2	2		r2
no response	4	1		3

The cultivated judge [æ] as old (2), new, correct and heard (3), the latter amplified as Negro, rural and incorrect. [ɜ] and [σ] are termed natural, and [ɨ] is termed old. The uncultural judge [æ] about equally old or heard but also natural (1) or Negro (2). [a] and [ɔ] are judged old, though the latter is also termed new, and [ɪ] is considered natural. Though its phonemic status is doubtful (Kurath and McDavid 1961: 134), [ɜ] is by far the most common form, and it frequently alternates with [ɛ]; in cultivated speech the two occur twice as frequently as all other variants combined. In cultivated speech [ʌ] is confined to Beaufort (18, 19) and Greenville; [ɒ] is most likely to be found in Charleston. [ɛ] and [ɜ] are also the most common variants in common speech, but [æ] is missing from few communities, mostly concentrated in the low country. [ɪ] and [ɨ] are distinctly less common and are also most characteristic of the low country; [ɔ] and the low vowels are most characteristic of the Pee Dee and the uppermost section of the state, though they do occur along the coast in the low country. [ʌ] and [ɐ] are absent only in a rather wide band of communities near the fall line.

(48) *vittles*

	I,II	N	2N11	III
[β]	2 r2	1		r1
[b]	2 r7	r1		r4

Phones other than [v] initially in *vittles* are judged as Negro by the cultivated, all from the coast but one, who further specifies coastal Negro usage. The uncultivated informants, also all in the coastal region, say these are Negro forms. The Charleston Negro folk informant specifies [b] as rural. The two whites who say [β] say the stop is the Negro form.

(50) *chew*

	I,II	N	2N11	III
/ɔ/	8 r23	1 r1	r1	1 r12
no response	5	1		5

Half the cultivated judges state that /ɔ/ in *chew* is used only in the expression *chew of tobacco*; the remainder give it as a heard form, with the additional specification of rural (4) or old (1). The folk informants say this form is restricted to tobacco (7), generally specifying it as old as well. /ɔ/ is also cited as a heard form (6) or rural (3) or humorous (3). Most of the instances of /ɔ/ are found in the Pee Dee, but it occurs above the fall line as well.

(55) *tomato*

	I,II	N	2N11	III
/ɒ ~ ɔ/	3 r20	1	1	4 r1
/ɑ/	r3			2 r1
/æ/	5 r11			7 r8
no response	4			1

Cultured informants in the low country say that /æ/ is an old form, but some still use it anyhow. The up-country informants report the variants as heard, /ɒ/ being further characterized as rural or Charlestonian, /æ/ as Negro. The folk judges consider /æ/ old (10) as a rule but also as heard, Negro or humorous. Old is also the general characterization of /ɒ/, and heard is general as well, but humorous and Negro are also applied. /e/, of course, is virtually universal, and cultivated variants are found only on the coast. Though /ɒ ~ ɔ/ and /æ/ are widely reported in the up country, they are seldom found there.

(77.3) *deaf*

	I,II	N	2N11	III
/ɪ/	7 r3	1		r1
/i/	27 r27	4	r1	r5
no response	13	3		8

The cultivated opinion, all from the low country, is that the variants /i/ and /ɪ/ are heard forms and rural (1) or rare (1). For about two-thirds of the folk judges, these are heard forms, and half the remainder characterize them as old. Occasionally the forms are said by the folk to be Negroisms (4). /i/ and /ɪ/, though not especially common, are rather evenly dispersed over the state.

(77.5) *boil* 'furuncle'

	I,II	N	2N11	III
/ai/	7 r7	3		r5
no response	28	3		13

/ai/ in *boil* is considered by the cultured judges as heard but also old (2). A similar consensus exists among the folk judges, though they also characterize /ai/ as Negro usage (2) or more natural (1). /ai/ occurs most frequently in the Pee Dee but is also found elsewhere; it is generally the usage of the least cultured informants.[24]

(90) *haunt* (*ed*)

	I,II	N	2N11	III
/æ/	70 r16	5	1 r1	6 r13
/e/	6 r2			
no response	16	4		11

Half the cultured informants report /æ/ as heard; the remainder are equally divided between Negro, old and humorous. Most of the uncultured cite this as a heard form as well, though about half say it is heard from Negroes. /e/ is cited as old or Negro. Though not prevailing in cultivated speech, /æ/ is not lacking there either and is rather general among other speakers. /e/ is scattered in the Pee Dee and above the fall line.

(97) *stamp*

	I,II	N	2N11	III
/ɔ/	85 r5	5	1	5 r8
/æ/	3 r4		1	5 r5
no response	17	5		6

The cultivated informants judge /ɔ/ in *stamp* as a heard form .5' and elaborate to deny the use of it (3) or to point out that /æ/ is correct (2). The judgments of the uncultured are generally divided between heard, or that one or the other of the forms was correct. /ɔ/ is universal in the speech of the uncultured – even those few who say /æ/ have both forms. Exclusive use of the latter is confined to cultivated informants.

(104) *hoist*

	I,II	N	2N11	III
/ai/	35 r13	5		2 r8
no response	31	4		6

The general opinion of the cultivated on /ai/ in *hoist* is that it is a heard form; they elaborate to specify that it is a Negroism (2), rural or what a dog does with his hind leg. The latter is also the opinion of the uncultured (5) or that /haist/ is what a boil does; somewhat more commonly it is a heard term (6), elaborated as old (2), Negro or rural; and finally, it is said to be incorrect (3). /haist/ is found in all areas of the state, especially among the most rustic informants.

GRAMMAR[25]

(3) *rise* (preterite)

	I,II	N	2N11	III
/rɪz/	14 r10	r1		r4
/raiz/	3	r1		
/raizd/	4	3		
no response	22	5		11

For the cultivated informants, /rɪz/ is a heard form, also further described as Negro (1) or predominantly Negro (1). The majority of the folk who judged *rise* were relatively more cultivated. The opinion of the folk, as a rule, is that /rɪz/ is a heard form, especially Negro (2) or rural; a minority characterize the form as incorrect (3). The zero preterite was considered old-fashioned. /rɪz/ is most common in the Pee Dee and along the fall line but absent only in the lower coastal region.

(12.4) *ain't* stressed, (12.5) *ain't* unstressed 'have'

	I,II	N	2N11	III
ain't not recorded	19		1	22 r4
no response	5	2		3

Ain't[26] is reported as a heard form by the cultivated, though two of them use it anyhow in informal contexts. *Ain't* is general among the uncultivated, except for those with social aspirations.

(25.3) *I ain't*, (25.4) *ain't I?* 'be'

	I,II	N	2N11	III
ain't not recorded	10 r2			4 r9
no response	4	2		13

The judgments of the cultivated are varied: taught to avoid *ain't* (2), informal (2), old, common, rare, careless and heard frequently. The spouse of one informant who avoids *ain't* uses it regularly, as does one informant taught to avoid it. One uncultured judge gives *ain't* as heard; the other admits to occasional use of it. The most striking fact about *ain't* 'be' is that it is rejected much less often, especially by the cultivated informants. Furthermore, the judgments of the cultivated are much less emphatic than for *ain't* 'have'.

(27) *shrink* (preterite)

	I,II	N	2N11	III
/ʃrʌŋk/	61	3	1	23 r3
/ʃræŋk/	8 r3			7 r1
/ʃrɪŋk/	5 r1	4		
/ʃriŋk/	9 r5	4		r1
no response	22	4		3

The opinion of the cultivated informants is that /ʃræŋk/ is correct, though one declares /ʃrʌŋk/ is natural; /ʃrɪŋkt/ is reported as a frequently heard form. On the latter form, the uncultured informants offer the judgment heard (4), with the additional qualification that it is a Negroism (2) or old-fashioned. The uncultured find /ʃræŋk/ less natural, and the zero form is reported as heard. /ʃrʌŋk/ is the predominant form in cultivated speech in South Carolina, as it is throughout the Atlantic Seaboard (Atwood 1953:21). The weak preterites are found in uncultured speech below the fall line, as are the majority of the zero preterites.[27]

(48) *eat* (preterite)

	I,II	N	2N11	III
eat	51 r2	5		1 r1
et	38 r6	4	r1	9 r5
no response	3	2		3

The judgment of the cultured is that *et* is heard (4) or old (3), though it is also characterized as natural. *Eat* is also a heard form. The uncultured characterize *et* as heard or old or ignorant, and *eat* is termed old. *Ate* is a heard term for one cultivated informant who states *et* is natural; the uncultivated judge *ate* as new (1) or proper (1). *Ate* is the form preferred by most of the better-educated informants; *et* is found in cultivated speech only below the fall line, and it is always paired with participial *eaten*. There is considerable mixed usage in all communities, though *eat* is somewhat more rustic in the low country and appreciably more rustic in the up country, where *et* occurs less often. The participial *eaten* is a much better touchstone of social acceptability than the preterite.

(95) *dive* (preterite)

	I,II	N	2N11	III
dived	53 r1	1 r1	1	11 r2
dove	14 r4	1 r1		14 r2
div	15 r5	1 r1		r1
dive	8	4	1	
no response	17	4		8

The cultivated judged all forms as heard; both *dived* and *dove*, however, are cited as correct by two of the cultivated. The prevailing judgment of the uncultured was that all the variants were heard forms, though *div* was cited as Negro, old and incorrect. A form not attested in usage, /duv/, was once cited as a Negroism. *Dived* is current everywhere, but *dove* is chiefly a low country form (*cf.* Atwood 1953, Fig. 6), *div* is current everywhere but in the tidewater. Though *dived* is the commonest form, *dove* is slightly more used by the cultivated. *Dive* and *div* are chiefly found in the speech of the least cultivated.

(96) *climb* (preterite)

	I,II	N	2N11	III
/kłʌm/	20 r8		r1	r6
/klæm/	3 r3			
/klɪm/	7 r5			r1
/kłom/	3 r2			
no response	16	4		9

The cultivated judged all forms as heard, though /klʌm/ is further identified as old (1) or Ne̯gro (1). /klɪm/ and /klʌm/ are characterized as heard forms, though the latter is also identified as old-fashioned, natural and incorrect. /klom/ is identified as old-fashioned, uneducated usage, and /klæm/ was judged a Negroism (2) or old. /klæmd/ was also judged heard, but no examples were found in actual usage. *Climbed* is the only form used by the cultivated and predominates in the speech of better-educated or urban informants. All other forms were found in rural communities below the fall line except two instances of /klɪm/ in the northwest corner of the state and one /klʌmd/ just above the fall line.

(104) *fight* (preterite)

	I,II	N	2N11	III
/faut/	12 r14	1 r1		r3
/fɪt/	5 r9	1		r2
/fait/	1 r1	2		
no response	9	5		5

The cultivated informants reported only heard judgments; for /faut/ the judges were from the low country, for /fɪt/ they were from the up country. The uncultured judged the former as heard (10), sometimes old (3) as well. Half the uncultivated judgments of /fɪt/ were that it was old-fashioned; the remaining attributions were equally divided between Negro and poor white. /fɔt/ was judged as correct or less natural (2), and the zero preterite was judged as Negro and rustic by the same informant. /fɔt/ is predominant at all social levels in all parts of the state; the other forms are confined to the speech of the least educated, with /faut/ being found only below the fall line.

CONCLUSION

The 144 South Carolina field records for the *Linguistic Atlas of the Middle and South Atlantic States* were systematically examined for the currency and generally ascribed status of 45 items about which a significant number of the 32 cultivated informants had offered judgments of acceptability.

Judgments were made most frequently where there were a large number of competing forms, e.g., synonyms for (54) *peanut* and (7) *living room*, or the pronunciations of (45.7) *yolk* and (45.8) *yellow;* yet a large number of judgments does not necessarily indicate either a large number of variants or a frequently occurring variant, e.g., the pronunciations of (48) *vittles* and (17) *vase.* Lexical variants reflecting cultural change are usually accurately evaluated, e.g., the innovations (7) *living room*, (8) *andirons*, (45) *doughnut* and (79) *casket*, or the older (3) *sunup,* (8) *fire dogs,* (17) *spider,* or (27.3) *breeches.* There is somewhat less accuracy in judgments on pronunciation, especially with (24) *kerosene.* For grammatical items, the most striking fact is the scarcity of comments on uninflected preterites, among the clearest touchstones of non-standard usage.[28]

Since the informants' attitudes were obtained indirectly, the number of judgments varied greatly from one interview to another. Moreover, the indirect approach often evoked such judgments as (1) two or more forms may be equally acceptable; (2) certain forms may be judged as unnatural or affected, as well as old-fashioned or rustic; and (3) even though an alternate form may be widely current or generally held to be correct, informants often prefer their own usage to the dictates of external standards.

With respect to the number of judgments on a given item, like the cultivated informants, the uncultivated most often judge lexical items and least often judge grammatical items. Still, a large number of cultivated judgments does not necessarily predict a large number of uncultivated judgments. One direction further research should take is the determination of items which the uncultivated find most interesting, but which excite little or no interest in the cultivated. As for the quality of the judgments, it is hardly rare for the uncultivated to be at least as perceptive as the cultivated, particularly for lexical items. Finally, of particular interest to scholars concerned with intercultural relations, forms are rarely labelled unequivocally as Negroisms – by informants of any class or region in South Carolina. Those forms that are labelled Negroisms are not infrequently widely distributed in white speech and are not necessarily predominant among Negroes.

The evidence from the regional linguistic atlases – both recorded forms and judgments – thus constitutes a useful supplement to other studies of acceptability. Even though language and usage continually change, it may not be safe to assume that attitudes change at the same rate, *cf.* (27) *shrank*. Atlas evidence can be used to establish benchmarks from which change can be measured.

Conclusions about usage are best drawn from systematically executed surveys of actual usage, of whatever design. The future researcher cannot be too skeptical of preconceived notions, whether those of his informants or his own.

NOTES

1. We gratefully acknowledge the permission of the American Council of Learned Societies to quote from the unpublished archives of the Linguistic Atlas of the United States and Canada, which has enjoyed since its inception the good offices of the Council. We also acknowledge the continuing support of our respective institutions, the University of Chicago and the University of South Carolina, for the editing and publication of the Linguistic Atlas of the Middle and South Atlantic States.
2. Informants were, of course, life-long residents of their respective communities; in the longest-settled regions (though certainly unrepresentative, if not impossible in more recently settled regions, *cf.* Allen 1973–76) their families had been resident two or more generations back as well, *cf.* Kurath and McDavid (1961:23–27).
   In locating informants and ascertaining their social rank, field workers paid close attention to the opinions of local contacts familiar with the class structure of their communities and to the position of individuals within the class structure. The informants' *vitae* take note not only of these comments but the educational and occupational histories, membership in churches and other organizations, social contacts, intellectual pursuits and the like of the informants, and, where available, of their immediate and more remote ancestors; salient points of the character of the informants are also noted. In the course of eight hours face-to-face contact during a typical interview, normally in the informant's home, there was ample opportunity to revise and refine preliminary judgments about social rank.
   Though aware that no single factor is an adequate indicator of social rank, linguistic geographers have paid close attention to education since it deals specifically with usage and attitudes towards usage, often fostering usages and attitudes towards usage contrary to the oral traditions. Correspondingly, the folk informants are typically minimally educated, the cultivated of generally superior education, and users of common or popular speech represent a distinctly intermediate level of education. Still, the three types are more or less rough classifications; for the study of social differences in speech, Kurath has always insisted that the *vitae* be consulted (Kurath *et al.* 1939: 44; *cf.* McDavid and O'Cain 1973).
3. Field workers varied in their practices: some were more interested in the temporal succession of forms, some were more attentive to careful distinctions in various semantic fields, etc. The character and temperament of the informant himself and the

interplay between informant and field worker are significant as well (Kurath *et al.* 1939: 46–47, 143–145).

4. Kurath *et al.* (1939:48): 'The views of the informants must be accepted with caution, but they are significant even when they are wrong.'
5. The North American surveys comprising the Linguistic Atlas of the United States and Canada are a group of autonomous regional surveys sharing a common methodology, though modified as local conditions and resources dictate. In addition to the full phonetic presentation of LANE (Kurath *et al.* 1939–1943), there exists a full treatment in normal orthography of the lexicon and grammar of the Upper Midwest (Allen 1973, 1975); for pronunciation, Allen (1976) is avalogous to Kurath and McDavid (1961). There are also summary volumes for the entire Atlantic Seaboard, Kurath (1949), Atwood (1953), and Kurath and McDavid (1961). V. McDavid (1956) is analogous to Atwood for the North Central States and the Upper Midwest. Similar summary volumes for the North Central States have been recommended (Payne forthcoming). For the Middle and South Atlantic States (Kurath, McDavid and O'Cain 1977) the full phonetic record will be published in list manuscripts. Lee A. Pederson expects to make the transcribed Gulf States field records on microfiche. The transcription of the responses is considered merely a protocol of the basic records, all tape recorded (Pederson **[1976]**).
6. Kurath *et al.* (1939–1943) and Allen (1973–76) contain lists of significant comments by the informants for each item as well as conventional designations for the status of forms in the general presentations.
   No scholar has ever been denied access to the regional collections in our custody, and we know of no restrictions on the use of the other LAUSC collections.
7. McDavid was interviewed for LAMSAS by Bernard Bloch in 1937. For the judgments in the record see McDavid (1974).
8. McDavid made 119 field records for LAMSAS in South Carolina alone and over 500 for various regional surveys. O'Cain made 20 records (each about three times the length of a typical Atlas interview) in South Carolina for Cassidy (forthcoming), as well as 100 brief records for his survey of Charleston (O'Cain 1972).
9. There are 144 field records from South Carolina. Guy S. Lowman, Jr. made 19 (1933–1934, 1937); Bloch, 1 (1937); Lee A. Pederson, 5 (1965); O'Cain, 1 (1967); and McDavid, 119 (1941, 1946–48, 1964). The records by Pederson and O'Cain were tape recorded and were re-transcribed by McDavid to minimize field worker differences in LAMSAS, for which fewer than one percent of the records were transcribed by workers other than Lowman or McDavid.
10. Even some incomplete records have rather substantial numbers of judgments, e.g., 24e, 38c.
11. According to Albert H. Marckwardt, Marjorie Daunt summarized a report on the teaching of English in the United States by saying that there were three possible attitudes toward grammar and usage: indifference, assurance and anxiety. No Americans were indifferent, and the only assured ones were two maiden ladies from Charleston.
12. Historical and sociological evidence aside, there are ample indications in Kurath (1949), Atwood (1953) and Kurath and McDavid (1961) that this approach is reasonable. We have excluded any marginal cases from group III.
13. Kurath (1949) was completed before the McDavid records became available and is based on the 20 records by Lowman and Bloch. Of the items treated herein, numbers 2, 3, 9, 27.3, 48, 54, 79, 98 and 100 are not treated by Kurath. *Cultivated* and *cultured* are

used interchangeably with no difference in sense; *folk* is likewise interchangeable with *uncultured* or *uncultivated.*

14. There are 102 uncultivated white informants, 10 uncultivated Negro informants, 1 cultivated Negro informant and 31 cultivated white informants.
15. Numbers following judgment labels in parentheses give the number of judgments. Where there are no numbers the figures are derivable or of no particular significance.
16. Statements about the social and geographical distribution of forms are strictly limited to those forms actually current in the speech of the informants.
17. *Stoop* has some currency in the Savannah River valley but is quite marginal elsewhere.
18. The *fall line* is the head of navigation on the rivers and sets off the *low country* from the *up country* (piedmont). Communities 21, 22, 25 and 29 are situated more or less on the fall line. The *Pee Dee,* a separate cultural subdivision of South Carolina (*cf.* Kurath 1949: Fig. 3), is set off from the low country by the river of that name, which empties near communities 6 and 7. The *tidewater* extends from the mouth of the Pee Dee southward and includes the lands within about 30 miles of the coast.
19. *Folk* is used in a somewhat broader sense than heretofore to mean all the uncultured informants, groups I, II and N.
20. There are also 24 occurrences of other terms, all of which are distinctly minor variants, few occurring more than once. In several of the items there are minor variants that resist summary treatment, and about which expressions of opinion are non-existent or insignificant.
21. Matter following a single parenthesis gives the context in which a form was elicited or instructions to the field worker.
22. Phonetic details are of necessity greatly abridged; phonemic transcriptions are consistent with Kurath and McDavid (1961). Items 24, 26 and 48 are not treated by Kurath and McDavid (1961).
23. Additional phones of the stressed vowel in *yellow* were taken from pages (56) *yellow corn,* (60) *yellow bellied cooter,* (60A) *yellow jacket* and (79) *yellow jaundice.*
24. (46) *boiled egg,* (24) *oil,* and (89) *joined,* from another etymological source than (77.5) and (104) *hoist,* also very rarely have /ai/; the distribution of /ai/ in the former does not alter the conclusions about the latter.
25. The number of grammatical items treated is smaller for two reasons: the judgments were less frequent because the items were recorded from free conversation and the number of grammatical items in the work sheets is proportionately smaller.
26. *Ain't,* even more than other grammatical items, is best recorded from free conversation. The principle is that by which one never asks a stranger if he is from Virginia: if he is, one will learn within ten minutes; if he isn't, one should avoid embarrassing him.
27. Interestingly, there was no commentary on the incidence of /ʃr-/ and /sr-/; the latter is dominant in South Carolina.
28. Surprisingly, the multiple plurals (54) /mætesɨz/ 'tomatoes' and (64) /tʃɪlenz/ 'children', and such double comparatives as (26) *more prettier* pass without comment.

REFERENCES

Allen, H. (1973–76), *Linguistic Atlas of the Upper Midwest.* Minneapolis, University of Minnesota.

American Heritage Dictionary (1969), Boston, American Heritage Publishing Co. & Houghton Mifflin Co.

Atwood, E. B. (1953), *A Survey of Verb Forms in the Eastern United States*. Ann Arbor, University of Michigan.

Cassidy, F. G. (in progress), Dictionary of American Regional English.

Creswell, T. J. (1974), 'Usage in dictionaries and dictionaries of usage'. University of Chicago dissertation. [Microfilm]

Kurath, H. (1949), *A Word Geography of the Eastern United States*. Ann Arbor, University of Michigan.

Kurath, H., *et al.* (1939), *Handbook of the Linguistic Geography of New England*. Providence, Rhode Island, American Council of Learned Societies. [2nd ed. 1973. New York, AMS Press]

– (1939–1943), *Linguistic Atlas of New England*. Providence, Rhode Island, American Council of Learned Societies. [Reprinted 1972, New York, AMS Press]

Kurath, H., and McDavid, R. I., Jr. (1961), *The Pronunciation of English in the Atlantic States*. Ann Arbor, University of Michigan.

Kurath, H., McDavid, Jr., R. I. and O.Cain, R. K. (1977–), *Linguistic Atlas of the Middle and South Atlantic States*. Chicago, University of Chicago.

McDavid, R. I., Jr. (1974), 'The failure of intuition'. Unpublished paper delivered before the Henry Lee Smith, Jr., Memorial Symposium, Buffalo, New York.

– (forthcoming), Review of *The Study of Social Dialects in American English* (1974), *American Anthropologist*.

McDavid, R. I., Jr., and O'Cain, R. K. (1973), 'Sociolinguistics and linguistic geography', *Kansas Journal of Sociology*, 9, pp. 137–156.

McDavid, V. G. (1956), 'Verb forms in the north central states and upper midwest'. University of Minnesota dissertation. [Microfilm]

Mencken, H. L. (1963), *The American Language*. [One-volume abridged edition; 4th ed. & 2 supplements, edited with new material by R. I. McDavid, Jr. with assistance of D. W. Maurer] New York, Alfred A. Knopf.

O'Cain, R. K. (1972), 'A social dialect survey of Charleston, South Carolina'. University of Chicago dissertation. [Microfilm]

Payne, R. C. (forthcoming), 'The Linguistic Atlas of the North Central States: Plans and Prospects', *American Speech*.

Pederson, L. (1974 [1976]), 'Tape/Text and Analogues', *American Speech* 49, pp. 5–23.

B. A. MOHAN

9

Acceptability Testing and Fuzzy Grammar

Lakoff (1973) proposes a model of grammar called 'fuzzy grammar'. Asking how this model might be endangered by data raises questions of acceptability testing. The goal of this paper is to examine theoretical and empirical issues which arise when claims for this model are tested on judgments by speakers. These issues relate to assumptions of the fuzzy grammar model and to assumptions of measurement procedures.

1. FUZZY GRAMMAR

In fuzzy grammar the well-formedness of sentences is viewed as a scale ranging from 1 (completely well-formed) to 0 (completely ill-formed), rather than the standard dichotomy of well-formed/ill-formed. The degree of well-formedness of a sentence depends on the rules which have applied in its derivation. Thus a rule in fuzzy grammar will have associated with it a rule function defining the degree of well-formedness of its output. The degree of well-formedness depends on the rule involved and on factors entering into the rule. It is claimed that 'hierarchies' or ordering relations exist within factors and that these hierarchies will be largely constant from speaker to speaker. However, different speakers will have different acceptability thresholds.

Lakoff's conception of rule function can be illustrated (with some simplification) for rules of Adverb-preposing and Topicalization, rules which move surface adverbials and surface nominals, respectively:

1(a) Adverb-preposing: $wf = f_1$ (A category, island, trigger)
(b) Topicalization: $wf = f_2$ (N category, island, trigger)

where f_1 and f_2 represent two different rule functions and wf represents a well-formedness value between 1 and 0. In 1(a) there are three relevant factors contributing to the well-formedness of the resultant output: the adverb category, island and trigger hierarchies. In 1(b) the factors are the noun category, island and trigger hierarchies. The island hierarchy consists of predicates (such as *possible* and *realize)* whose complements have different degrees of 'islandhood', i.e., form units which resist the movement of elements from them in varying degrees. The trigger hierarchy consists of predicates (again, such as *possible* and *realize*) which differentially 'trigger' adverb-preposing or topicalization in their complements, i.e., promote the movement of certain elements in varying degrees. Lakoff identifies a number of predicates common to both hierarchies and claims that the common predicates are identically ordered in each hierarchy. Sentences 2(a–d) show variation along the island hierarchy, across Adverb-Preposing and Topicalization. 3(a-d) show variation along the trigger hierarchy, across the two rules. Italics indicates stress.

2(a)	Tomorrow it's possible that Matilda will eat.	(Adv.)
(b)	Tomorrow I realize that Matilda will eat.	(Adv.)
(c)	*Vases* it's possible that Matilda hates.	(Top.)
(d)	*Vases* I realize that Matilda hates.	(Top.)

3(a)	It's possible that tomorrow Matilda will eat.	(Adv.)
(b)	I realize that tomorrow Matilda will eat.	(Adv.)
(c)	It's possible that *vases* Matilda hates.	(Top.)
(d)	I realize that *vases* Matilda hates.	(Top.)

The fuzzy grammar model bears various formal similarities to Labov's model of variable rules. In each case, the model for a rule is a function having input from linguistic environments with continuous variables associated with them and yielding a continuous variable as output. In each case variability is claimed to be an aspect of linguistic competence. On the other hand, the output of a fuzzy grammar function is a well-formedness value while the output of a variable rule function is a rule application probability; a variable rule incorporates its relevant linguistic features and their input probabilities, whereas the items in a hierarchy and their relative values are specified in the grammar as a whole, since the same hierarchy is considered to show up in different rules; the data base for variable rule studies has been speech samples whereas the most obvious data base for fuzzy grammar is judgments of sentences; the input of a variable rule may include non-linguistic parameters such as the socio-economic status of the speaker.

Comparison with the variable rules model reveals certain unspecified areas in the fuzzy grammar model. Cedergren and Sankoff (1974) have proposed a general form for the variable rule function. No general or specific form has been proposed with respect to fuzzy grammar rule functions. For the present it will simply be assumed that the fuzzy grammar functions examined here preserve the rank order within a hierarchy, that well-formedness is monotonically related to the scale values for each hierarchy (*cf.* Lakoff 1973: 282).

Cedergren and Sankoff relate the social grammar of the speech community and the individual grammar of the speaker by incorporating a speaker's non-linguistic parameters in the input probability and by setting the strictly linguistic parameters at fixed values for the whole community. It is not clear how the fuzzy grammar model would characterize a social grammar in relation to individual grammars, yet this issue is important if one wishes to work with data from groups of speakers. A weak claim would be that all members of a speech community will order the predicates of, say, the trigger hierarchy in the same way; that is, that they will share the same ordinal scale for this hierarchy and similarly for other hierarchies. A stronger claim would be that they will not only agree on the ordering of the predicates but will also agree on the ordering of the differences between the predicates, i.e., they will share the same interval scale for this hierarchy and for others. This stronger claim will be assumed as a working hypothesis in this study.

On either claim, there is no prediction that the members of a speech community will agree in dichotomous judgments as to whether a particular sentence is well-formed or not. This is reflected in Lakoff's claim, mentioned above, that different speakers may have different acceptability thresholds. Accordingly, where dichotomous grammar must give central importance to acceptances of sentences, fuzzy grammar gives central importance to the ordinal or interval scaling of sentences as an underlying constant, and individual acceptances become a matter of possibly superficial variation. Nevertheless, the pattern of individual acceptances across a speech community should not be random but should reveal an implicational scale, the basis of which is the shared ordinal or interval scale, for it would be inconsistent for an individual to rank sentence A as more well-formed than sentence B, but to accept B and reject A.

The prediction of an implicational scaling in the pattern of sentence acceptances is, of course, made by those who would claim that the patterning is due to the presence of distinct dichotomous individual grammars related in an implicational series (*cf.* Elliott et al. 1969). This implicational scale model therefore supplies an alternative account for the same data.

If an implicational pattern of acceptances cannot be demonstrated for our data, both the fuzzy grammar model and the implicational scale model can be falsified. If an implicational pattern can be demonstrated, the next task is to choose between the two models. Fuzzy grammar claims that at least an ordinal scaling of the sentences at issue is shared by the members of the speech community and that this would be the basis for the implicational pattern found. The implicational scale model would claim no such commonality and would view the implicational scale as external to the grammar of each individual in the speech community. Failure to find evidence for at least a shared ordinal scale would therefore falsify the fuzzy grammar model. The implicational scale model makes a measurement assumption that, where an implicational scale exists, a distinct number of acceptances is evidence of a distinct individual grammar, i.e., if speaker A accepts five sentences and speaker B accepts six, then this constitutes evidence that A and B have distinct grammars. The fuzzy grammar model makes no such assumption. If this assumption can be shown to be false, the implicational scale model can be falsified. This will be discussed in greater detail in the next section.

In sum, then, if we wish to use acceptability judgments from members of a specific speech community to test the fuzzy grammar model, our experiments eliciting their judgments on an appropriate set of sentences should provide evidence for or against:

(a) an implicational scaling of dichotomous judgments of the well-formedness of the sentences where one hierarchy is varied and other factors are held constant;
(b) a shared ordinal scaling of the sentences under the same conditions;
(c) a shared interval scaling of the sentences under the same conditions;
(d) the measurement assumption associated with the implicational scale model;
(e) specific forms for the fuzzy grammar rule functions under consideration.

2. MEASUREMENT PROCEDURES

There seems to be no good reason not to regard acceptability testing as a particular case of psychological measurement. Accordingly, assumptions of acceptability testing should be instances of assumptions discussed in the extensive literature of psychometric theory (*cf.* Nunnally 1967). Nunnally makes a convenient distinction between consideration of measurement theory relating to measurement techniques and considerations of contingent variables likely to bias measurement.

Considerations of measurement theory have received little attention in acceptability testing. Yet assumptions dealt with explicitly in measurement theory are made implicitly whenever the numerical results of an acceptability study are interpreted so as to provide a representation or model of the relations holding between a given set of speakers and sentences. The representation is in effect a miniature theory, and, if this theory is to be falsifiable, the assumptions implicit in the representation should be evaluated by consistency checks (for a discussion of representational measurement, see Coombs, Dawes and Tversky 1970). For example, the representation of a set of acceptability results as an implicational scale may be evaluated by using the Guttman scalogram technique in which the consistency check is fundamentally an evaluation of the degree to which contrary implications are present in the data. Another technique used in this study derives from functional measurement theory (see Anderson 1971) where internal consistency is evaluated using the analysis of variance with a factorial design. Various acceptability studies may be criticized for failing to use a measurement technique incorporating consistency checks and thereby failing to provide support for assumptions of the representation they present. Assumptions underlying certain acceptability testing procedures may be stated explicitly in the theory of the appropriate measurement technique. The implicational scale model of grammar assumes that a distinct number of acceptances is evidence of a distinct individual grammar. This depends on the more fundamental assumption that the probability of acceptance for any given sentence is either one or zero, which is a particular case of the general assumption of the Guttman technique that characterizes that technique as a deterministic scaling model (*cf.* Nunnally 1967: 61 ff.).

Contingent variables have received some attention in the acceptability testing literature. Thus Greenbaum (1973) found that order of presentation had a significant effect on acceptability results. The question of contingent variables has a bearing on the measurement assumption associated with the implicational scale model. If variability in the number of sentences accepted can be accounted for by a contingent variable, it is not necessary to posit the existence of distinct individual grammars to account for it. Just such a contingent variable has received considerable attention in psychometric studies in the investigation of individual tendencies to agree to questionnaire items, which would correspond in acceptability testing to individual tendencies to accept sentences. The initial postulation of a very general personality trait of 'agreement tendency', 'acquiescence' or 'yea-saying' has not been supported (*cf.* Nunnally 1967: 615) but it remains to be seen whether there is a significant yea-saying factor in the specific area of acceptability judgments.

A second issue which can be viewed as a matter of contingent variables relates to the validity of rating methods for acceptability testing. Acceptability testing has typically used rating methods: a speaker is asked to rate the well-formedness of a sentence on a two-point (yes/no) or perhaps a five-point scale. A ranking method might require a speaker to place a set of sentences in rank order of well-formedness. The first requires an absolute judgment, the second a comparative judgment. Subjects have been found to be notoriously inaccurate when judging the absolute magnitude of stimuli but notoriously accurate when making comparative judgments (see Nunnally 1967: 40). This study will use a ranking method as well as a rating method as a check on the validity of the latter.

In this study, consideration of the validity of rating versus ranking methods, of the possible presence of a yea-saying factor and of consistency checks for the measurement techniques used all serve to examine assumptions made in the present measurement procedures.

3. DATA COLLECTION

96 subjects were chosen from students at the University of Wisconsin-Milwaukee; 64 were from freshman level linguistic classes, 32 were from freshman level anthropology classes. The two groups' results were combined after statistical analysis showed no significant difference between them. The subjects were considered to be representative of the local speech community with additional homogeneity in age and education.

The subjects' main task was to judge the well-formedness of sentences in which two rules and two hierarchies were varied using both ranking and rating methods. The stimulus design consisted of 44 sentences (4 sets of 11 sentences) which were produced by expanding the design shown in 2(a-d) and 3(a-d) above by adding more points on each hierarchy. Thus the two points on the island hierarchy illustrated in 2(a-b) were expanded to 11, which were, in order from weakest island to strongest island, (1) no embedded S, followed by ten predicates: (2) *possible;* (3) *expect;* (4) *think;* (5) *say;* (6) *know;* (7) *realize;* (8) *find out;* (9) *be surprised;* (10) *regret;* (11) *mention.* 2(c-d) were similarly expanded to 11 points. Comparable expansions were made of 3(a-b) and 3(c-d) to 11 points along the trigger hierarchy, which were, in order from strongest trigger to weakest trigger: (1) a deleted performative, followed by (2)–(11), the above ten predicates in the same order. Details of the analyses of these sentences are given in Lakoff (1973), where it is claimed that the ordering along each hierarchy is associated with decreasing well-formedness of the resultant sentence. The total design is shown in Figure 1 and consists of two row × column factorial designs, with the row factor being a rule factor and the column factor being the island hierarchy in one case and the trigger hierarchy in the other.

Figure 1.

	Hierarchy	
	Island (11 points)	Trigger (11 points)
Adverb-preposing	11 sentences	11 sentences
Topicalization	11 sentences	11 sentences

Subjects performed two specific tasks, a rating task and a ranking task. The rating task was to rate the well-formedness of each of the sentences on a 10-point scale which was anchored at each end by an example sentence, a rating of 1 meaning 'completely well-formed' and a rating of 10 meaning 'completely ill-formed'. The ranking task was to place the 11 sentences of a given set in rank order down a page, giving the most well-formed sentence the highest rank, and then to draw a line across the ranking to divide it into well-formed and ill-formed sentences. This was repeated for each set. Appropriate randomization procedures were used to control for order effects. All subjects performed both tasks with a two-week interval between them, half of each group of subjects performing rating first, the other half performing ranking first.

To provide data on a possible yea-saying factor, a third task was devised by choosing a 'mish-mash' set of 50 sentences which bore no obvious relation to the rules and hierarchies mentioned above. They ranged over a number of syntactic points (including pronominalization, conjunction, relative clauses, determiners and *dare* and *need*) and in previous experiments had evoked divergent responses from speakers.

Subjects were asked to accept or reject each sentence. The basic instructions for each of the three tasks were identical,[1] and all sentences were presented simultaneously in written and spoken form.

4. IMPLICATIONAL SCALE

A first issue is whether the results show a pattern of acceptances which conform to an implicational scale. Acceptances and rejections were provided directly in the ranking task when the subjects divided the ranked set into well-formed/ill-formed. With the rating data, a rating of 1–5 was treated as an acceptance and a rating of 6–10 as a rejection. The acceptances for each set of 11 sentences for each task were analyzed by the Guttman scalogram technique, using the Biomed computer program BMDO5S. The scalogram technique provides three measures which can be used to evaluate the scalability of the sentences. The Coefficient of Reproducibility (CR) measures how far an individual's total number of acceptances predicts the pattern of his acceptances; the Minimum Marginal Reproducibility (MMR) indicates the minimum CR that could have occurred, given the proportion of the subjects accepting and rejecting each of the sentences; and the Coefficient of Scalability (CS) combines these two measures (CS = CR – MM/1 – MM). CR and CS range between 0 and 1. If the items constitute a scale the CR value should be higher than .9 and the CS value higher than .6, but the statistical theory of those measures is incomplete, and these are rule-of-thumb standards. Table 1 shows the results. On the whole these results provide fair evidence of the existence of an implicational scale for each set of sentences, although no precise test of significance is available.

Table 1.

	Rating			Ranking		
	CR	MM	CS	CR	MM	CS
Adv. Is.	.88	.70	.60	.92	.75	.68
Adv. Tr.	.96	.91	.51	.90	.67	.69
Top. Is.	.92	.78	.61	.90	.75	.58
Top. Tr.	.89	.73	.61	.90	.77	.57

5. SHARED ORDINAL SCALE

Both the fuzzy grammar model and the implicational scale model could account for the implicational patterns found, but the fuzzy grammar model would claim that the ordinal scaling of the sentences is part of the competence of the individual speaker. The rank ordering results from the ranking task can be used to test this claim, since speakers should give similar rank orderings if they share the same ordinal scale. An appropriate statistical measure of agreement between rankings is Kendall's Coefficient of Concordance W, which ranges from zero to one; the higher the value, the greater the degree of concordance or agreement. The null hypothesis is that the rankings are unrelated, and the significance of a given value of W is determined by taking it together with the number of judges (96) and number of objects ranked (11) and deriving a chi-square value, whose significance, with 10 degrees of freedom, is given in Table 2. Since each of the W values is significant, the null hypothesis can be rejected.

Table 2.

	Ranking data			Averaged rank data		
	W	χ^2	p	W	χ^2	p
Adv. Is.	.61	434.9	$<.001$	.19	182.4	$<.001$
Adv. Tr.	.38	211.8	$<.001$	.06	57.6	$<.001$
Top. Is.	.28	124.7	$<.001$	.11	105.6	$<.001$
Top. Tr.	.25	62.2	$<.001$	.02	19.2	$<.05$

However, it could be argued that the concordance between the rankings is an artifact of the Guttman scale present in the data. Assume a dichotomous grammar, and suppose that a subject judges sentences as clearly acceptable or clearly unacceptable. Given a set of sentences to rank, one would expect him to rank any acceptable sentence higher than any unacceptable sentence but to rank order the subset of acceptable sentences arbitrarily and to rank order the subset of unacceptable sentences arbitrarily. Where a Guttman scale exists, a sentence acceptable to all subjects will receive the highest average rank, a sentence acceptable to some will receive a lower average rank and a sentence unacceptable to all, the lowest average rank. Kendall's concordance measure might well give a significant result for this data, but one could not conclude from this that the subjects shared the same ordinal scale for these sentences.

It was decided to calculate the degree of apparent concordance which might have arisen by this process. For each subject and each set of 11 ranked sentences, the sentences the subject accepted were assigned their average rank, and the sentences the subject rejected were assigned their average rank, in order to provide a simple analogue of arbitrary choice within these two subsets. Kendall's measure was applied to the averaged rank data produced, and the results are shown in Table 2. If it were true that the concordance found in the ranking data was due solely to the implicational scale relations in the data, one would expect the W values for the averaged rank data to be similar to those for the original ranking data. Comparison shows that the W values for the original data are markedly higher. It is therefore concluded that the results for the original data do provide evidence that the subjects share an ordinal scale for these sentences.

6. YEA-SAYING FACTOR

A measurement assumption of the implicational scale model, that a distinct number of acceptances constitutes evidence for a distinct individual grammar, can be falsified if a yea-saying factor can be shown to account for variation in the number of sentences accepted by individuals. If acceptances are solely a function of the well-formedness of sentences for the individual, there should be no correlation between a subject's total number of acceptances on the diverse set of sentences which made up the third task and his total acceptances on either the rating task or the ranking task, for the two sets of sentences involved are not related. On the other hand, if there is a significant positive correlation between the diverse set acceptances and each of the rating and ranking acceptance totals, this is evidence for the possible presence of a yea-saying factor in acceptability testing, i.e., for the hypothesis that there is a tendency to accept sentences regardless of the particular sentences judged. If this positive correlation were very high, it would suggest that a yea-saying factor could account for all of the individual differences in number of acceptances in the present data.

A count was made of the number of sentences accepted by each individual on the rating task for the test set of sentences, the ranking task for the test set and the acceptance task for the diverse set of sentences. The product moment correlations between the totals are shown in Table 3. There is a significant but moderate positive correlation between the number of acceptances on the diverse set of sentences and the number of acceptances on the rating task and the ranking task. This suggests the presence of a yea-saying factor, but, since the correlation is not high, it cannot be argued that this factor can account for all individual differences in acceptances. The correlation between the rating and ranking acceptances of the test set of sentences is not very high, despite the fact that the same sentences and individuals are involved, which implies that acceptance data contain important sources of error other than a yea-saying factor.

Table 3.

Acceptances	Correlation	Significance
Diverse & Rating	.43	.0001
Diverse & Ranking	.32	.0016
Rating & Ranking	.57	<.0001

The data indicate that acceptances are not solely a function of the well-formedness of sentences for the individual, which argues against the validity of the implicational model for these data. The evidence for a yea-saying factor can only be tentative, but it points to a possible source of bias in measurement, which should be identified so that it can be controlled.

7. SHARED INTERVAL SCALE AND RULE FUNCTION SPECIFICATION

The questions of shared interval scale and of the form of fuzzy grammar rule functions are best taken together, for the measurement technique used to test a proposed form for rule functions assumes (and tests for) a shared interval scale (hence the convenience of the assumption of an interval scale shared by members of a speech community). The results of the rating task provide the data for examining these questions, since the sentence ratings may yield an interval scaling of the sentences.

The suggested form for rule functions is an application of a more general model of information integration proposed by Anderson 1971. The framework for rule functions given in 1(a-b) above indicates that the item entering into the rule from each hierarchy contributes a scale value to the rule. An interpretation of one variant of Anderson's model would assign a weight to each of the hierarchies and sum the result in each case. Assuming that each rule function assigns different weights to its hierarchies, the two rule functions would be reformulated as in 4(a-b):

4(a) Adverb-preposing: wf = (w1 × A category + w2 × island + w3 × trigger);

(b) Topicalization: wf = (w4 × N category + w5 × island + w6 × trigger).

4(a-b) claims that the rule functions have the same general form while allowing them to differ in the weights, or relative importance, they assign to each hierarchy. The hierarchy values are each between one and zero. An objection to this formulation is that it may yield wf values outside the range 1 to 0 and thus needs to be constrained to this range, perhaps by a truncation convention (*cf.* Cedergren and Sankoff 1974: 337). An averaging variant of Anderson's general model (see Anderson 1971: 181) would offer a more elegant solution to this problem, but the choice between the two variants would require experimental testing beyond the scope of this study.

Anderson claims that the assumptions of an interval scaling of the data and the proposed form of the function can be tested simultaneously using a test of goodness of fit which makes certain predictions with respect to the results of the analysis of variance applied to a factorial design. The present data design consists of two factorial designs with the row factor being a rule factor, and the column factor being a hierarchy factor. Assuming the rule functions of 4(a-b), the variation in the column factor will be along the scale values for a hierarchy; the variation in the row factor will be in the two differing weights assigned to that hierarchy by the two different rules. For this design the goodness of fit prediction is that there will be significant interaction between the two factors, but that only the bilinear component[2] of the interaction will be significant (for details of this analysis, see Mohan 1975).

The analysis of variance results is shown in Tables 4–6 (Note that this analysis is for 4 sets of 10 sentences each, the original first sentence of each set having been eliminated for technical reasons.) The results for the island hierarchy factorial design are as predicted: there is significant interaction between the rule factor and the island hierarchy factor (Table 4), and when the interaction is partitioned into a bilinear component and a remainder, only the former is significant (Table 6). On the other hand, the results for the trigger hierarchy design are not as predicted: the interaction between the rule factor and the trigger hierarchy factor is not significant (Table 5). It may be that each rule assigns much the same weight to the trigger hierarchy, in which case this result could be accounted for. Consequently, the evidence is not completely convincing that these results provide for the assumptions that there is an interval scale shared by all the subjects for each set of sentences and therefore for each hierarchy, and that the rule functions have a summated weighting form. Nevertheless, it is considered sufficient to establish these assumptions as tenable working hypotheses for further investigation.

Table 4. *Summary analysis of variance for Island hierarchy*

Source	F-ratio
Rules	132.2*
Hierarchy	24.2*
Rules × Hierarchy	23.2*

Table 5. *Summary analysis of variance for Trigger hierarchy*

Source	F-ratio
Rules	317.8*
Hierarchy	8.7*
Rules × Hierarchy	1.7

Note: For tables 4 and 5 all degrees of freedom for f-ratios reduce to 1/95 with Geisser-Greenhouse correction. Each source has its own error term with 95 degrees of freedom. Significant F-ratios are indicated by asterisks ($p \leqslant .05$).

Table 6. *Interaction components for Island hierarchy*

Source	Mean square	F-ratio
Rules × Hierarchy	1016.1	
Bilinear component	887.4	119.1*
Remainder	128.7	3.8

8. HIERARCHIES

General predictions of the fuzzy grammar model have been examined above. There are also some specific predictions for the two hierarchies tested which, if confirmed, would add weight to the general results. Lakoff (1973) predicts a specific order for each of the hierarchies and claims that the two orders are identical for the items being tested. Table 7 shows the predicted order and the ordering observed in the rating and ranking results. Ties are indicated by +, and * marks tau values significant at the .05 level or better. The first column labeled 'tau' indicates the correspondence between observed order and the predicted order as measured by the Kendall rank correlation coefficient, tau. Since only half of these tau values are significant, it appears that the observed orders do not correspond well to the predicted order. It might be argued that this reveals error in the rating and ranking procedures. This view would be supported if the rating orderings and the ranking orderings did not correlate well with each other. The second column marked 'tau' gives the correlation between the rating order and the ranking order for each of the four sets of sentences. All of these tau values are highly significant, which argues that some confidence can be placed in the observed orderings derived by either method and that the discrepancies from the predicted order cannot be dismissed. Table 8 presents the ordering for each hierarchy in the ranking results when averaged across Adverb-preposing and Topicalization. The tau value is not significant, indicating that the orders for the island hierarchy and the trigger hierarchy were not the same in these data.

Table 7.

		Predicted order												
		1	2	3	4	5	6	7	8	9	10	11	τ	τ
Observed Orders														
Adv. Is.	Rating	1	3	6	4	7	2	10	5	9	8	11	.60*	
	Ranking	1	3	6	4	7	10	2	8	9	11	5	.49*	.82*
Adv. Tr.	Rating	1	8	5	6	3	11	4	7	10	9	2	.16	
	Ranking	1	5	8	3	4	6	11	7	9	10	2	34	.44*
Top. Is.	Rating	1	6	+9	8	4	2	7	5	+10	+11	3	.09	
	Ranking	1	6	8	3	9	4	7	10	2	5	11	.30	.82*
Top. Tr.	Rating	1	6	3	5	2	8	7	10	4	11	9	.53*	
	Ranking	1	6	3	8	5	4	7	10	11	2	9	.38*	.71*

Table 8.

Ranking												τ
Island Adv. & Top.	1	6	3	4	7	8	10	2	9	11	5	.27
Trigger Adv. & Top.	1	5	8	3	6	4	11	7	9	10	2	

Thus, while there is good evidence of ordering in these results, the observed orders do not correspond well to Lakoff's predictions. How can the observed orders be accounted for? Lakoff offers no explicit justification for the order he predicts, or for any parts of it, so that it is not clear how an explanation of deviations from this order might proceed, and no obvious explanation of the deviations suggests itself. A more explicit theory of fuzzy grammar should provide motivation for the hierarchy orderings predicted.

9. CONCLUSION

The fuzzy grammar model has survived various tests. The data indicate that variation in acceptances of the test sentences by speakers is systematic, that the fuzzy grammar model may be chosen over the implicational scaling model and, less strongly, that the hypotheses of interval scale hierarchies within a speech community and a summated weighting model for rule functions are tenable. On the other hand, Lakoff's specific predictions for these data have not been confirmed, raising the question of the theoretical motivation for ordering in hierarchies. Regarding acceptability testing as a special case of psychological measurement made it clearer what standards should be applied to these tests and what were likely sources of measurement error. Consideration of the two grammatical models led to the use of two measurement models, the Guttman model and Anderson's functional measurement model, the importance of which was that they made measurement assumptions explicit and provided consistency checks. In examining contingent variables which might be sources of measurement error, evidence was found for a yea-saying factor and for the validity of the rating method in comparison with the ranking method.

Recently there has been a tendency for work in acceptability testing and work in sociolinguistics to develop in isolation from each other. But in this study the mutual relevance of acceptability testing and sociolinguistic considerations emerges rather clearly. On the one side, it is more practical to test sentences with a group of speakers rather than with a single speaker and to choose those speakers from the same speech community. Hence the sociolinguistic assumptions of the model being tested have had to be made explicit. On the other side, it has been shown how acceptability testing can incorporate various empirical checks. This may help to persuade those who believe otherwise that acceptability data can play a valid role in sociolinguistic work.

ACKNOWLEDGMENTS

The College of Letters and Science, University of Wisconsin-Milwaukee, kindly provided research assistance and computer facilities for this study, and the staff of the Social Sciences Research Facility and Fred Ostapik were most helpful in statistical programming. I am very grateful to Marshall Dermer, Sidney Greenbaum, Robert Remstad and Walter Zwirner for discussion of various issues, and to Donnie Dean for assistance in many phases of this research.

NOTES

1. The instructions were: 'Consider each of the sentences and decide if it would be possible that you would say this in conversation. An example of an obviously possible sentence is:
   'John plays golf.' It is clearly normal and natural. An example of an obviously impossible sentence is:
   'John will chasing me.' It is clearly abnormal and unnatural.
2. For discussion of this claim, see Anderson 1971: 179–180; and for a discussion of bilinear (or linear × linear) components and of trend components of interaction generally, see Winer 1971: 388ff.

REFERENCES

Anderson, N. H. (1971), 'Integration theory and attitude change', *Psychological Review*, 78, pp. 171–206.

Cedergren, H., and Sankoff, D. (1974), 'Variable rules: Performance as a statistical reflection of competence', *Language*, 50, pp. 333–355.

Coombs, C., Dawes, R., and Tversky, A. (1970), *Mathematical Psychology*. Englewood Cliffs, N. J., Prentice-Hall.

Elliott, D., Legum, S., and Thompson, S. (1969), 'Syntactic variation as linguistic data', *Papers from the fifth regional meeting of the Chicago Linguistic Society*, pp. 52–59.

Greenbaum, S. (1973), 'Informant elicitation of data on syntactic variation', *Lingua*, 31, pp. 201–212.

Lakoff, G. (1973), 'Fuzzy grammar and the performance/competence terminology game', *Papers from the ninth regional meeting of the Chicago Linguistic Society*, pp. 271–291.

Mohan, B. (1975), 'Testing rules in fuzzy grammar' in A. Makkai and K. V. B. Makkai, Eds., *The First LACUS Forum 1974*. Columbia, S.C., Hornbeam Press.

Nunnally, J. (1967), *Psychometric Theory*. New York, McGraw-Hill.

Winer, B. J. (1971), *Statistical Principles in Experimental Design*. New York, McGraw-Hill.

CHAIM RABIN

10

Acceptability in a Revived Language

Hebrew, as spoken today in Israel, is the result of an effort, started almost one hundred years ago, to turn what was then a purely written language in a diglossia situation into an all-purpose national language.[1] It is now for more than 50% of the Jewish population of Israel, about 1.25 million, mother-tongue and often sole language and for a large percentage of the rest the main language of communication; most of them are not conscious, or perhaps unaware, of it not having been spoken three generations ago. What may be called the Linguistic Establishment, on the other hand, is acutely aware of the revival situation and identifies itself with slogans such as calling today's Hebrew 'a language in the course of being revived' *(lashon mitḥaya)* or describing Israel as 'a society of language learners' *(ḥevra lomedet)* and engages collectively in a sustained campaign to change the language as used at present so that it will conform with the usage of the Sources, i.e., the groups of literary texts on the basis of which the revival was started. The present study sets out to describe some of the problems of acceptability created by this situation. However, as the effort to bring the language back to fuller dependence on the Sources in fact tries to restore to it the main characteristic it had as the upper language of the diglossia situation, the acceptability problems resemble those found in diglossia situations as such.

The 'upper' language in a diglossia situation is either the living language of some other community or a language or language form that is no longer spoken anywhere. We may call the second type the classical language, since some of its most outstanding examples are known under that name. In either case the upper language will be learned as a second language, and like all second languages its standards derive from outside the learner's society, from some body of users or corpus of texts, written or oral, regarded as authoritative by the diglossic group, such as the Attic writers for the Romans or the *auctores* of Golden and Silver Latinity for the user of medieval Latin. A classical language is not taught from contemporary texts but from a well-defined body of ancient texts, in most cases works of cultural, moral or religious value, which we may call the Sources. There may be periods when adherence to the linguistic standards of the Sources is lax and others, often referred to as renaissances, when close imitation of the Sources is widespread. Since with time the concepts and ways of thought that need to be expressed in the diglossic classical language become quite unlike those found in the Sources, and direct imitation is rarely feasible, it becomes necessary to establish a system of rules as to what constitutes proper adherence to the language of the Sources. This is the main sociological matrix for the rise of grammars and dictionaries. Such rules tend to become independent of the Sources, especially as any larger body of Source literature will rarely be entirely uniform in language, and there are several cases in which the text of the Sources is known to have been revised in order to conform to the normative rules ostensibly derived from it.[2] The Sources in most cases present only a very narrow range of registers, and these tend to become blurred in the usage of the diglossical classical language, and the latter develops registers of its own by rearrangement of the linguistic materials found in the Sources. This is sometimes achieved by a somewhat arbitrary assignment of different periods of Source language to present registers.[3]

This situation demands an army of language pundits familiar with the written and unwritten laws of writing and speaking the classical language. These may partly be identical with those who teach that language, especially in those cultures where that teaching includes training in practical composition; but it seems this class recruits itself from various sources, such as theology students, writers with good style and lack of imagination, translators, etc. Their sense of mission and authority, and the corresponding willingness even of men of great intellectual and literary power to accept corrections from them, are a sociolinguistic phenomenon well worth studying. The highly conscious and socially exhibitionist character of linguistic competence in this type of linguistic society leads to stylistic artistry being valued more highly than content, towards the *rhetorische Funktionslosigkeit* so well described by Erich Auerbach (1958, p. 158).

During the time that Hebrew was part of a diglossia situation, its Sources derived from the two stages of religious literature: the Bible on the one hand, and the rabbinic literature of ca. 100–600 of the Christian Era, starting with the monumental law collection of the *Mishnah*.[4] The language of these two corpuses differs considerably in vocabulary, grammar and syntax, though the phonetical and grammatical difference is obscured by historical spelling and by the writing system which leaves most vowels unexpressed and expresses the others rather vaguely.[5] When Hebrew ceased to be spoken in the third century, literary activity in Mishnaic Hebrew went on, and the Bible continued to be studied. Before long, a mixed Biblical-Mishnaic language came into being for liturgical poetry (the so-called Piyyut). Aramaic, which had replaced Hebrew as spoken and written language of part of the Jewish communities, also entered into this mixture, and so did to some extend Greek. In the ninth and tenth centuries, under the influence of Arab classicism, Hebrew artistic prose, and later also poetry, began to be written in Biblical Hebrew, with extensive use of direct quotation. Biblical-type Hebrew, becoming increasingly purer and grammatically more regulated, remained the language of artistic writing until ca. 1880, while the language of utilitarian prose of all kinds retained the Mishnaic type of Hebrew, with growing admixture of Aramaic influences from surrounding languages and developments and reorganization of its own but also with extensive literal borrowing from both Bible and rabbinic literature. The situation changed when in the second half of the eighteenth century, under the influence of Western European classicism, Biblical-type Hebrew penetrated into scientific and narrative prose as written by the westernizing followers of the Enlightenment or *Haskalah* movement, while in traditional circles the prose language remained unchanged, but poetry – now tainted by its Enlightenment associations – ceased to be written or read, and the study of the Bible was proscribed, except for those parts recited as part of the religious ritual. A further turning-point came in the 1880's, when, at the same time as the beginnings of the movement for spoken Hebrew, but quite independently, Mendele Mokher Sefarim (1836–1917) in Russia introduced in his stories a style freely mixed of Biblical and Mishnaic Hebrew but completely different from the medieval mixture. As Hebrew writing now spread and was applied to new fields, such as newspapers, politics and modern science, medieval Hebrew was also increasingly incorporated into the written idiom, and Aramaic words were used to help fill gaps in the vocabulary, so that present-day Hebrew effectively absorbed material from all periods. At the same time not only were new words created by the thousand, involving also some innovations in the grammatical structure, but the spoken language developed usages that were in some cases opposed to the rules of traditional Hebrew.

As a result of its history, Hebrew has thus three areas in which differences of acceptability are concentrated: (1) linguistic items in which there are differences between Biblical, Mishnaic and sometimes medieval Hebrew; (2) developments which are in conflict with the language of the 'Sources'; (3) innovations for which there is no guidance in the 'Sources'. This enumeration already reveals the main feature which sets acceptability in Hebrew apart from acceptability in most western languages where studies on this subject have been undertaken: to the usual factors influencing acceptability judgments, such as habit, *Sprachgefühl,* 'logic', aesthetics, normativist authorities and 'best authors', there is here added another, the Sources, which is taken over from the diglossia stage of the language. In the consciousness of the community, this is the main factor, the only one that really matters, as described at the beginning of this article.

In this respect, there is some similarity with acceptability in a classical-diglossic situation, and there can be little doubt that this attitude in present-day Hebrew is a survival from the period when Hebrew was part of diglossia situations. The difference is that the average Israeli Hebrew speaker has not learned Hebrew from the Sources but as a spoken language from his surroundings. This applies to the normal immigrant Hebrew as much as to the native Hebrew speaker. The institutions which teach the immigrant Hebrew do so by means of material from everyday life, though in a register somewhat closer to written than to spoken Hebrew, and use material from the Sources only as occasional supplementary illustrations of usage and for the sake of cultural and national veneer. The native speaker meets the Sources through his or her education, as material of national or religious education. Although the quantity to which he is exposed is rather large, these texts are not offered to the child as linguistic exempla but as sources of information. There is only sufficient explanation to ensure contextual understanding. Some children are influenced by Biblical style and start using it in essays, but this is not encouraged. On the contrary, the tendency in education nowadays is to discourage the active use of phraseology from the Source texts, which is condemned as *melitza,* the term used to denote the use of direct quotation during the diglossia period. The educated Israeli knows the Bible, and many are able to quote from it fairly extensively, but its language has no direct influence upon his speech or writing.

The link with the Sources is established by the activity of normativists, and, to understand their influence, it is necessary to give here a brief description of the way in which this group functions.

Since about 1905, Israel has had a Language Academy.[6] This has done very important work in standardizing and enlarging the vocabulary and in doing so has of course drawn on the Sources. Its decisons (which since 1953 have legal force) have on the whole been accepted by the public. The Israeli public also firmly believes that the Language Academy legislates on matters of grammatical and stylistic acceptability; but actually its role in this sphere is rather restricted. The plenum, which makes the official decisions, has so far discussed and decided only a small number of morphological and syntactical points and even on these has in some cases, where the Sources differed among themselves, confined itself to pointing out that more than one set of forms was permissible. A more ambitious undertaking, to rule on the declension of all Hebrew nouns, is at the time of writing still in progress, and its effect on public usage cannot yet be assessed. In 1968 the Academy established a spelling system, but this is so far in use only in the Academy's own publications and has only a year ago started being taught in schools, while in those respects which the system intends to regulate, anarchy still rules in newspapers and books without impairing the functioning of the language. The real influence of the Academy on acceptability is through its Scientific Secretaries and other employees, who reply to inquiries from the public and in some cases point out to news media and public figures mistakes they made. There is also a committee of Academy members for influencing the news media and public bodies, which, however, is not active except insofar as its members act individually. The Academy also appoints, and partly finances, the linguistic adviser to the radio. It publishes, apart from a research quarterly, a popular periodical which occasionally contains normativist material and an illustrated wall-newspaper mainly normative in character. The responsibility for the normative statements in these publications lies with their editors – who are Academy employees – and not with the Academy as a body. It should be added that employees and members of the Academy (as distinct from the adviser to the radio) generally restrict themselves to statements either universally recognized or confirmed by the Academy plenum and refer points on which there is controversy to the Academy's member committees, where they may or may not be authoritatively settled, usually after a considerable lapse of time.

The real normativists are free-lancers. Some of them have regular columns in the press; the adviser to the radio has a twice-daily 'Minute of Hebrew' at top listening times; some are attached to government offices and issue official or unofficial internal publications of linguistic advice, the most interesting one being the stylistic editor of the parliamentary record, who circulates among the members of the Knesset a sheet entitled 'From the Speaker's Stand' in which he quotes mistakes they make with his corrections; there also exists a number of books, some of them collections of the author's press items, which are dictionaries or encyclopaedias of correct Hebrew. Many of these were or are best-sellers.[7] Two of them achieved some sort of official status: *Wedayyeq* by J. Bahat and M. Ron (1960), which became through the official matriculation examinations the standard textbook in schools; and A. Bendavid and H. Shay, *Madrikh lashon la-radio vela-televisia* (1974), written, as the title shows, especially for the broadcasting services, where the first author is language adviser on behalf of the Language Academy. It is perhaps significant that these two books are also the ones which state rules and do not provide arguments or (with rare exceptions) proof-passages from the Sources,[8] while the usual normativist publications are written on the pattern of scientific articles, and many passages shed valuable light on linguistic details in the Sources.

The essential variability of acceptability judgments is reflected in Hebrew, as elsewhere, in differences of opinion between the normativists.[9] One interesting feature is the absence of discussion, except in the work of R. Sivan (*cf.* note 7). The normativist writer, as distinct from the scientific researcher, addresses himself to the public and does not refer either with approval or polemically to the views of his fellow normativists. The educated public which reads these works is of course aware of the differences, but characteristically tends to concentrate on the distinction between rigorists *(maḥmirim)* and permissivists *(meqillim)* – terms taken from Jewish religious law – in other words, those who insist on following strictly the usage of the Sources and those who make concessions to popular language. The public pays little attention to the much more frequent differences of opinion which derive from conflict between the Sources, different interpretation of Source evidence or views on linguistic features of more recent origin. It appears that the familiarity of the educated Israeli with Source texts 3,000–1,500 years old, and the relative ease with which he understands them, make him oblivious of the differences between them. This is abetted by school teaching, which minimizes such differences as matters of 'style' and as slight variations in a Hebrew thought to be essentially one and the same throughout the ages. As for differences of analysis and interpretation, the average intellectual has been conditioned by school grammar teaching that there can be only one truth, while there may be differences in men's readiness to accept that truth and act upon it. In conversation, forms in Source literature which are not in accordance with school grammar are often said to be mistakes, or are even taken as evidence that in ancient times people could not have known Hebrew grammar because it had not been sufficiently investigated!

A study made in the late 1960's by one of the present author's students on 16 students of the Hebrew University of Jerusalem showed that the knowledge of standard normative prescriptions was best among students of Hebrew Language (as was to be expected), less good among students of humanities in general and poor amongst students of the natural sciences. As against this, the attitude towards normativism among the Hebrew Language group varied from negative to mildly tolerant, while at the other end of the scale the science students believed in the necessity of regulating the language by prescriptive rules, which they thought ought to be established by the Language Academy. Though carried out upon a small sample, the results of this investigation are confirmed by observation: the Israeli public feels that language ought to be strictly regulated, and only among those who have been in contact with linguistics, modern or traditional, is there at times a consciousness that the language as it actually is may have a value at least comparable with the image of a Hebrew language laid down by normativism.

While from the normative activist's point of view, the entire body of normative rulings is an attempt to preserve and purify a homogeneous entity, the Hebrew Language, and any new normative discovery is merely a further step in covering the whole field, the body of normative rulings is not all of one piece from the point of view of the public. There is a comparatively small number of generally recognized rules – research undertaken by students suggests it is somewhere around 25 – which are known to educated people.[10] The individual may hold any one of these rules to be obligatory or may reject it; he may even think it obligatory but decide that it is too complicated for him to observe it – but he is aware of the existence of these rules. Any survey of normative literature, however, shows that there are many more rulings which appear in some of them (perhaps even in all of them) but are largely unknown to the wider educated public. These additional rules form an open series, and their number grows continually. The additional items are published in books or articles, sometimes in out-of-the-way publications, and invariably reach only a small section of the public. Among those that see such a new ruling there may well be some enthusiasts for normativism, who will then start publicizing it by the process of correcting others. Lately the 'Minute of Hebrew' on the radio has become a fertile producer of such new rulings. The Hebrew speaker is thus constantly faced with normative rules he did not know before and becomes aware that a form which he used without hesitation so far may in fact be 'wrong'. Not being able to check the basis of such normative statements, he accepts them as evidence that Hebrew is a language full of pitfalls and that only owing to the patient and devoted labor of the experts will it one day become possible to know all the mistakes one can make.

The Israeli is often faced with this situation at a particularly critical time, during his matriculation examinations. It is a constant complaint that in that section of the paper in Hebrew Language which presents sentences for normative correction, there appear 'mistakes' which were not discussed in school. The veteran teachers who set these papers, of course, are strict normativists and keen on new normative insights; but no one thinks of warning the teachers in advance or restricting the corpus of rules.

The majority of educated Israelis is perfectly able to write a Hebrew which follows the generally accepted normative rules. It normally appears as a register in which conformity with this standard normativism is combined with the use of a literary vocabulary. This register is variously referred to as 'Good Hebrew' *('ivrit ṭova),* 'Rich Language' *(lashon 'ashira)* and in familiar parlance as 'Sabbath Hebrew' *('ivrit shel shabbat).* The literary vocabulary has its own problems of acceptability which are quite distinct from those of morphology and syntax and a great deal more complicated. It is entirely derived from the Sources, and, at least theoretically, a phrase or word of this group is acceptable only if it used as in the Sources. In practice, many phrases are employed in a sense different from the one they have in the passage from which they are taken, but these new senses were established in literary usage in the middle ages or in the early modern period. The existing dictionaries are only of limited help in this matter, as at best they give both the original Source meaning (sometimes several, because of different interpretations of one and the same passage) and the meaning used today; but in many cases they will only indicate the Source meaning. Those accustomed to writing a great deal, mainly professional writers and journalists, will be familiar with the use of these phrases, in the sense that they either use them as prescribed by recognized usage or do not mind using them somewhat differently, knowing that many of their contemporaries use them the same way. The position is different with politicians, scholars and the like. They are aware of the pitfalls but do not trust themselves to avoid them. Moreover, editors of periodicals and book publishers do not trust their authors to handle the approved literary style efficiently and therefore use style editors. A system justified in the case of those who learned Hebrew as adults and have no full command of it is thus extended to a whole writing population. The authors generally accept correction by style editors, and many even demand it.

The Israeli stylistic editor may be looked upon as the front-line soldier of normativism and seems in many cases to be fully aware of his role. There is no professional course for style editing in Hebrew; university departments of Hebrew Language (which are organizationally quite separate from departments of Hebrew Literature) deal with theory and history, though some provide exercises in 'style' at a level rather different from the rest of the course. Because of the lack of agreement on so many points of normative grammar, and the relative paucity of normative occupation with syntax, the style editor has largely to provide his own guidelines. He thus becomes a creative normativist, though few style editors, to the best of my knowledge, have ever tried to present their practice in print. The instances that are available distinguish themselves by purist extremism and lack of contact with the linguistic research that has been done on present-day written Hebrew. It is, however, clear, and has been confirmed to the present writer by stylistic editors of his acquaintance, that the professed ideal is to cast the text into the patterns it would have had in the Sources. There is a kind of mystical belief that Hebrew has ways of its own to express trends of thought, and that it is possible to recover these from the ancient sources. This may be to some extent due to confusing syntax and stylistics. It is notable, however, that in contrast to morphological normativism, which is mainly based on Biblical Hebrew, syntactical-stylistic normativism is almost entirely based on Mishnaic Hebrew. There is a widespread belief that only extensive reading of sources of Mishnaic Hebrew, such as is provided by a traditional 'Yeshiva' education in Talmudic studies for religious training, is a guarantee for a good Hebrew style.

The prevalence of stylistic editing has a feedback effect. Seeing his own efforts at unambiguous and circumspect expression receiving scant respect from the style editor, and watching choice idioms from the Sources replace his own dry westernized collocations, the writer soon feels that his own manuscript is merely a rough draft for the language expert to get working upon. He will therefore invest little effort in phrasing his thoughts. Writing for publication becomes a combined product of two experts, the expert on the subject and the expert in style, and they are not supposed to interfere with each other's work. At least one well-known publishing firm has in its contracts a section in which the author agrees to style correction, and in case he objects to any of the editor's corrections and cannot persuade the latter to rescind it, consents in advance to having the differences settled by an impartial arbitrator.

The dichotomy, by which the native speaker delegates acceptability to the expert, runs deep throughout the life of present-day Hebrew. It is inherent in the authoritative tenor of teaching 'usage' *(shimush ha-lashon)* in schools and of 'language improvement' *(tiqun ha-lashon)* in adult education and in the tone of normativist newspaper columns, books and radio programs. The daily 'Minute of Hebrew' features a man and a woman, who take it each week in turn to be the omniscient corrector who exposes the mistakes in perfectly ordinary Hebrew sentences uttered by the other and almost always 'remembers' a quotation from the Sources. A well-known stylist, who taught 'style' to university students, once summed up his activity by saying that he had not much success in improving his students' performance but that he had succeeded in making them conscious that they did not know. The statement 'I do not know Hebrew' is frequently heard from people with good education and actively engaged in very effective use of the language. One of the most embarrassing aspects of being an academic teacher of the Hebrew language is that people one meets will apologize for their Hebrew or remark 'I suppose you notice that I speak with mistakes'.

However, the malaise of the educated Hebrew speaker about his non-normative speech does not result in an effort to adopt the norms, at least not in ordinary conversational style. In fact, just as most educated speakers manage perfectly well to write without normative mistakes in official letters or for publication, so most of those who have to make a set speech can do so without errors in grammar. But to speak in this style in friendly conversation is not only felt to be slightly affected, but also somehow unfriendly. This seems also to apply to private letters. A survey of 100 letters by ten people with high-school education or beyond showed that all of them used non-normative forms, sometimes both the normative and the non-normative varieties. Conversational Hebrew is a well-established form of language, expressive, forceful and pliable. It has a range of registers and a scale of social varieties. And it has, of course, its own full set of acceptability judgments, except that these are repressed into some linguistic subconscious and replaced by another set, unrelated to the language as spoken or written, and mysterious because in its fullness that set is not revealed to anyone except the expert.

It is almost impossible to get the average educated Israeli to make statements about his actual usage, whether spoken or written. Questions about acceptability will elicit formulations – sometimes quite incorrect – of normative rules and will soon reach a stage at which the subject will hesitate or refuse to answer. A frequent reaction to the lecturer's remarks in first- or second-year classes in the university about features of colloquial Hebrew is: 'Do you mean to justify this?' Colloquial

Hebrew is normally referred to by the name of *sleng,* and that this is not merely a question of name is proved by the fact that students asked to collect slang words for seminar essays or in examination questions invariably include common grammatical colloquialisms.

One of the most remarkable phenomena is the view of normativists that any attempt at linguistic description of colloquial Hebrew is unscientific because it describes a state of language that does not exist. Thus, when a well-known literary critic opened a scathing review of the pioneer study of H. B. Rosén, 'Our Hebrew' by asking 'Who speaks like that?',[11] a leading normativist, who was also Professor of Hebrew Linguistics, wrote an article in a daily paper, in which he illustrated by a diagram that the speech of every non-Israeli-born speaker was influenced by his or her home language and that therefore there were as many kinds of colloquial Hebrew as there were countries of origin;[12] A. Ben-david (1967: 303–325) discusses at length his contention that, since all Hebrew speakers are still learning the language, there is no sound linguistic method in a descriptive study of their mistakes. In all three cases this is combined with the thesis that scientific description lends to colloquial Hebrew a status which will make it difficult to combat it.[13] In private conversation, however, it is often stated that the population, and especially young people, do not really want to accept normative Hebrew. The conclusion mostly is that the situation can only be saved by a united front of unbending normativism and that any show of 'permissiveness' or interest in the colloquial on the part of those belonging to the Linguistic Establishment is a betrayal of the cause and may have dire consequences. This may be interpreted as growing awareness of the emergence of a colloquial register and other not fully normative registers, such as private letters and newspaper language.

The phenomena described here can all be found in other language communities, though not in the same combination or with the same intensity. There appears to be a connection between them and the presence of an influential literary heritage and a heightened consciousness of the past. Since language revival – even in the limited sense of reversing a process of recession, or of westernization, of a traditional literary language – is necessarily connected with intensified interest in the past of the community, it may be difficult to separate the two factors in their influence on normativism and acceptability. The situation in such cases, however, allows us to study in concentration one of the most intriguing features of the societal aspects of language, namely normativism. It seems to the present writer that normativism is an inherent property of language as a medium of communication within a society and that by understanding its causes, processes and effects we might contribute not only to more efficient language planning but also to a better grasp of the mechanics of social dialects and other phenomena.

NOTES

1. For a description, see Chomsky (1957: 231–44), Fellman (1973), and Rabin (1974). The diglossia situation, previously covering Jews everywhere, had by the latter part of the nineteenth century become restricted to Eastern Europe (from where those who revived Hebrew mainly hailed) and the Islamic countries. Elsewhere Hebrew was restricted to prayer and religious studies. The attempt of Parfitt (1972) to show that Hebrew was fully alive in Palestine during the earlier part of the 19th century fails to distinguish between a *lingua franca* and a normal group language.
2. Thus in the offical collections *(diwans)* of pre-Islamic Arabic poetry, deviations discussed by Arab grammarians with regard to passages from those poets have often been replaced by impeccable expressions. The Samaritan text of the Pentateuch is grammatically much more regular than the Massoreic text used by Jews.
3. Thus in medieval Hebrew writing, Biblical Hebrew for poetry, Mishnaic Hebrew for prose (see below). The novelist A. Mapu in the 1850s employed Biblical Hebrew for the speech of his Enlightenment heroes, a semi-Mishnaic Hebrew for the non-westernized enemies of Enlightenment. A well-known instance of this tendency is Sanskrit drama, in which different classes of people speak different Indian dialects.
4. There is controversy as to whether the texts in Mishnaic Hebrew reflect a spoken language or Hebrew speech had died with Biblical Hebrew in the 6th century and the background of Mishnaic Hebrew is spoken Aramaic. For Bibliography, see Rabin (1970: 320).
5. The indication of all vowels by signs placed under and over the letters was only introduced in the 7th or 8th centuries. *Cf.* Chomsky (1957: 93–106), Morag (1962).
6. A first foundation in 1880 soon lapsed and was revived only in 1905, under the name of Language Council. The present Academy replaced it in 1951. There is no history of this institution; Eisenstadt (1967) is biobibliographical. For a brief account; see Medan (1969).
7. A good account of the history of Hebrew normativism is given by Ben-Asher (1969). Since then there have appeared Reuben Sivan, *Lexicon le-shipur ha-lashon* (Tel Aviv, 1969) and A. Bendavid.
8. In his other writings, Bendavid does adduce proofs and arguments.
9. See Ben-Asher (1969), who also deals with the problem of consensus formation.
10. More precisely, they are aware of what forms to avoid; few educated speakers would be able to verbalize the rules.
11. S. Zemach, *Isfu Yedeykhem,* in *Davar* daily, March 9 and 16, 1956; *cf.* Rabin (1970: 333).
12. Yitzḥaq Peretz, 'Language policy and linguistic research' (Hebrew), in *Davar,* December 10, 1965. Peretz actually advocated permitting deviations in the spoken register, in Peretz (1961).
13. This is an interesting case of the principle stated by Mathesius (1932) that 'codification' (in grammars and dictionaries) is an important ingredient in establishing the status of a language. *Cf.* also Garvin and Mathiot (1960). The negative attitude to research on

contemporary Hebrew is neatly summed up in the 'Minute of Hebrew' of April 22, 1975, in branding the colloquialism *kazoti* (= *ka-zot-hi'*) 'such' fem., for normative *kazot*. After being reproved, the speaker who had used the colloquial form asks the one who corrects him: 'I wonder how such a form came into being?' and gets the reply: 'Never mind how such forms come into being! You just remember the rhyme *kazoti ze idioti* ('*kazoti* is idiotic')'. Interestingly enough, *ze idioti* contains three colloquialisms.

REFERENCES

Auerbach, E. (1958), *Literatursprache und Publikum in der lateinischen Spätantike und im Mittelalter*. Bern, Francke Verlag.

Ben-Asher, M. (1969), *Hitgabshut ha-diqduq ha-normativi*. Merhavia, Ha-Kibbutz ha-me-'uḥad.

Bendavid, A. (1967), *Biblical Hebrew and Mishnaic Hebrew* (Hebrew), I. Tel Aviv, Dvir.

Chomsky, W. (1957), *Hebrew, The Eternal Language*. Philadelphia, Jewish Publication Society.

Eisenstadt, S. (1967), *Sefatenu ha-'ivrit ha-ḥaya*. Tel Aviv, Tequma.

Fellman, J. (1973), *The Revival of a Classical Tongue*. The Hague, Mouton.

Garvin, P. L., and Mathiot, M. (1960), 'Urbanization of the Guaraní language', in A. F. C. Wallace, Ed., *Men and Cultures*. Philadelphia, University of Pennsylvania Press.

Mathesius, V. (1932), 'O požadavku stability ve spisovném jazyce', in B. Havránek and M. Weingart, *Spisovná čestina a jazyková kultura*. Praha, Pražský Linguistický Kroužek.

Medan, M. (1969), 'The Academy of the Hebrew Language', *Ariel*, 25. [Also in French and German]

Morag, S. (1962), *The Vocalization Systems of Arabic, Hebrew, and Aramaic*. The Hague, Mouton.

Parfitt, T. (1972), 'The use of Hebrew in Palestine 1800–1882', *Journal of Semitic Studies*, 17, pp. 237–252.

Peretz, Y. (1961), *'Ivrit ka-halakha* (2nd ed.). Tel Aviv.

Rabin, C. (1970), 'Hebrew', pp. 304–346 in *Current Trends in Linguistics VI: Linguistics in South West Asia and North Africa*. The Hague, Mouton.

– (1974), *A Short History of the Hebrew Language*. Jerusalem, The Jewish Agency.

CATHERINE SNOW and GUUS MEIJER 11

On the Secondary Nature of Syntactic Intuitions

Recent linguistic theorizing is largely based on syntactic intuitions, i.e., on intuitions about the grammaticality of sentences. We would like to argue that these syntactic intuitions are secondary to other kinds of language behavior and even to other kinds of linguistic intuitions in three senses: developmentally, pragmatically and methodologically.

DEVELOPMENTALLY SECONDARY

It is obvious that children develop the ability to use language before they develop the ability to give linguistic intuitions. Although children as young as two years can judge sentences as 'silly' (Gleitman, Gleitman and Shipley 1972), these judgments seem to be elicited exclusively by semantic anomaly or uninterpretability (deVilliers and deVilliers 1972). Judgments that semantically acceptable sentences are wrong on purely syntactic grounds do not occur reliably before children are about six years old, and even older children and adults sometimes explain their rejection of syntactically deviant sentences on incorrect semantic grounds. It seems clear that a child's spontaneous speech forms a much more reliable and dependable source of information about what he knows than his linguistic intuitions and that a child's linguistic intuitions are more-or-less automatically directed at the semantic content of sentences, not at its syntactic form. This is entirely understandable if one accepts the semantic primacy theory of language acquisition, i.e., that a child starts learning language with the assumption that the sentences addressed to him will be meaningful and will be interpretable on the basis of what is going on around him (see Macnamara 1972 for a discussion of semantic primacy). The child assumes semantic content and uses the utterances he hears to collect information about syntax. Young children cannot reject sentences on syntactic grounds because all input sentences are still serving as sources of information about the syntax of the adult language.

PRAGMATICALLY SECONDARY

The primary function of language is communicative. Trying to understand a sentence is a normal activity for a language user but trying to determine whether a sentence is grammatically correct is a derived and secondary function. This is reflected in the fact that 'What did you say?' is a commonly heard question in normal conversation, but 'You said that incorrectly' is much more infrequent and sounds pedantic. Giving linguistic intuitions about the meaning of sentences, e.g., whether one sentence is a paraphrase of another or whether a sentence is ambiguous, lies fairly close to the normal activity of the average speaker-hearer, who is trying to convey and receive meaning. But producing syntactic intuitions and ignoring the message conveyed by the sentence in question is an activity which has very little to do with the everyday function of language. Moreover, given the social character of such notions as 'grammatical' and 'correct' (and by 'social' we mean 'man-made', 'conventional', 'shared', etc.), one can never be certain of really reaching the system that underlies this everyday function without distortions stemming from social correction, prejudice, rationalization, etc.

METHODOLOGICALLY SECONDARY

Primary data about language consist of utterances and texts. Syntactic intuitions are secondary, but not unimportant, sources of information about the system of language. They become especially interesting when they provide information about sentences which rarely occur in normal language use or when they deviate from the data available from the primary sources. But in cases of deviations, there is no reason to assume that the syntactic intuitions reveal the competence more directly than the primary data do.

Syntactic intuitions can also be said to be secondary to semantic intuitions in the sense that the interpretability of a sentence seems to be a crucial factor determining whether it will be called grammatical. If contexts which make rather strange sentences interpretable are provided, then the judgments of grammaticality increase greatly (Heringer 1970). Judges seem to be trying to find a situation in which they would use the test sentence; if they cannot find one, then they call it ungrammatical.

Syntactic intuitions have been relied on to a great extent by linguists precisely because they have been thought to be free of the disturbing performance factors which make the primary data so difficult to interpret. However, recent experiments suggest that syntactic intuitions are also less than perfect in terms of reliability (Snow 1975), consensus (Levelt 1972) and insensitivity to effects of order and context (Greenbaum 1973, 1977, Heringer 1970, Labov 1973, Snow 1975). Syntactic intuitions have even been questioned on grounds of validity (Bever 1970, Labov 1972). Despite these drawbacks, it is inevitable that linguistic intuitions will continue to be an important source of information to theoretical linguistics. The following experiments were performed in order to explore differences between different methods of eliciting syntactic intuitions and to determine to what extent syntactic intuitions reflect the language system one uses in the primary linguistic functions of conveying and receiving information and to what extent they reflect an independent, secondary linguistic function.

EXPERIMENT 1

Subjects

Twenty-five native Dutch-speaking students majoring in linguistics served as subjects. The subjects were in their first or second year of linguistics. None of them had taken courses in transformational grammar and/or syntactic theory.

Materials

Sentences were chosen to represent the interesting cases with respect to three questions of word order in Dutch (word order being the most purely syntactic phenomenon):

1. The order of direct and indirect object (DO and IO) relative to one another and to the verb (V).
2. The order of infinitives in sequences of tense auxiliary (Aux), modal auxiliary (M_1), modal auxiliary (M_2), main verb (V).
3. The order of verb (V) and direct object (DO) in verb complement constructions governed by 'proberen' (try) and the form (past participle or infinitive) of this verb in these constructions.

All the crucial constructions were presented in subordinate clauses which, unlike main clauses, have normal S-O-V word order. The four major variants of each of the three word-order problems studied are presented in Table 1, with translations and indications of their superficial structure.

Table 1. *Examples of the test sentences used in Experiments 1, 2 and 3*

		Sentence	Structure
1.	a.	Bea had zondag geprobeerd het gras te maaien	PastPart-DO-*te*-V
	b.	Bea had zondag het gras geprobeerd te maaien	DO-PastPart-*te* V
	c.	Bea had zondag proberen het gras te maaien	Infin-DO-*te*-V
	d.	Bea had zondag het gras proberen te maaien (Bea had tried to mow the grass Sunday)	DO-Infin-*te*-V
2.	a.	Dirk vond dat ze hem moeten laten lopen hadden	M_1-M_2-V-Aux
	b.	Dirk vond dat ze hem hadden moeten laten lopen	Aux-M_2-M_1-V
	c.	Dirk vond dat ze hem hadden moeten lopen laten	Aux-M_1-V-M_2
	d.	Dirk vond dat ze hem hadden laten lopen moeten (Dirk thought they should have let him walk)	Aux-M_2-V-M_1
		The most neutral 'correct' order was not tested. It would have been: Dirk vond dat ze hem hadden moeten laten lopen	Aux-M_1-M_2-V
3.	a.	Floortje zei dat ze haar moeder het beeldje beloofd had	IO-DO-V
	b.	Floortje zei dat ze het beeldje haar moeder beloofd had	DO-IO-V
	c.	Floortje zei dat ze haar moeder beloofd had het beeldje	IO-V-DO
	d.	Floortje zei dat ze het beeldje beloofd had haar moeder (Floortje said that she had promised the figure to her mother)	DO-V-IO

Four alternative versions of each of the test sentences were written, differing from those shown in Table 1 only lexically. The 48 sentences were then divided into two groups, such that each of the 12 structures was represented twice in each group, and the lexical variants were distributed evenly over the groups. One of these groups was then used for the Rank-ordering (RO) condition and the other for the Absolute Judgments (AJ) condition.

For the AJ condition, the 24 sentences were typed on separate sheets. Each subject was given his own test booklet, containing the separate sentences in a unique, random order. The instructions for the AJ condition read (in Dutch, of course):

> On each of the following pages you will find one sentence. Will you please read the sentence, then indicate whether you think it is a good Dutch sentence (by 'good' we mean 'acceptable in spoken language' and not 'grammatically correct'). Write + if the sentence is good, – if it isn't good, and ? if it is in-between or if you don't know. Do not look back once you have completed a page.

For the RO condition, the 24 sentences were divided into four groups, such that each group of six contained a different combination of six structures and three problems. The groups of six were typed in one of two random orders on separate pages, and test booklets were made up of these four pages in all possible orders. Each subject received a unique combination of page-order and sentence-order. The instructions accompanying the RO test booklets read:

> On each of the following four pages you will find six sentences in a random order. Will you please rank these sentences within the groups of six by rewriting them at the bottom of the page with those sentences which are good Dutch, or the best Dutch, at the top and those sentences which are the worst Dutch at the bottom. Sentences which are equally good or bad can be written on one line. You can make as many groups of sentences as you wish, between one and six, as in the example given below. Once you have finished a page, do not look back.

Procedure

Subjects were tested during one of their introductory classes. 13 received the RO condition first and 12 the AJ condition first. As no differences were found as a result of the order of the test sessions, this variable will be ignored in the discussion to follow. One week elapsed between the two sessions. At both sessions, subjects were told to work on their own pace and were not timed.

Results

The results can be analyzed both for agreement between subjects and for agreement within subjects. We will discuss the intersubject agreement first.

Intersubject agreement in the RO condition. The degree of agreement between the subjects in assigning ranks to the sentences was calculated with Kendall's coefficient of concordance W (Siegel 1956) over 25 subjects for each group of six sentences. The coefficients ranged from .466 to .670 and were in all cases significant ($\chi^2 = 55.92$ for the smallest way W, df $= 5$, $p < .001$; see Table 2, column for naive native speakers). However, although significant, the W values were not extremely high (W ranges from 0.0, indicating minimal agreement, to 1.0, indicating perfect agreement), and no sentence was scored by all the subjects as being either the best or the worst out of its group of six. The sentence which received the most unanimity, 'Barend had in de vakantie geprobeerd een rekord te vestigen' (Barend tried to set a record in the vacation), is in fact a perfectly normal Dutch sentence; yet it was scored as less than perfect by three out of 25 subjects, and its alternate version 'Bea had zondag geprobeerd het gras te maaien' (Bea tried to mow the grass Sunday) was placed below the top line seven times out of 25. The other 'best' and 'worst' sentences of each group of six, as based on their mean ranks, showed an average of seven disagreements, i.e., subjects who did not score them as the best or the worst. The four nonextreme sentences of each group of six showed even greater disagreement.

Table 2. *Coefficient of concordance values for naive native speakers, linguists and non-native speakers*

Sentence set	Naive native speakers	Linguists	Non-native speakers
I	.670***	.844**	.631**
II	.639***	.581**	.476**
III	.585***	.736**	.295*
IV	.466***	.705**	.177

$^{*}p<.05$ $^{**}p<.01$ $^{***}p<.001$

Intersubject agreement in the AJ condition. Since two sentences were inadvertently omitted from the booklets for the AJ condition, the analysis to follow will be based on those ten sentences that were scored in two versions. The data given for a sentence type take the form of ++, ––, +–, ??, +? and –?. The complete data are presented in Table 3. It can be seen that no sentence received a unanimous judgment; 1c and 3d come closest to being generally judged acceptable and 1a, 2d and 3c to being judged unacceptable. If we ignore ?s and subjects who were inconsistent in their judgments, then five out of the ten sentences were judged as either ++ or –– by everyone, while five received both ++ and –– judgments. It may be that these five are subject to true idiolectal variation, which resulted in subjects giving consistent judgments which nonetheless disagreed with one another.

Two of the ten sentences (1b and 2b) were extreme 'unclear cases', in the sense that they received approximately equal numbers of plusses and minusses. This proportion is comparable to the 18 percent unclear cases found by Spencer (1973).

Half of the sentences tested occasioned enough consistent disagree-

Table 3. *Results from the AJ condition in Experiment 1*

Sentence	++	--	??	+-	+?	-?
1a	23	0	1	0	1	0
1b	7	6	2	5	2	3
1c	2	20	0	1	1	1
1d	15	2	0	4	4	0
2a	(presented in only one version)					
2b	7	5	0	5	7	1
2c	0	12	2	5	0	6
2d	0	17	1	2	1	4
3a	21	0	0	1	3	0
3b	3	7	0	9	3	3
3c	(presented in only one version)					
3d	0	24	1	0	0	0
Total	78	93	7	32	22	18
%	31.2	37.2	2.8	12.8	8.8	7.2

ment among the judges that their status as 'acceptable' or 'unacceptable' would have been seriously obscured had they been checked only with a few native speakers. One of the interesting problems for linguists is to explain such consistent, non-dialectal disagreement between speakers.

Intrasubject consistency in the AJ condition. A subject showed a consistent response if he scored both versions of a given sentence type +, – or ?. The 25 subjects produced an average of 70.8 percent consistent judgments, i.e., about three out of the ten sentence pairs were inconsistently judged. Of these inconsistent judgments, however, only 44 percent were combinations of + with –, the rest being somewhat less serious +? or –? combinations. This degree of consistency appears to be relatively high, but we must be cautious in attempting to relate these results to an underlying theoretical distribution based on chance. Few subjects showed an equal tendency to score plus and minus and some showed a strong preference for one or the other judgment (one subject scored plus only three times out of 20, and another 14 times out of 20). The greater the preponderance of one judgment, the greater the chance of spurious agreements within subjects. A subject who scores – for every sentence has no chance to be inconsistent, whereas a subject who scores precisely one third +, one third – and one third ? has the greatest chance to produce conflicting judgments. Thus, the asymmetrical scoring tendencies of the subjects inflate their apparent reliability. Carden found that 105 of 125 subjects tested gave consistent responses of 8 test sentences (reported in Labov 1972). Our results suggested a somewhat lower degree of consistency; only one of the 25 subjects was consistent on all 10 sentences, and 2 were consistent on only 5 of the sentence pairs.

Comparison of the AJ and RO conditions. The results for each subject consisted of a set of ranks plus two sets of +, – and ? judgments for each group of six sentences. Each group was scored with the following rules for the arrangements of AJs which produced maximal agreement and for the arrangement which produced maximal disagreement. The mean of these two was then taken as the subject's score on that group of sentences. The scoring rules were as follows:

> If plusses, question marks and minusses are assigned to sentences in order 1 to 6, no matter where the transitions are, then the subject receives a score of 0, indicating perfect consistency. If sentences that had received the same RO received different AJs, then the subject loses one point for a combination of + with – and ½ point for a combination of + or – with ?. If a ? is out of order (i.e., before a + or after a –), the subject loses one point for each rank displaced. If a + or a – is out of order, the subject loses two points for each rank displaced.

The mean AJ-RO consistency score over all 25 subjects was – 1.6 (calculated as the mean of the four sentence set scores per subject), which indicates an inconsistency somewhat less serious than one plus-minus reversal per sentence set. The maximum negative score possible was –18, which would result from scoring sentences 1, 2 and 3 minus, and sentences 4, 5 and 6 plus. However, the maximal disagreement score is possible only if the number of plusses and minusses is equal; as mentioned above, most subjects showed considerable asymmetry in their use of plus and minus, which raised their consistency scores considerably.

Large variation was apparent between subjects in their degree of AJ-RO consistency, as was the case with the plus-minus consistency scores. The best score was 0 (scored by one subject), and the worst score was 4.6. In order to see whether it is possible to identify generally consistent subjects, the Pearson product-moment correlation coefficient r was calculated for the AJ-RO consistency scores and the plus-minus consistency scores. The correlation between consistency measured in these two ways was very small ($r = .21$) and nonsignificant, suggesting that there is no easy way to identify 'good', consistent, reliable producers of syntactic intuitions.

Individual subjects' AJs did not correspond perfectly to their ROs, nor did the sets of judgments for the group as a whole show perfect consistency between how high a sentence was ranked within its own set and the number of times it was scored plus. Table 4 shows the sentences in order of acceptability based on the percentage of plusses assigned by all subjects in the AJ condition. It can be seen that the mean rank assigned to the same sentences in the RO condition does not indicate the identical order of acceptability. There was at least one reversal in each set, and in one case two, as indicated in the last column of Table 4.

Table 4. *Inconsistencies between pooled judgments in the AJ and RO conditions*

Sentence set	Sentence	AJ condition		RO condition	Reversed judgments
		Percentage plusses[1]	Percentage minusses	Mean rank	
I	1a	94	0	1.87	1a – 3a
	3a	92	2	1.67	
	1b	42	40	3.54	
	2c	10	70	3.69	
	2d	6	80	4.62	
	3d	0	96	5.60	
II	1a	94	0	1.19	
	2b	52	32	2.48	
	1c	12	84	4.67	
	2c	10	70	3.17	1c – 2c
	3c	4[2]	96[2]	4.44	1c – 3c
	3d	0	96	5.06	
III	3a	92	2	1.83	
	1d	76	16	1.90	
	1b	42	40	3.08	
	3b	36	52	4.90	
	2d	6	80	4.38	3b – 2d
	2a	0[2]	96[2]	4.92	
IV	1d	76	16	1.44	
	2b	52	32	2.33	
	3b	36	52	3.81	
	1c	12	84	4.50	
	3c	4[2]	96[2]	4.27	1c – 3c
	2a	0[2]	96[2]	4.65	

1. The percentage is calculated on the basis of total responses, including question marks.
2. The percentage is based on presentation of only one version of the sentence.

We can conclude that testing even a relatively large group of subjects, all of them relatively intelligent and language-conscious, does not assure internally consistent judgments concerning the relative acceptability of sentences.

EXPERIMENT 2

In Experiment 1 information was collected concerning the reliability and consensus in the syntactic intuitions from a group of intelligent, language-conscious native speakers without extensive training in linguistics. Unfortunately, such normal native speakers are little called upon to supply syntactic intuitions by linguists, who prefer to rely on their own judgments. We wished to examine whether the judgments linguists produce are representative of the judgments produced by such normal native speakers. We therefore repeated Experiment 1, using precisely the same sentences, procedure, scoring methods, etc., with a group of eight working linguists whose research is primarily directed to problems of syntax and whose primary data consist of their own intuitions.

Results

The most striking finding was the degree to which linguists gave reliable judgments. Their mean plus-minus consistency score was 94.3 percent (significantly higher than in Experiment 1, as tested with a Mann-Whitney U, $z = 3.26, p < .001$), and their mean AJ-RO consistency score was –0.24 (significantly higher than in Experiment 1, as tested with a Mann-Whitney U, $z = 3.42, p < .0002$). The linguists' greater consistency may be partly ascribable to their preference for minusses in the AJ condition, which was even greater than that of the nonlinguists in Experiment 1 (tested with a Mann-Whitney U, $z = 1.96, p < .05$). Not only was intra-subject consistency greater among linguists than among nonlinguists, but linguists showed greater agreement with one another as well, as indicated by the coefficients of concordance for agreement within the RO condition. Values of W for linguists ranged from .581 to .844 and were in three cases out of four higher than the values for nonlinguists (see Table 2).

Given that linguists are more reliable producers of linguistic intuitions than nonlinguists, and that they show less idiolectal variation, the most important question is whether their judgments agree with those of nonlinguists. A correlation between the mean rank assigned to each of the 24 sentences in the RO condition by linguists and by nonlinguists reveals a high, though not perfect, agreement (Spearman's $\rho = .89$). A correlation of the number of plusses assigned to each of the ten sentences presented doubly in thc AJ condition is almost as high (Spearman's $\rho = .84$). Both these correlations are significant ($p < .01$). These findings would seem to conflict with those of Spencer (1973), who found that nonlinguists disagreed with the judgments of linguists concerning 73 of the 150 sentences he tested. However, he was comparing a fairly large group of nonlinguists with an individual linguist, and he accepted disagreement within the nonlinguist group as deviance from the linguist's judgment. If we compared individual linguists with our entire group of nonlinguists in the same way, a similar pattern of disagreement would emerge.

EXPERIMENT 3

The difference between linguists and nonlinguists in the consistency and reliability of their syntactic intuitions suggests that the ability to produce syntactic intuitions is in some sense secondary to the ability to speak a language, if we assume that the linguists and the nonlinguists are equally fluent speakers of Dutch. Producing syntactic intuitions may be a skill that must be learned and refined independently of, though of course not entirely detached from, the skills of speaking and understanding. In order to test this hypothesis more directly, the experiment was repeated with a group of eight speakers of Dutch as a second language. These eight non-native speakers were more-or-less equivalent to the group of native speakers in social classes and interests, though they were somewhat older and were all finished with their university training. They had been living in Holland at least five years, and two for as many as twenty years.

Results

In terms of consistency, non-native speakers resembled the group of normal native speakers more than the linguists did. The non-native speakers' AJ-RO scores did not differ significantly from those of native speakers (tested with a Mann-Whitney U, $z = 0.17$) and their AJ-consistency scores were slightly, but significantly, better (Mann-

Whitney *U*, $z = 2.52$, $p < .02$). Non-native speakers did not differ from native speakers in the number of plusses assigned (Mann-Whitney *U*, $z = 0.74$).

Agreement within the group of non-native speakers was somewhat lower than among the normal native speakers, with Kendall *W* values ranging from the nonsignificant .177 to .631 (see Table 2). This degree of disagreement is not surprising when one considers that the non-natives varied considerably in how long they had been speaking Dutch and in their skill in the language.

Nonetheless, the pooled judgments of this group agreed reasonably well with the pooled judgments of native speakers (Spearman's $\rho = .65$ for mean ranks over 24 sentences, and $\rho = .88$ for number of plusses over ten sentences). The correlation for number of plusses is higher between native speakers and non-native speakers than between native speakers and linguists (for linguists and native speakers, $\rho = .84$). Chi-square tests performed on the number of plusses assigned per variant within each of the three problem sets of four sentences showed a significant deviation from the normal pattern only for sentence set 1, the 'try' sentences. In the other cases the non-native speakers distributed their plusses over the four sentences within the set as the native speakers did.

The degree of agreement between these non-native speakers and native speakers is the more surprising when one considers that only one of the non-native group could be said to be a perfect bilingual. Two more were very good bilinguals, and the other five spoke Dutch considerably less well than their native language (English in all cases). Yet the correlation between the mean ranks of the group of three excellent bilinguals and the native speakers was not higher than the correlation for the poorer Dutch speakers with native speakers. This suggests that skill in speaking a second language can be developed without developing 'better' (i.e., more native-like) syntactic intuitions about that language. Similarly, skill in producing syntactic intuitions about a language can be developed in the absence of skill in speaking that language, as no doubt occurs, for example, in some classics scholars. The results from the non-native speakers strongly support the notion that syntactic intuitions in a second language are produced by a linguistic faculty which is separate from the faculty of speaking and understanding. There is no reason to think that this is not equally the case for one's first language, and in fact the large differences among native speakers in ability to produce consistent and correct syntactic intuitions strongly suggests that it is.

DISCUSSION

It is obvious that syntactic intuitions are an important source of data to the theoretical linguist. The fact that we believe that syntactic judgments are developmentally, pragmatically and methodologically secondary, both to the primary data of spontaneous speech and to semantic judgments, does not imply that we think they should be abandoned. We do, however, think that they should be collected with more attention to methodological principles and that relatively more attention should be paid to those factors which produce inconsistency, unreliability and lack of consensus among normal native speakers, rather than excluding these factors from consideration by collecting syntactic intuitions only from a few linguists.

In general, we entirely agree with the views expressed by Labov (1972, 1973) that present-day linguistics lacks a notion of 'validity', and that the basis for a linguistic theory which can be called 'empirical' must be found in everyday speech. In Labov's conception of a 'secular linguistics' the primary data consist as much as possible of spontaneous speech productions, and all other sources of information about the underlying linguistic system are seen in relation to this primary one. What we tried to do in this paper was clearly not a 'secular' study of the three syntactic structures we used in the experiments. But since the use of syntactic intuitions about unclear or complex structures seems inevitable, at least in the near future, it is only realistic to look for sampling procedures which assure some degree of reliability.

Our results suggest that the RO procedure for collecting linguistic intuitions is very usable. It provides more information than the AJ procedure, with its three categories (+, – and ?), since most judges distinguish at least four, and often six, levels of acceptability. It is clear that normal native speakers sometimes make unaccountable mistakes, and it is thus crucial to require at least two, preferably more, judgments of a given sentence. Some judges are more prone to making mistakes than others; some check on the quality of the judge can be obtained by including one or more clearly good and clearly unacceptable sentences in each set submitted for reordering. If a given subject makes a mistake with these check-sentences, then his results for the test sentences should be discarded. An alternative procedure would be to require both ROs and AJs for all test sentences, and then base one's conclusions on only those judgments which are consistent. However, it may be the case that some sentences elicit inconsistent judgments more than others and that these inconsistencies indicate interesting aspects of the sentence in question, which should be further pursued.

The remarkable reliability of linguists in producing syntactic judgments can be explained in a number of ways. Linguists argue that they have trained themselves to make these judgments and that they are therefore better at it than nonlinguists. But precisely what have they learned to do? Have they learned to ignore minor differences of a semantic nature, e.g., differences in how probable the event described is or differences in the interpretability of the sentence? Or have they learned to let their linguistic theory determine their judgments of unclear cases? This would not in itself be objectionable if they did not pretend that those judgments were data in favor of the theory. If the second alternative is the correct one, then it is clear that, in Labov's words, 'linguists cannot continue to produce theory and data at the same time' (1973: 199) and that they must start collecting their syntactic intuitions from normal native speakers. If the former alternative is correct, then linguists are not cheating by using their own intuitions, but they are excluding from consideration information about pragmatic, stylistic and communicative aspects of language which are at least as interesting as the syntax on which they are concentrating.

REFERENCES

Bever, T. G. (1970), 'The cognitive basis for linguistic structures', pp. 279–362 in J. R. Hayes, Ed., *Cognition and the Development of Language,* New York, Wiley.

de Villiers, P. A., and de Villiers, J. G. (1972), 'Early judgements of semantic and syntactic acceptability by children', *Journal of Psycholinguistic Research,* 1, pp. 299–310.

Gleitman, L. R., Gleitman, H., and Shipley, E. F. (1972), 'The emergence of the child as grammarian', *Cognition,* 1, pp. 137–164.

Greenbaum, S. (1973), 'Informant elicitation of data on syntactic variation', *Lingua,* 31, pp. 201–212.

– (1977), 'Contextual influence on acceptability judgements', *International Journal of Psycholinguistics.*

Heringer, J. T. (1970), 'Research on negative quantifier dialects', Papers from the 6th Regional Meeting, Chicago Linguistic Society, pp. 287–296.

Labov, W. (1972), 'Some principles of linguistic methodology', *Language in Society,* 1, pp. 97–120.

– (1973), *Sociolinguistic Patterns.* Philadelphia, University of Pennsylvania Press.

Levelt, W. J. M. (1972), 'Some psychological aspects of linguistic data', *Linguistische Berichte,* 17, pp. 18–30.

Macnamara, J. (1972), 'Cognitive basis of language learning in infants', *Psychological Review,* 79, pp. 1–13.

Siegel, S. (1956), *Non-Parametric Statistics for the Behavioral Sciences.* New York, McGraw-Hill.

Snow, C. E. (1975), 'Linguists as behavioral scientists: Towards a methodology for testing linguistic intuitions', pp. 271–276 in A. Kraak, Ed., *Linguistics in the Netherlands, 1972–1973.* Assen, Van Gorcum.

Spencer, N. J. (1973), 'Differences between linguists and nonlinguists in intuitions of grammaticality-acceptability', *Journal of Psycholinguistic Research,* 2, pp. 83–98.

JAN SVARTVIK and DAVID WRIGHT

The Use of *ought* in Teenage English

1. FIELD OF STUDY

In English, main (or lexical) verbs have *do*-periphrasis in non-assertive contexts, i.e., (a) in most questions and (b) in sentences negated by *not:*

(1) John likes the play.
(1a) *Does* John *like* the play?
(1b) John *doesn't like* the play.

Modal auxiliary verbs, however, do not take *do*-periphrasis in these cases:

(2a) *Will* John *like* the play?
(2b) John *won't like* the play.

In addition to the 'central' modal auxiliaries *can, could, may, might, will, would, shall, should* and *must,* there is a group of verbs that may be called 'marginal' auxiliaries in that they are constructed sometimes like lexical verbs (with *do*-periphrasis and a following *to*-infinitive), sometimes like central modals (without *do*-periphrasis and *to*-infinitive). The marginal auxiliaries are *need, dare, have (to), use(d) to* and sometimes *ought;* for example *need:*

(3a) *Does* John *need to come?*
(3a¹) *Need* John *come?*
(3b) John *does not need to come.*
(3b¹) John *needn't come.*

When, as here, two or more constructions are available to users of the language, we refer to this area as one of 'divided usage' (Quirk and Svartvik 1966: 100). Of course, some speakers use one of the constructions exclusively or much more frequently than the other. Nevertheless, even when two or more constructions are available, they are rarely, if ever, fully interchangeable. While the term 'divided usage' is useful in statements at a very high level of generalization, it only inadequately represents usage in actual speech situations. The choice of alternatives is conditioned by semantic, stylistic and, above all, syntactic factors (see Quirk *et al.* 1972: 53f).[1]

For lack of space, this paper has to be restricted to an account of the techniques employed in two sets of elicitation experiments and the results for a single auxiliary, *ought.* (The experiments in fact investigated, in addition to *ought,* usage with *dare, have (to), have got to, may, need* and *use(d) to.*)

The experiments were carried out with 425 English school-children as informants. Unfortunately, very little is known about the grammar of 'teenage English'. We may assume, however, that the usage of young speakers will be particularly interesting in grammatical areas where usage is unstable among the speech community as a whole (such as the marginal auxiliaries). Here the usage of the younger generation is more likely to throw light on immediate future usage than in areas where usage is relatively fixed (such as the central auxiliaries).

2. EXPERIMENTAL GROUPS

The subjects in the first experiment, which took place in July 1971, were 208 school-children between the ages of 14 and 17 living in South-West Essex about 20 miles from London. In the second experiment, which took place in July 1974, the subjects were 217 school-children aged 15 or 16 living in the same area and attending the same schools as in the first experiment.

The only information the subjects were asked to give about themselves was age, sex and whether they had spent any part of their lives outside South-West Essex. Since, however, none of these factors has in the event produced any discernible differences in response as regards the verb *ought* (not even the regional factor – 37 out of the total number of 425 subjects had spent some part of their lives outside South-West Essex), they will not be discussed further here.

Of the school authorities we inquired only about the average standard in relation to public examinations of the total group tested at each school. The examination referred to here is GCE (General Certificate of Education), a national examination taken at the age of 15 or 16 by pupils at selective entrance schools and the top ability range at non-selective schools.

In view of the considerable differences in academic standard among the schools, it was thought advisable to subdivide the five schools into three major groups to see whether there was any connection between academic standard and linguistic usage with regard to the verbs being investigated. These groups are referred to in the discussion as Groups A, B and C:

Groups A, B and C:	*No. of pupils* 1971	1974
Group A, a selective grammar school, where all the pupils had passed GCE (1971) or were about to take GCE (1974)	33	86
Group B, non-selective schools plus one private school, all or predominantly GCE candidates	62	87
Group C, non-selective, few or no GCE candidates	113	44
	208	217

Since the informants can largely be regarded as being members of a geographically limited speech community (the five schools are located within a radius of only three miles), any variation that may occur among the three groups will be of particular interest. Among several possible interpretations of such variation the most obvious would be that there is a link between academic standard and 'social' dialect.

3. TYPES OF ELICITATION TESTS

The study was carried out by means of the elicitation test technique, which has been devised to establish degrees and kinds of acceptability of sentences. Four types of tests were used: performance, judgment, rating and rationalization. Rationalization is an addition to the test batteries described in Quirk and Svartvik (1966) and Greenbaum and Quirk (1970).

3.1. The performance test

The performance test was used in both the 1971 and the 1974 experiments (and the items are referred to as Pa1, Pa2, and Pb1, Pb2, etc., respectively). The test consisted of one of the following two simple operations:

(Que) turning a sentence into a question, and
(Neg) making a sentence negative.

In explaining the operations to the pupils, the experimenter said:

> I'm going to read some sentences to you. After each sentence I'll ask you to change the sentence in some way. Look at the blackboard. [Writes: *Mr. Smith works in London.*] Now, I might ask you to make that into a question. What would you say then? [Waits for answer. Writes: *Does Mr. Smith work in London?*]
> Let's do one more. [Writes: *English is an easy language.*] How would you make that into a question? [Waits for answer. Writes: *Is English an easy language?*] All right, sometimes I'll ask you to make the sentence into a question like that.
> Sometimes I'll ask you to make the sentence negative. What does that mean? [Waits for answer.] Yes, it means using the word *not* or *n't*. Look at the blackboard again. How would you make *Mr. Smith works in London* negative? How would you put it into the *not*-form? [Waits for answer. Writes: *Mr. Smith doesn't work in London.*] Let's look at the other sentence, too. How would you make that negative? [Waits for answer. Writes: *English isn't an easy language.*].

Several of the Performance items (including one with *ought*) consisted of making negative a sentence that was already a question. An example of this type of item was given in the instructions, but even so the pupils in 1971 seemed to find the operation extremely difficult to perform correctly, and less than one-third were able to produce a negative question in their answers. As a result, care was taken in 1974 to preface each such item with the reminder 'This is already a question; what you write should be a negative question.' This resulted in over three-quarters performing the operation successfully.

3.2 The judgment test

The judgment test (items referred to as Ja1, Ja2, etc.) was used in the 1971 experiment only. After the performance test papers had been collected the informants were required to state (in writing) for a number of sentences read out to them whether they found them 'acceptable', 'unacceptable' or 'doubtful'. The instructions given to the informants were as follows:

> The second part of this exercise is very short. I'm going to read 16 sentences to you and ask you what you think of them. I want you to decide for each sentence whether it's something you would say yourself or not. Look at your paper. There are three answers you can give. You can write 'Yes', '?' or 'No':
> 'Yes' means 'This is what I would probably say myself'.
> '?' means 'I might say it, but I would probably say something a bit different'.
> 'No' means 'I wouldn't say this at all'.

These explanations of 'Yes', '?' and 'No' were printed at the top of the answer paper for easy reference during the test.

3.3 The rating test

The rating test (items referred to as Rb1, Rb2, etc.) was used only in the 1974 experiment, and required the informants to state their preference among two or more alternatives of the following type:

Rb2 (a) Oughtn't we to send for the police?
(b) Oughtn't we send for the police?
(c) Didn't we ought to send for the police?

The test was given in written form but the informants were asked to choose the form which would come most naturally to them to *say*. The following example was given on the blackboard:

(a) Who did you see?
(b) Whom did you see?

The experimenter then said:

> Which of those two would you say? You would say *Who did you see?* Even if you may feel that *Whom did you see?* is more correct in some way – you may have been taught to write *whom* in sentences like that – you would never actually say it, would you? All right, I want you to do this next exercise in the same way. Choose what you yourself would actually *say*.
> In some cases you may find that more than one alternative sounds all right. In those cases try to decide which one would come *most* naturally to you.
> In other cases you may find that none of the alternatives sounds really natural. Look at the blackboard. [Writes:
> (a) *To whom did you speak?*
> (b) *Whom did you speak to?*]

> You wouldn't say either of those, would you? What would you say? [Answer: *Who did you speak to?*] All right, even if you have questions like that, I want you to try and make a choice.

When the informants had completed the test, they were asked to go back to the beginning and look at each of their selected sentences in turn. In those cases where they felt they would not actually *say* the form they had chosen (they were reminded of the second set of examples on the blackboard) they were asked to put a cross in the right-hand margin. These will be referred to in the results (4.3) as rejections.

3.4 The rationalization test

The rationalization test was used in the 1971 test only. The test was designed for this particular experiment to investigate a very hazy area of information – namely, the informants' own subjective attempts at explaining their queries or rejections of particular sentences in the judgment test. This is how the task was explained immediately after the judgment test:

> Now, I expect all of you have written '?' or 'No' for some of these sentences. What I'd be interested to know is *why* you've done so. There are several reasons why you might not say one of these sentences – you might think it sounded old-fashioned, you might think it sounded bad grammar or American or just straight-forward un-English – you'd never heard anything like it before.

The experimenter wrote the following examples on the blackboard:

(a) 'Old-fashioned':	*Thou art foolish.*
(b) 'Ungrammatical':	*I is English.*
(c) 'American':	*He sure can run.*
(d) 'Never heard anything like it':	*Time is walking slowly.*

Since the term 'ungrammatical' was not clear to some, it was explained as meaning 'breaking a *rule* of English':

> What I want you to do now is to listen to the sentences again and against the ones where you've written '?' or 'No' put one of the letters (a), (b), (c) or (d). I'll leave the examples on the blackboard. You can give more than one answer if you like.

4. OUGHT (TO)

The handbooks on English grammar tell us that *ought* is constructed as an auxiliary verb. This means that questions and negations are expressed not by means of the *do*-periphrasis but through inversion *(ought we?)* and plain *not* or enclitic *n't (we ought not, we oughtn't).* What according to the grammars distinguishes *ought* from all the other auxiliaries (except *have to* and *used to*) is the necessity for *to* before a following infinitive. This is in especial contrast to usage with *need* and *dare,* where the lack of *to* is a characteristic of the auxiliary construction (compare auxiliary usage *he needn't do it* with lexical usage *he doesn't need to do it*). In line with this, Fowler (1952) gives a prescriptive warning against combining *ought* with auxiliaries without *to* (as in *ought and can go*). Hornby (1974) gives the following examples of negative and interrogative usage: *Such things ought not to be allowed, ought they?* and *Ought I to go?*

However, the Evanses (1957) assert that in the United States 'the simple form of the verb is sometimes used instead of the *to*-infinitive after *ought not,* as in *'You ought not stay',* though 'the construction with *to* is generally preferred'. In elicitation tests with American college students, Hirschland (1969) has indicated that *ought not* without *to* is more acceptable than with *to*-infinitive. Greenbaum (1974: 248) states: 'For Wisconsin, the home state of most of the informants, educated speakers are divided on the use of *ought not* with a bare infinitive or *to*-infinitive, most expressing an explicit preference for the bare infinitive. It is therefore correct to say that American English has also the bare infinitive for *ought* in negative sentences, though the elicitation experiment, confined mostly to speakers of one region, does not provide evidence on how widespread this variant is.'

The tendency to drop *to* in such constructions has, however, not been shown to be true for English outside the United States. In fact, most British native speakers who have been asked informally about this usage claim to be unfamiliar with it. In this paper we will show that the tendency to prefer *to*-less *ought* in certain non-assertive contexts exists also in British English, at least among teenage speakers. It will be suggested, however, that this preference may be largely a product of the elicitation tests themselves and may have little bearing on actual usage.

4.1 Performance test results

The following test sentences in the two sets of experiments are relevant for the discussion ('Neg' = 'negative sentence', 'Que' = 'question', 'Pos' = 'positive sentence'; 'Pos → Neg' for example, means 'positive sentence which the informants were asked to negate', see 3.1; Performance tests are denoted 'Pa' for the 1971 and 'Pb' for the 1974 tests, respectively):

1971 items:
Pa1 (Pos → Neg): You ought to tell him today.
Pa2 (Pos → Que): We ought to send Margaret some flowers.
Pa3 (Que → Neg): Ought we to visit Peter today?
1974 items:
Pb1 (Pos → Neg): You ought to tell him today.
Pb2 (Pos → Que): We ought to send for the police.
Pb3 (Que → Neg): Ought we to give him another chance?

The answers indicating the following major aspects are given in Table 1:

Aux + *to:* Auxiliary construction, i.e., without *do*-periphrasis, with *to*-infinitive, e.g., Pa2:
Ought we to send Margaret some flowers?
Aux - *to:* Auxiliary construction without *to*-infinitive:
Ought we send Margaret some flowers?
Lex: Lexical construction, i.e., with *do*-periphrasis:
Did we ought to send Margaret some flowers?
Other: Other construction, e.g., replacing *ought to* with *should:*
Should we send Margaret some flowers?

The results of the two sets of experiments (1971 and 1974) with entirely different subjects and somewhat different test sentences are rather similar (see Tables 1 and 2).

The auxiliary construction is on both occasions more highly represented in negative sentences (Pa1, Pb1) than in positive questions (Pa2, Pb2) and in negative questions (Pa3, Pb3). This probably does not mean more than that straightforward negation is the simplest of the three operations to perform mechanically, for no such bias is found in the rating test results (see 4.3).

It is clear from Table 1 that of those who retained the verb *ought* in their responses the vast majority (643) preferred the auxiliary verb construction to the lexical verb construction (24). The *do*-periphrasis is not here a real alternative construction with *ought,* which is somewhat surprising in view of the considerable support given to *did ought* forms

Table 1. *Performance test results**

		Aux			Lex	Other	Total
		+to	*-to*	Aux total			
Pos → Neg	Pa1	83	57	140	4	63†	207
	Pb1	85	75	160	5	50	215
Pos → Que	Pa2	63	20	83	4	120	207
	Pb2	50	41	91	7	119	217
Pos + Que → Neg + Que	Pa3	33	21	54	0	153	207
	Pb3	40	75	115	4	98	217
All Pa		179 (28.8%)	98 (15.8%)	277 (44.6%)	8 (1.3%)	336 (54.1%)	621 (100%)
All Pb		175 (27.0%)	191 (29.4%)	366 (56.4%)	16 (2.5%)	267 (41.2%)	649 (100%)
Total		354 (27.9%)	289 (22.8%)	643 (50.6%)	24 (1.9%)	603 (47.5%)	1270 (100%)

* When the total is less than 208 and 217 in the 1971 and 1974 tests, respectively, the difference is due to cases of 'no answer'. The unusually large number of 'Other' responses here is a result of the fact that many subjects (notably the majority of Group C) were unable to handle the 'Pos + Que' → 'Neg + Que' operation and instead produced a negative statement in their answers.

† This figure comprises 60 replacements for *ought* (see Table 3) and 3 'wrong operations'.

Table 2. *Performance test results (conflated with percentages)*

Pos → Neg	Pa1, Pb1	168 (39.8%)	132 (31.3%)	300 (71.1%)	9 (2.1%)	113 (26.8%)	422 (100%)
Pos → Que	Pa2, Pb2	113 (26.7%)	61 (14.4%)	174 (41.0%)	11 (2.6%)	239 (56.4%)	424 (100%)
Pos + Que → Neg + Que	Pa3, Pb3	73 (17.2%)	96 (22.6%)	169 (40.0%)	4 (1.0%)	251 (59.2%)	424 (100%)

in the rating test (see 4.3). However, of those who used the auxiliary construction, as many as 289 (45.0%) dropped the *to* of the original sentence, producing *You oughtn't tell him today,* etc. Even more striking is the result that of the total number of subjects almost half (603, i.e., 47.5%) used an entirely different construction from *ought.* From previous work with performance testing we know that subjects have a remarkable capacity for manipulating even highly unacceptable sentences (see Quirk and Svartvik 1966) and that a substitution for the original item is a clear indication of dissatisfaction with any readily available construction with that item.

The most common substitute for *ought* in the answers is *should.* In test sentences Pa2 and Pb2 there are actually more occurrences of *should* (67 and 52, respectively) than of the auxiliary construction with *ought to* (63 and 50). As in the experiment with American college students (Hirschland 1969), these performance tests suggest that *should* is the natural modal auxiliary expressing obligation in non-assertive sentences. Unless non-assertive *ought to* is taken to be a largely unfamiliar syntactic form, how is one to account for the extensive dropping of *to* and the replacement of *ought* by *should* and a number of other auxiliaries (*shall, must, need,* etc.)? In Table 3 all *ought*-replacements are given for one test sentence (Pa1).

Table 3. *Replacements for* ought *in test sentence* Pa1

You shouldn't tell him today.	14	You didn't have to tell...	1
You should not tell...	10	You don't have to tell...	1
		You do not have to tell...	1
You needn't tell...	9		
You need not tell...	3	You will not tell...	1
You don't need to tell...	1		
He doesn't need to tell...	1	You should have asked...	1
There is no need to tell...	1		
		You don't tell...	4
You had better not tell...	2		
You better not tell...	1	You should not ought to tell...	1
You'd better not tell...	1	Shall we tell...?	1
You must not tell...	1	You should tell...	3
You mustn't tell...	1		
		You should wait a while.	1
Total			60

The wording of the performance test sentences was deliberately not identical in the two experiments. The unexpected nature of the 1971 results, specifically the large number of *should* substitutions, led us to suspect that the choice of words in Pa2 and Pa3 was in some way unsuitable – 'sending flowers to Margaret' and 'visiting Peter' may not be '*ought* situations'. There seemed to be less doubt on this score with the new sentences, especially the more formal-sounding *We ought to send for the police* (Pb2). Even so there was only a slight drop in the proportion of *should* substitutions here (52 *should* to 91 *ought (to)* for Pb2 against 67 *should* to 83 *ought (to)* for Pa2), and this could to a large extent be accounted for by the higher academic standard of the experimental group in 1974 (see 4.5).[2]

In the 1974 experiment, we added an *ought* sentence without *to* but otherwise like Pb3:

Pb3	(Que → Neg):	Ought we to give him another chance?
Pb3′	(Que → Neg):	Ought we let him try again?

The results for these two sentences are very similar in terms of the distribution of auxiliary/lexical/other constructions. However, as can be seen from Table 4, there is no tendency to add *to* in Pb3′ parallel to the tendency to drop *to* noted for Pb3 and the other sentences above, as appears from Table 4. Whereas 75 out of the 115 subjects that used an auxiliary construction for Pb3 dropped *to,* only 10 out of 108 added *to* for Pb3′.

Table 4. *Change or no change in* to-*usage in two parallel test items*

Original / Answer	Aux + *to*	Aux - *to*	Total
Pb3: + *to*	40	75	115
Pb3′: - *to*	10	98	108
Total	50	173	223

The 1974 battery also included a sentence with *should:*

Que → Neg: Should we tell them everything?

Again the preference for *should* was clearly documented: here, not one of the informants replaced *should* by *ought.*

Table 5. *Judgment test results*

		'Yes'	'?'	'No'	Total	Groups
Ja1	Oughtn't we to light a fire?	19 (19.6%)	43 (44.3%)	35 (36.1%)	97	ABC
Ja2	Ought we to send Margaret some flowers?	19 (17.8%)	48 (44.9%)	40 (37.4%)	107	BC
Ja3	They didn't ought to do that sort of thing.	17 (15.0%)	26 (23.0%)	70 (61.9%)	113	BC
Ja4	We oughtn't to tell him, ought we?	4 (12.1%)	17 (51.5%)	12 (36.4%)	33	A
Ja5	Did we ought to tell him the truth?	13 (12.1%)	41 (38.3%)	53 (49.5%)	107	BC
Ja6	They ought to give him a reward, didn't they?	8 (12.1%)	13 (19.7%)	45 (68.2%)	66	BC
Ja7	He hadn't ought to blame himself for it.	6 (8.8%)	20 (29.4%)	42 (61.8%)	68	BC
Ja8	You ought to take a coat, oughtn't you?	5 (7.9%)	24 (38.1%)	34 (54.0%)	63	AB
Ja9	Didn't he ought to clear the table.	4 (4.0%)	18 (17.8%)	79 (78.2%)	101	AC
Ja10	You oughtn't to tell him today.	3 (3.9%)	20 (26.0%)	54 (70.1%)	77	BC

Groups B and C were each composed of classes from more than one school. Discrepancies in the above totals depend on the fact that only some of these classes were tested on each item, never the whole of either Group B or Group C.

4.2 Judgment test results

The judgment test (used in the 1971 experiment only) consisted of 16 sentences.[3] Since it would have been undesirable to include too many *ought* items in this part of the test, and yet at the same time we wanted to test as many constructions with *ought* as possible, only four of the total ten judgment test items (listed in Table 5) were given to any one group of subjects. (This is in contrast to the performance test, where the same items were given to everybody.)[4] In the table the test sentences are listed in order of most to least acceptable. As the column on the extreme right shows, the number and type of pupils giving judgments concerning the different test sentences varied considerably. ('Type' of pupils refers here to the ability groups A, B and C.) As a result, therefore, only very general conclusions can be drawn.

One thing at least stands out. What was suspected in the performance test responses (namely, that non-assertive *ought to* is not a familiar form) is now quite clear. Not one of the ten constructions has an acceptance rate above 20%, and six of them have an outright rejection of over 50%. That this is a genuine response can safely be assumed if we compare those results with the results for such sentences as the following which were given in the same test:

Did you use to catch the 8.20?
Didn't you use to sing in the choir?
Peter used to live in London, didn't he?

all of which were accepted by 70% or more of the subjects tested.

As important as the above finding was the extreme variation in response among the ability groups (A, B and C). Group A consistently favored *ought to* as an auxiliary, whereas Group B and especially Group C consistently rejected it. This point is discussed in detail in 4.5. Here it will suffice to note that the anomalous results for Ja4 and Ja10 are entirely a result of the fact that the former was tested on Group A and the latter on members of Groups B and C.

4.3 Rating test results

The results of the rating test (in 1974) are given in Table 6. The table demonstrates three things. Firstly, the *to*-less *ought* construction is not only extremely popular but is, in fact, the preferred form in the negative (Rb1) and negative-interrogative (Rb3) sentences. (In assertive contexts

(Rb4 and Rb5) there is, however, still a safe majority for the *ought to*-construction.) Secondly, the *do*-construction is more frequent than in the Performance test results. Thirdly, and this must be the most important finding, at least three-quarters of the subjects rejected *all* the non-assertive constructions with *ought*. (Rejections (see 3.3) of a form already selected as being 'the most natural' within a group of items must be interpreted as an implicit rejection also of the other items in that group.)

Table 6. *Rating test results* [a]

		Selections	Rejections
Rb1	(Neg):		
(a)	They ought not to do that sort of thing.	55	37
(b)	They oughtn't to do that sort of thing.	21	14
(c)	They ought not do that sort of thing.	43	36
(d)	They oughtn't do that sort of thing.	50	46
(e)	They didn't ought to do that sort of thing.	68	48
		237	181
Rb2	(Que):		
(a)	Ought we to have done it?	108	93
(b)	Ought we have done it?	65	53
(c)	Did we ought to have done it?	65	57
		238	203
Rb3	(Neg + Que):		
(a)	Oughtn't we to send for the police?	70	60
(b)	Oughtn't we send for the police?	106	92
(c)	Didn't we ought to send for the police?	62	47
		238	199
Rb4	(Neg tag):		
(a)	You ought to work a bit harder, oughtn't you?	228	178
(b)	You ought work a bit harder, oughtn't you?	10	8
		238	186
Rb5	(Pos):		
(a)	We ought to give him another chance.	233	78
(b)	We ought give him another chance.	6	4
		239	82

[a]The order of these constructions was shuffled in the actual experiment.

Rejections totalled 181 (74.9%) for the negative, 203 (83.8%) for the interrogative, 199 (86.6%) for the negative-interrogative and 186 (76.9%) for the negative tag groups of *ought* items. Rejection on this scale did not occur on any of the other groups of items tested. For example, there was a total of only five rejections for all three alternatives of interrogative *have:*

		Selections	Rejections
(a)	Has Tony an MG?	14	1
(b)	Does Tony have an MG?	19	2
(c)	Has Tony got an MG?	184	2
		217	5

Here the subjects show clear preference for a single form *(have got)* and do not subsequently reject it.

With *ought,* on the other hand, not only is there a large-scale rejection of all forms, there is not even a clear or consistent preference among non-assertive constructions. The rejection of non-assertive *ought* corroborates the information gained from the 1971 judgment test. It is interesting to note that the teenagers are not too happy about the verb *ought* even in a straightforward assertive context, as the 78 rejections (i.e., 32.3%) for Rb5 show.

4.4. Rationalization test results

Since the unreliability inherent in answers to all introspective questions is magnified in the face of a sophisticated question of the type presented in the rationalization test (see 3.4), little faith can of course be put in the test answers as such. On the other hand, even if we cannot find out *why* the subject finds a given sentence unacceptable, it may be of considerable interest to know why he *thinks* he finds it unacceptable.

Table 7 shows the number of votes (including cases where the subjects voted for more than one alternative) for queries and rejections in the judgment test (see 3.4) of the four *ought* sentences with lexical verb construction with *do (They didn't ought to do that sort of thing,* etc.), the single *had* constructions *(He hadn't ought to blame himself)* and the five auxiliary verb constructions (*You oughtn't to tell him today,* etc.). The subjects were given four alternatives to choose from: (a) 'Old-fashioned', (b) 'Ungrammatical', (c) 'American' and (d) 'Never heard anything like it'.

Table 7. *Rationalization test results*

Lexical *(do)*		a	ⓑ	c	d	?	Total
(Ja3)	Neg	36	36	2	15	4	93
(Ja6)	Neg tag	5	43	1	11	5	65
(Ja5)	Que	22	32	3	11	3	71
(Ja9)	Neg + Que	31	53	1	18	5	108
		94 (27.9%)	164 (48.7%)	7 (2.1%)	55 (16.3%)	17 (5.0%)	337 (100%)
Lexical *(had)*		**a**	**ⓑ**	**c**	**d**	**?**	**Total**
(Ja7)	Neg	21 (28.8%)	31 (42.5%)	4 (5.5%)	15 (20.5%)	2 (2.7%)	73 (100%)
Auxiliary		**ⓐ**	**b**	**c**	**d**	**?**	**Total**
(Ja10)	Neg	23	25	3	4	2	57
(Ja4)	Neg + Pos tag	11	9	1	5	7	33
(Ja8)	Neg tag	12	23	0	13	11	59
(Ja2)	Que	41	13	2	9	2	67
(Ja1)	Neg + Que	35	27	0	7	14	83
		122 (40.8%)	97 (32.4%)	6 (2.0%)	38 (12.7%)	36 (12.0%)	299 (100%)

a = 'Old-fashioned' c = 'American'
b = 'Ungrammatical' d = 'Never heard anything like it'

The 'correct' answers have been circled.

The answers are clearly not random: note the uniformly (and correctly) low scores for the option 'American'. Accepting then that the pupils have taken the test seriously, it is surprising to find that in neither the lexical nor the auxiliary category have more than half given the 'correct' answer, i.e., the explanation which can be found in grammars (option (b) for 'lexical' and option (a) for 'auxiliary'). The figures 27.9% for option (a) 'Old-fashioned' on the lexical constructions and 32.4% for option (b) 'Ungrammatical' on the auxiliary verb constructions are high, the latter especially so considering that all grammars prescribe only the auxiliary verb construction.

For a tentative interpretation of the unexpectedly high 'old-fashioned' response to lexical *ought,* see the end of section 4.5.

4.5 Groups of schools

The *to*-dropping phenomenon has been noted in both performance and rating test results. Table 8 shows that the three groups of schools set up on the basis of academic standard (Section 2) vary considerably in their performance test results in this respect.

Table 8. To-*dropping in performance tests (1971 and 1974) by groups (in percentages)*

	A	B	C	Total
		Pa 1, 2, 3, (1971)		
ought to	81.4%	74.4%	47.0%	64.6%
ought	18.6%	25.6%	53.0%	35.4%
Number of Subjects	70	90	117	277
		Pb 1, 2, 3 (1974)		
ought to	56.0%	45.8%	20.9%	47.5%
ought	44.0%	54.2%	71.9%	52.5%
Number of subjects	166	155	43	364

On both occasions Group A favors *ought to* and Group C *ought,* with Group B adopting an intermediate position. A general shift towards *to*-less *ought* for all groups in 1974 does not affect this A-to-C polarity.

Similarly, *should*-substitution is far more common in Group C than in Group A. As with *to*-less *ought,* there is a general shift toward *should*-substitution in 1974, but here again the A-to-C polarity is not affected. In the negation of *You ought to tell him today* (the identical sentence occurring in both experiments), the ratio of *should* to *ought* (+ *to*) on the two occasions is for Group A 1 to 14 and 1 to 4, respectively, and for Group C 1 to 9 and 1 to 2. On both occasions Group B adopts an intermediate position.

As regards *to*-dropping a very similar tendency is apparent in the rating selections (see Table 9 and Figure 1). For Group A the *ought to* form is the most popular in all three cases (Rb1, 2, 3). It is the least popular, however, for Group C, who are fairly evenly divided between the other two options. The polarity between these two groups can be seen at its clearest in the interrogative item (Rb2), where the *ought to* construction is four times as popular in Group A as in Group C. Group B, as before, adopts an intermediate position with a slight overall preference for the *to*-less construction.

Table 9. *Rating test results for Groups A, B and C*

		Group A	Group B	Group C	Total
Rb1:					
(a,b)	*ought not (oughtn't) to*	38 (44.2%)	26 (29.9%)	7 (16.7%)	71 (33.0%)
(c,d)	*ought not (oughtn't)*	34 (40.0%)	33 (38.0%)	16 (38.1%)	83 (38.6%)
(e)	*didn't ought to*	14 (16.3%)	28 (32.2%)	19 (45.2%)	61 (28.4%)
Rb2:					
(a)	*ought we to?*	62 (72.1%)	32 (36.8%)	8 (18.6%)	102 (47.2%)
(b)	*ought we?*	15 (17.4%)	23 (26.4%)	20 (46.5%)	58 (26.9%)
(c)	*did we ought to?*	9 (10.5%)	32 (36.8%)	15 (34.9%)	56 (26.0%)
Rb3:					
(a)	*oughtn't we to?*	41 (47.7%)	23 (26.4%)	5 (11.6%)	69 (32.0%)
(b)	*oughtn't we?*	34 (39.5%)	38 (43.7%)	19 (44.2%)	91 (42.1%)
(c)	*didn't we ought to?*	11 (12.8%)	26 (29.9%)	19 (44.2%)	56 (26.0%)

It is interesting to note the relatively high incidence of *do*constructions with *ought to* in the Rating test compared with the Performance test (1974, same subjects), where the total number of *do*constructions for Pbl, 2, 3 is only 16 (2 for Group A, 11 for Group B, and 3 for Group C). The most likely explanation of this discrepancy between the results in the two types of tests would seem to be the following: being generally unfamiliar with the verb *ought,* the pupils either carried out a simple mechanical operation (often dropping *to* in the process) or replaced the unfamiliar item by another, more familiar, such as *should.* In the Rating test, however, where the pupils were presented with a number of options, the academic difference between the groups came into play. Whereas Group A generally follow prescriptive usage, Group C, in particular, having less prescriptive bias, are naturally less inhibited in their choice. As a result, their answers are more evenly distributed.

A further point might also be made. We saw that the rationalizations showed a high 'old-fashioned' response (26%) for the lexical *did(n't) ought* forms, a response which we have suggested was 'incorrect', since these forms are rather to be classed as ungrammatical. However, a breakdown of these 'old-fashioned' responses shows that, seen as a proportion of the total number of rationalizations for each group, these were nearly four times as common for Group C as for Groups A and B combined (see Table 10). We also see (in Table 11) that it is notably Group C who have selected the lexical constructions in the rating test before subsequently to a large extent rejecting them.

Table 10. *Rationalizations by groups*

	a	b	c	d	?	Total
Lexical (do)						
Group A	3	24	1	9	2	39
Group B	10	55	4	14	4	87
Group C	81	85	2	32	11	211
Total	94	164	7	55	17	337
Auxiliary						
Group A	28	19	1	8	24	80
Group B	40	52	-	12	8	112
Group C	54	26	5	18	4	107
Total	122	97	6	38	36	299

Table 11: *Acceptance of* ought-*forms in rating test by groups (selections minus rejections)*

	A	B	C
Aux + *to*	29	13	6
Aux - *to*	14	13	10
Lex	8	15	17
Rejections or no answer	207	220	99
Total	258	261	132

It is tempting to suppose that there is a connection between these two phenomena, and that, for the less academic pupils, 'old-fashioned' was after all the 'correct' explanation of their rejection of the *did(n't) ought* forms. For if these forms ever were as common as oral tradition insists, it would certainly have been among this category of pupils rather than among those of higher academic status. We see, for example, in Table 10 that Group A overwhelmingly give the correct textbook reason ('ungrammatical') for rejecting the lexical construction (24 of 39 votes). What is perhaps more interesting is that in the case of 'their own' auxiliary constructions, though the largest single vote (28 out of 80) is also 'correct', viz 'old-fashioned', a remarkably high number (24) fall back on the '?' option. This may in fact reflect the true position at present of many in this academic category. In view, however, of the apparent overriding dislike of the verb *ought,* the whole of this 'social' aspect of the question is now of little more than historical interest. The little that is left of the rating selections when the rejections have been deleted is seen in Table 11. This does suggest a remnant of some such academic class distinction.

5. CONCLUSIONS

The first impression that one gets from the results of the elicitation tests given on the two occasions is that spoken English usage with *ought* is considerably less fixed than appears from current descriptions of the language.

The performance tests and the selections in the rating test show that the teenage subjects have a marked (and expected) preference for the auxiliary over the lexical *(did ought)* construction. This is particularly obvious in the case of the academically superior Group A. What is less expected is that, with this auxiliary construction, there seems to be a tendency for *ought* + bare infinitive to be preferred to *ought to,* thus bringing the verb into line with the central auxiliaries (see Section 1), perhaps specifically with *should:*

They {shouldn't / oughtn't} do it.

{Should / Ought} they do it?

This tendency is seen most clearly in the responses of the academically lower groups, B and C. There is, however, virtually no evidence in any of the three groups of *to*-dropping after *ought* in assertive contexts, where the options are:

They {should / ought to} do it.

The force of analogy, as regards the non-assertive forms, may have been strengthened by the fact that the remaining auxiliaries with *to* (*have to* and *use(d) to*) are both nowadays primarily treated as lexical verbs (of which we have recent experimental evidence): *You don't have to, he didn't use(d) to,* thus leaving *ought to* out on a limb. Even so, the magnitude of the *to*-dropping phenomenon (increasing markedly from 1971 to 1974) is at first sight surprising, since these forms have not previously been noted in British English.

The massive rejections, however, of all forms of *ought* in the rating test explain the anomaly. Rejection on such a scale can mean only one thing. The verb is now very little, if at all, used in non-assertive contexts by these informants.[5] What we are seeing in the verb *ought* may in fact be not so much a simple case of divided or changing usage as one of disappearing usage. The disappearance of *ought* can probably be attributed in part to the eroding influence of divided usage, the preferred *should* being by comparison grammatically straightforward and stylistically unmarked.

The results of these experiments are interesting also from the point of view of elicitation test technique, since they give warning that an incomplete battery of tests could well lead to quite wrong conclusions. Performance and rating selection tests alone might have led us to the conclusion that *to*-less *ought* was a common form. The rejections, however, tell us that, in non-assertive contexts, the verb is uncommon (perhaps even non-existent for many speakers) and suggest that the choice of the *to*-less form was largely a 'test choice', bearing little relation to reality. A corpus-based study of *ought* would probably have been methodologically inferior to elicitation tests because of the extremely large corpus required for a study of an infrequent item like *ought* and because of the lack of information about subjects' dislike of *ought* and their preference for other constructions.

We can only speculate as to whether *to*-less *ought* (in as far as it exists) merely constitutes an interim form pending complete disappearance of the verb in non-assertive contexts, and whether the ultimate stage may not possibly be that it also disappears in assertive contexts. For how else is one to explain the rejection of the innocent-looking sentence *We ought to give him another chance* by nearly a third of the teenagers in the 1974 experiment?

NOTES

1. Other studies in this field of research include Bolinger (1942), Quirk and Duckworth (1961), Twaddell (1965), Ehrman (1966), Kalogjera (1966), Svartvik (1968), Greenbaum and Quirk (1970), Jacobsson (1974) and Greenbaum (1974). For help with the present paper, our thanks are due to many people: to Alvar Ellegård, Sidney Greenbaum, Göran Kjellmer and Peter Wright for comments on an earlier version, to the local education authorities in South-West Essex, the individual school heads and teachers who through our experiments suffered a totally uninvited disruption of their time-tables and, not least, to the school-children who, quite in the dark as to the object of the exercise, gamely submitted to the unconventional demands of our elicitation experiments.
2. Since *should* substitution was proportionately higher in Group C than in Group A on both tests, the fact that Group C was the largest in 1971 and the smallest in 1974 tends to conceal the considerable swing towards *should* substitution from the one occasion to the other. In fact, Group A produced only 1 *should* for Pa2 (out of 33 subjects) against 19 for Pb2 (out of 86 subjects).
3. It will be seen that all the judgment test sentences are *ought* + *to* constructions. The reason for not including any *to*-less items was that, since we had had no prior experience of this form in British English, we felt that there were other more relevant constructions that should be tested. Just how mistaken we were on this point became immediately apparent in the answers to the performance test.
4. The advantage of the performance test, i.e., that the aim of the test can be concealed, is almost inevitably lost in the judgment test, particularly if it includes too many instances of the same test item.
5. The scope of these experiments was already so large that no concurrent investigation of adult usage was made. The teenage results for *ought,* however, were so striking that it was felt that some kind of comparison with adult usage, at least for this verb, was

almost essential. Forty-six adults over the age of 30 living within commuting distance of London were, quite informally, given the rating test only. No strict comparison can be made with the teenage experiments, but the results may even so be interesting from the point of view of tendencies.

For Rb1 and 2 the *to*-forms were chosen by as many as four-fifths of the adults. The figure for Rb3 (the negative question) was somewhat lower on account of a relatively high score for *didn't we ought to* (nearly one quarter). The *to*-less forms so favored by the teenagers received in each case only about one-eighth of the votes. Rejections were high (about 50% on average) but nowhere near as high as for the teenagers. Among spontaneous rationalizations of *ought*-rejection were 'sounds old-fashioned', 'sounds Victorian', 'has always been a middle-class word', '*should* is easier to say'. Adult usage on this showing would appear to represent an intermediate stage between what the handbooks still tell us and what the young of today are actually saying.

REFERENCES

Bolinger, D. (1942), '*Need,* auxiliary', *College English,* 4, pp. 62–65.

Ehrman, M. (1966), *The Meanings of the Modals in Present-Day American English.* The Hague, Mouton.

Evans, B., and Evans, C. (1957), *A Dictionary of Contemporary American Usage.* New York, Random House.

Fowler, H. W. (1952), *A Dictionary of Modern English Usage.* London, Oxford University Press.

Greenbaum, S. (1974), 'Problems in the negation of modals', *Moderna Språk,* 68, pp. 244–255.

Greenbaum, S., and Quirk, R. (1970), *Elicitation Experiments in English: Linguistic Studies in Use and Attitude.* London and Coral Gables, Florida, Longman and University of Miami Press.

Hirschland, E. (1969), *'Ought (to)'.* A Seminar Report on Elicitation Techniques, Brown University. Mimeo.

Hornby, A. S. (1974), *Oxford Advanced Learner's Dictionary of Current English.* London, Oxford University Press.

Jacobsson, B. (1974), 'The auxiliary *need', English Studies,* 55, pp. 56–63.

Kalogjera, D. (1966), 'On the use of the verb *need', Studia Romanica et Anglica Zagrabiensia,* 21–22, pp. 147–153.

Quirk, R., and Duckworth, A. P. (1961), 'Co-existing negative preterite forms of *dare*', *Language and Society.*

Quirk, R., and Svartvik, J. (1966), *Investigating Linguistic Acceptability.* The Hague, Mouton.

Quirk, R., Greenbaum, S., Leech, G. and Svartvik, J. (1972) *A Grammar of Contemporary English.* London and New York, Longman and Academic Press.

Svartvik, J. (1968), 'Plotting divided usage with *dare* and *need', Studia Neophilologica,* 40, pp. 130–140.

Twaddell, W. F. (1965), *The English Verb Auxiliaries.* Providence, R.I., Brown University Press.

GUNNEL TOTTIE

Variation, Acceptability and the Advanced Foreign Learner: Towards a Sociolinguistics without a Social Context

As a Swede teaching in the English department of a Swedish university, I am constantly faced with the problem of choosing a suitable variant of English to teach to undergraduates. The choice is one involving several dimensions: British or American English, different styles of discourse and linguistic variants used by different social strata of the population, to mention the most obvious ones. Obviously, at university level, one does not normally have to face the naive learner who demands to be taught what is 'right' or 'wrong' in English. Most undergraduates have greater sophistication and are more sensitive to the subtler nuances of language than that. Yet the problem of finding a suitable variant to teach is not an easy one to solve.

Many grammar-books still tend to lump together variants of English as if they constituted a unified whole, thus presenting a falsely simplified picture. On the other hand, the teaching of variants, or parallel forms, poses immense pedagogical problems, in addition to making great demands on the foreign learner, who might, at an early stage at least, feel justified in demanding to be taught the most widespread variant. This is perhaps the core of the problem, for very often we do not know what *is* the most common variant. One often wishes that the Chomskyan ideal speaker-hearer would materialize and settle matters once and for all, instead of leaving us to grapple unaided with linguistic variation. At least, these days we are not fighting totally in the dark – variation is no longer regarded as a non-existent phantom but is being studied in its various aspects on both sides of the Atlantic and by no means only by sociolinguists but increasingly by theoretical linguists.[1]

Obviously, one cannot hope to teach a whole spectrum of variant forms at once even to the most gifted university student, but it is necessary to adopt for teaching purposes some kind of monolectal grammar, a variety of English that is at the same time coherent, widespread, socially desirable and suitable for eventual dissemination by the future graduates to vast number of learners in the schools. One major choice is obviously between British and American English. At the level of pronunciation, the policy of the English department of Stockholm University is to accept British and American accents alike, but to try to avoid as far as possible the nondescript mixture of both that seems to be all too easy to acquire.

Much subtler choices have to be made, however. Are we to aim at the pronunciation, vocabulary and syntax of any one particular group within the British or American linguistic communities or should we try to distil some sociologically undetermined *lingua franca* of a general American or British flavor? It is easy to argue for the latter point of view on the grounds that you can always tell a foreigner anyway and that the characteristics of any one well-defined social stratum are not merely unattainable but also undesirable for non-native speakers. Such an approach is currently being tried with an experimental group of students in the English Department at the Adam Mickiewicz University, Poznan, Poland (cf. Marton and Preston 1975). However, convenient as it may be to opt for such a language-in-the-abstract, it does not strike me as an attractive solution. How are we to determine the criteria according to which we should select the linguistic features suitable to impart to our students? It seems altogether necessary to choose the language of some existing group as a model.

In our search for such a norm, we may join forces with those who try to describe a variety of English that can serve as a norm also to native speakers – not those, of course, who do so impressionistically, pronouncing anathema and recommendations founded on private idiosyncracy and traditional precepts, but those who are concerned with investigating the language and intuitions about language of existing groups of speakers.[2] Such groups must be both large enough to produce sufficient data to base statistically-sound analyses on, and also sociologically determined in such a way as to use a variety of language that may be regarded as some kind of standard. I will leave aside the issue of normative grammar for native speakers here – the foreign learner obviously *must* have a model.[3]

In order to find this model we will have to engage in a branch of sociolinguistic research akin to that pursued by other investigators of the languages or 'lects' of groups. One characteristic of recent work in sociolinguistics (e.g., Labov 1969; Fasold 1972; Wolfram 1969; Berdan and Pfaff 1972) is that it has dealt, to a very large extent, with nonstandard varieties of English. Reference is often made to Standard English, a concept which seems to be taken for granted and which, although it has received so little attention from sociolinguists, is nevertheless a *sine qua non* as a foil for the nonstandard varieties.

There are, however, research projects whose object it is to investigate the standard language. One such project is the Survey of English Usage, started by Randolph Quirk at University College, London. The original purpose of the Survey was to collect a large enough corpus of English, written as well as spoken, to serve as a basis for a description of the 'common core' of English, and care was taken to include a wide spectrum of stylistic strata.[4] Even so, the written corpus, augmented with transcriptions of recorded English, proved insufficient, mostly because of the low order of frequency of some linguistic items or collocations of items but also because of the inconclusiveness of the data in certain cases of – what seemed at least – free variation. It was therefore decided to elicit data from speakers, and the researchers at the Survey were thus faced with the necessity of finding a group of informants actually speaking a standard variety of English. (This in itself is not merely a linguistic problem but one involving one's social convictions and beliefs about future developments in society, as well as practical difficulties.) Possibly this was not even considered as a problem by the Survey investigators, and the choice of informants that was in fact made was probably determined by the availability of large numbers of undergraduates in the immediate vicinity of the research group.

However this may be, the choice was a good one. The informants were young and about to embark on their academic careers and thus likely to be representative not only of the linguistic standards of the present but also of those of tomorrow, by virtue of their age and their future roles as educators, administrators and mass media workers. One objection that could be raised against this choice of informants would be their too-great awareness of existing grammatical precepts, most of them being undergraduates in an English department. However, not all of the informants were students of English, and, moreover, a subsequent comparative study undertaken by myself for the purpose of evaluating a different brand of informants – sixth-formers (i.e., senior high-school students) in a British Midland comprehensive school – showed that there was great consensus in usage as well as in straightforward evaluations between the two kinds of informants (*cf.* Tottie 1971.) My investigation, the purpose of which was to ascertain norms as well as behavior with respect to the *do*-periphrasis with *have to* in British English, was thus based on the responses of high-school students aged 16 to 17, intellectually a less-rigorously selected group than the ones used for the London experiments. School classes have great advantages as sociolinguistic populations, not only for reasons of convenience but because the informants have the merit of youth, their language thus being indicative of trends of change rather than of established norms of the past. Using school classes for sociolinguistic research is of course not unique – this has been done for a number of studies whose aim has been to investigate deviations from the standard language rather than the standard language itself.[5]

If youth is then a prerequisite for the subjects of the kind of investigation we have in mind, what is the optimal age level of informants? Recent psycholinguistic studies have shown that the acquisition of certain complex syntactic phenomena may go on well into the teens (*cf.* Margaret Omar's study of the acquisition of plural endings in Egyptian Arabic), and some sociolinguistically-oriented studies also support these observations. For instance, Berdan (1973) found widely divergent grammars in first-grade and sixth-grade school-children in the Los Angeles area. The late teens would therefore seem to be a suitable age-level for subjects chosen to exhibit a stabilized yet not stagnant language. (A major experiment using teenage informants is reported in this volume by Svartvik and Wright, who also discuss their choice of informants.)

Assuming then that we have established youth and some degree of education as important criteria for delimiting the groups whose usage would constitute an acceptable norm, what aspects of language are the ones most necessary to investigate? As in all kinds of research, intuition must obviously play an important part in deciding this. The linguist must have a 'feel' for such fluctuation as is indicative of changes in progress that may affect, or already have affected, the rules laid down in grammar books. It may be argued that such variables as cannot be observed in written texts or spontaneously produced speech are *per se* of such low frequency as to be of little use to the foreign learner. This is a spurious argument, however, and for several reasons. Competing forms may occur in abundance, yet in apparently free variation, and elicitation in fully controlled contexts, linguistic as well as extra-linguistic, may be the only means of getting beyond such theoretically dubious concepts as free variation or optional rules. If there is variation in language, the advanced foreign learner as well as the native speaker concerned about his own language has a right to know the rules that trigger different forms or he should at least be given quantitative rules. As little as possible should be left in the free variation waste-basket.

Another thing that must be investigated is precisely the difference between linguistic norms and behavior. If the precepts of the grammar-books differ markedly from the empirical observations of the observer, native or foreign, he is bound to want to find out what the actual usage is. A likely outcome of a controlled investigation is that this kind of discrepancy is reflected in individuals also – it is a well-attested phenomenon that speakers often fail to adhere to practices they claim to endorse (*cf.* Labov 1972: 292ff; Greenbaum and Quirk 1970: Ch. 9). Labov even goes so far as to state that 'it seems plausible to define a speech community as a group of speakers who share a set of social attitudes to language' (1972: 293, fn. 8), i.e., 'agreement in subjective reactions' would be a more important criterion than actual behavior for sociolinguistic stratification. As Labov also points out, such covert norms are extremely difficult to elicit. Until we have the psychological means to do this, the learner can only hope to become even a peripheral member of a foreign speech community by means of conforming to actual standards of performance.[6] It seems therefore that careful empirical observations in the case of sufficiently frequent data, and controlled elicitation experiments where such data are unavailable, are the only practicable ways of achieving even an approximately correct picture of actual usage and of establishing a model for the foreign learner. It is obviously necessary to guard against regarding percentages as God's truth, but it may at least be possible to set up a scale of complete – high – medium – low – zero frequency.[7]

As Labov has pointed out, it is the higher-level syntactic variables that are hard to investigate in their social context, one of the 'chief stumbling-blocks' being the 'low frequency of occurrence of the critical subcases' (Labov 1972: 291). Syntactic variables of higher orders of frequency as well as phonological variables are obviously best studied by field methods.[8] Very often, semantic problems are also best handled by elicitation methods, as can be seen in, e.g., Greenbaum (1969) or Tottie (1974). In order to study semantic phenomena or low-frequent syntactic variables, it is necessary to resort to a sociolinguistics without a social context, and to study them by experimental methods until we develop practicable field-work techniques.

By what methods can we study variation and acceptability? Obviously, we need testing methods of some kind, and, obviously, these methods must be adapted to the level of sophistication of our informants. In order to investigate the use of *have* vs. *got* in the speech of Anglo and Black children in the Los Angeles area, Robert Berdan used pictures of bugs with and without spots, asking the child that was being interviewed: 'What is the difference between this bug and that bug?' (*cf.* Berdan 1973: 8). While being perfectly adequate for working with younger children, such a technique might cause embarrassment if it were used with sixteen-year-olds or adults. What is needed is an experimental method that takes into consideration the level of maturity of the age-group we have in mind, preferably without appealing to the introspection of the informants or focusing their attention on the linguistic problem under investigation.

An ingenious method developed for these purposes is the *compliance test*[9] described by Quirk and Svartvik in *Investigating Linguistic Acceptability* (1966). This method is particularly well adapted to the testing of cases of doubtful acceptability. For example, subjects may be confronted with the sentence *He is regarded insane* and be asked to change it into a question. Obviously, the problem involved has nothing to do with the distinction affirmative/interrogative, but is a matter of the acceptability of *regard* without *as,* and it is likely that many informants will not only change the original sentence into a question but also, while doing so, insert *as* and produce *Is he regarded as insane?* One great advantage of this approach is of course the fact that the subjects' attention is turned to an irrelevant problem and that their reaction to the variable under investigation is registered at a quasi-subconscious level. Another is that the kind of 'rectification' undertaken by an informant will indicate *why* a sentence is not acceptable to him. Among problems that have been successfully investigated by this method one may mention adverb placement (Greenbaum 1969) and the choice of copula in English (Bald 1972). Needless to say, the compliance test can, and should, be complemented by an overt appeal to the conscious judgments of the informants. If the behavioral and attitudinal tests show good positive correlation (as they usually do; *cf.* Quirk and Svartvik 1966: 49 ff.) we may feel sure of having a reasonably accurate tool for establishing the acceptability of a given linguistic phenomenon. A lack of positive correlation is usually an indication that we are dealing with lexical or semantic unacceptability and is thus also valuable as an indicator of the nature of the unacceptability of certain sentences.

A similar procedure may be resorted to for the elicitation of forms in divided usage, the *selection test.* If the issue at hand is the negative of *have,* the informants may be asked to turn a sentence like *I have a dog* into its negative counterpart, producing either *I haven't a dog* or *I don't have a dog,* thus showing their preference for either of the two variants. Or a *forced-choice test* may be used, whereby subjects are asked to insert two (or more) forms in given slots, thus showing the preferred environments for specific items (*cf.* Quirk 1970; Kempson and Quirk 1970; Tottie 1971).

No more need be said about various types of tests here, as they have been well described in monographs devoted to methodology (see Quirk and Svartvik 1966; Greenbaum and Quirk 1970). Nor do I feel that such 'laboratory' methods of doing sociolinguistics are in need of further justification. Field studies of spontaneous speech are of course superior for the investigation of usage whenever they are practically feasible, and no one, I believe, has contended otherwise. Acceptability, however, can only be ascertained by appealing to the intuition of speakers and presupposes some kind of testing procedure. Such methods intrinsically involve psychological problems, such as subjects' fatigue, reactions to the sequential order of test items, timing of the tests, etc.[10] Even more important, it seems to me, are such questions as whether we are actually justified, from a psychological as well as from a linguistic point of view, in asking subjects to substitute one word for another or to produce negative or interrogative counterparts of affirmative sentences. Obviously, the sentences produced in that way cannot *a priori* be assumed to be equivalent to spontaneously produced linguistic structures of the same type (and nobody has, as far as I know, treated them as such). However, we need to know a good deal more about the psychology of speech production before we can arrive at anything more than a very tentative evaluation of such tests. On the other hand, a valuable spin-off product of this kind of test is precisely that they may provide valuable insights into the underlying psychological mechanisms of linguistic competence and performance.

One objection that has been directed at the kind of experiments discussed here concerns the presentation of the results. Although records are naturally kept of the responses of individuals, the results are usually presented in terms of averages across informants for each sentence. Legum *et al.* (1974: 39) contend that this kind of presentation is of no value except for methodological studies. They state that 'implicational scales involving informants and sentences are somewhat more interesting' but that an analysis of response patterns of the kind that they propose is 'much more likely to be of broad interest to linguists'.

It seems to me that Legum *et al.* (1974) define the notions *value* and *interest* from a too narrowly theoretical viewpoint. What are indeed shortcomings from the point of view of theoretical linguistics may have positive virtues for the purposes I have had in mind throughout the present paper. In other words, I would suggest, à la Halliday (1968: 191), that just as different linguistic theories 'may be regarded as appropriate to different aims', different goals also necessitate diversified levels of descriptive adequacy. The level of description involving gross averages shows us what is the most common variant used by the group under investigation when it is a matter of divided usage or the most widely accepted form in the case of acceptability judgments. Assuming that we have chosen to examine the linguistic habits and judgments of a group of people whose language behavior may be regarded as representative of current trends as well as being socially desirable, we may proceed to incorporate our findings into textbooks and grammars, thus serving the interests of the advanced foreign learner. An example of such an addition that now seems to be due is the setting up of a new pair of modals using different lexical items in positive and negative contexts, similar to the established pattern of *may/must not,* viz. the complementary distribution of *ought to/should not* discovered by Svartvik and Wright (this volume). There is a strong case to be made for recurrent testing in areas of fluctuation, with subsequent revisions of grammars whenever necessary.

Moreover, it is obvious that the use of the experimental techniques themselves should not be restricted to investigations of the standard language. As they are almost the only methods currently available for the study of low-frequent phenomena, their value as a research tool for the study of language variants within a socio-linguistic framework is also indisputable.

There is no reason, however, why the results achieved by the methods of investigation that I have dwelt on above could not be further elaborated for theoretical purposes, as a basis for the establishment of implicational scales, variable rules or linguistically determined groups (*cf.* Berdan 1973), according to one's objectives. All that is needed is a different treatment of the data. The question which experimental techniques are the most reliable requires further elucidation, but it is nevertheless certain that such methods of elicitation as have been described in this paper are capable of providing yet another starting-point for the ultimate goal of linguistics: the achievement of explanatory adequacy.

ACKNOWLEDGMENTS

I am grateful to Alan Dixon, Sven Jacobson and Inger Ruin for reading and commenting on this paper. Any mistakes or inadvertencies that remain are my own responsibility.

NOTES

1. Among works by theoretical linguists, one may mention Carden (1970), Elliott *et al.* (1969) and Legum *et al.* (1974) on interpersonal variation. See also Ross (1972, 1973 and 1974). Charles-James Bailey's introduction to Bailey and Shuy, Eds., *New Ways of Analyzing Variation in English* (1973) gives a broad overview of the study of variation in the United States since the 1960s but fails to record work done in Britain and Europe. I hope the present paper will help to fill some of the gaps.
2. *Cf.* Greenbaum (1975b), who gives good examples of the usefulness of elicitation.
3. For a full account of these problems, see Greenbaum (1975a). *Cf.* also Quirk (1972: 117), who states that although 'linguistics should not be involved in the interests of conservationism ... this does not mean that linguistics is committed on principle to any rigorous insistence on laissez-faire in matters of language use'.
4. The most comprehensive work so far that has been based on Survey data is *A Grammar of Contemporary English,* published in 1972 by Randolph Quirk, Sidney Greenbaum, Geoffrey Leech and Jan Svartvik.
5. See Baratz (1969), Berdan (1973), and Garvey and Dickstein (1970). An early investigation based on data collected from schoolgirls in their teens is Reichstein's study of the loss of phonological oppositions in the French of Paris, carried out in 1956–1957 and published in 1960.
6. An interesting problem in this connection is the acceptability to native speakers of the speech of foreigners and the relative importance of different linguistic variables in determining this kind of acceptability. (On the acceptability to native speakers of the English spoken by Swedes, see, for instance, the papers by Olsson and Johansson in Svartvik, Ed., *Errata,* 1973.) It seems likely that a comparison of the criteria used by native speakers to assess the acceptability of the speech of foreigners and other native speakers, respectively, could prove of interest for the study of linguistic competence.
7. This scale is similar to the use of a five-point scale proposed for acceptability by Quirk and Svartvik (1966). For a critique of their terminology see Tottie (1969), where the terms complete – high – medium – low – zero are proposed. It is interesting to note that Lakoff (1973: 284) also suggests that judgments on 'fuzzy grammar' 'fall into more or less five categories: GOOD, PRETTY GOOD, IN BETWEEN, PRETTY BAD, DEFINITELY OUT'. It is, of course, important to remember that usage and acceptability scales seldom show exact correspondence.
8. Good examples are for instance Labov's studies of *r*-deletion (Labov 1966), and of the copula (Labov 1969), and the Sankoff and Cedergren studies of *que*-deletion in Montréal French (*cf.*, e.g., Sankoff 1973).
9. I use this term anachronistically for greater clarity. Quirk and Svartvik used the term *operation test* to cover what was later (see Greenbaum and Quirk 1970) subcategorized into *compliance* and *selection tests.*
10. For interesting findings on the effects of timing, see Legum *et al.* (1974).

REFERENCES

Bailey, C. J., and Shuy, R. W., Eds. (1973), *New Ways of Analyzing Variation in English.* Washington, D.C., Georgetown University Press.

Bald, W. D. (1972) *'Studien zu den kopulativen Verben des Englischen',* in *Commentati-*

onis Societatis Linguisticae Europaeae. Munchen, Max Hueber.

Baratz, J. C. (1969), 'A bi-dialectal task for determining language proficiency in economically disadvantaged Negro children', *Child Development*, 40, pp. 889–901.

Berdan, R. (1973), 'The use of linguistically determined groups in socio-linguistic research', *SWRL Professional Paper*, 26. Los Alamitos.

Berdan, R., and Pfaff, C. W. (1972), 'Sociolinguistic variation in the speech of young children: An experimental study', *SWRL Professional Paper*, 21. Los Alamitos.

Carden, G. (1970), 'A note on conflicting idiolects', *Linguistic Inquiry*, 1.

Elliott, D., Legum, S., and Thompson, S. A. (1969), 'Syntactic variation as linguistic data', *Papers from the fifth regional meeting of the Chicago Linguistic Society*.

Fasold, R. W. (1972), *Tense Marking in Black English*. Washington, D.C., The Center for Applied Linguistics.

Garvey, C., and Dickstein, E. (1970), 'Levels of analysis and social class differences in language', Report No. 83. Center for Social organization of Schools, Johns Hopkins University, Baltimore.

Greenbaum, S. (1969), *Studies in English Adverbial Usage*. London and Coral Gables, Florida, Longman and University of Miami Press.

– (1975a), 'Language variation and acceptability', *TESOL Quarterly*, 9, pp. 165–172.

– (1975b), 'Grammar and the foreign language teacher', in R. Crymes and W. E. Norris, Eds., *On TESOL 74*. Washington, D.C., TESOL.

Greenbaum, S., and Quirk, R. (1970), *Elicitation Experiments in English: Linguistic Studies in Use and Attitude*. London and Coral Gables, Florida, Longman and University of Miami Press.

Halliday, M. A. K. (1968), 'Syntax and the consumer', in R. J. O'Brien, Ed., *Georgetown University Round Table, Selected Papers on Linguistics 1961–1965*. Washington, D.C., Georgetown University Press.

Kempson, R. M., and Quirk, R. (1970), 'Controlled activation of latent contrast by forced-choice selection tests', *Language*, 47, 715–769.

Labov, W. (1966), *The Social Stratification of English in New York City*. Washington, D.C., The Center for Applied Linguistics.

– (1972), 'The study of language in its social context', in P. O. Giglioli, Ed., *Language and social context*. Harmondsworth, Penguin.

Lakoff, G. (1973), 'Fuzzy grammar and the performance/competence terminology game', *Papers from the ninth regional meeting of the Chicago Linguistic Society*.

Legum, S., Elliott, D. E., and Thompson, S. A. (1974) 'Considerations in the analysis of syntactic variation', SWRL Professional Paper, Los Alamitos.

Marton, W. and Preston, D. R. (1975), 'British and American English for Polish university students', *Glottodidactica* 8, 27–41.

Omar, M. (1973), *The Acquisition of Egyptian Arabic as a Native Language*. The Hague, Mouton.

Quirk, R. (1970), 'Aspect and variant inflexion in English verbs', *Language* 46, 300–311.

– (1972), 'Linguistics, usage, and the user', *The English language and images of matter*. London: Oxford University Press.

Quirk, R. and Svartvik, J. (1966), *Investigating Linguistic Acceptability*. The Hague, Mouton.

Reichstein, R. (1960), 'Etude des variations sociales et geographiques des faits linguistiques', *Word* 16, 55–99.

Ross, J. R. (1972), 'The category squish: Endstation Hauptwort', *Papers from the eighth regional meeting of the Chicago Linguistic Society*.

– (1973, 'A fake NP squish', in C. J. Bailey and R. W. Shuy, Eds., *New Ways of Analyzing Variation in English.* Washington, D.C., Georgetown University Press.

– (1974), 'Nouniness', in O. Fujimura, Ed., *Three Dimensions of Linguistic Theory.* Tokyo, TEC Company.

Sankoff, G. (1973), 'Above and beyond phonology in variable rules', in C. J. Bailey and R. W. Shuy, Eds., *New Ways of Analyzing Variation in English.* Washington, D.C., Georgetown University Press.

Svartvik, J., Ed. (1973), *Errata.* Lund, Gleeriyis.

Svartvik, J., and Wright, D. (1977), [this volume] 'The use of *ought* in teenage English'.

Tottie, G. (1969), 'Review of R. Quirk and J. Svartvik, *Investigating linguistic acceptability', Moderna Språk,* 53.

– (1971), *'Have to. A study of usage and acceptability in present-day British English.'* Stockholm theses in English 4. Stockholm.

– (1974), 'On promising in Swedish and English', *Papers from the first Scandinavian conference on linguistics at Kungälv, March, 1974.* Göteborg, Department of Linguistics.

Wolfram, W. A. (1969), *A Sociolinguistic Description of Detroit Negro Speech.* Washington, D.C., The Center for Applied Linguistics.